DANCE AND THE BODY POLITIC
IN NORTHERN GREECE

PRINCETON MODERN GREEK STUDIES

*This series is sponsored by
the Princeton University Committee on
Hellenic Studies under the auspices of the
Stanley J. Seeger Hellenic Fund*

A list of titles in the series
appears at the back of the book

DANCE *and the* Body Politic in Northern Greece

JANE K. COWAN

PRINCETON UNIVERSITY PRESS
PRINCETON, NEW JERSEY

Library of Congress Cataloging-in-Pulbication Data

Cowan, Jane K., 1954–
    Dance and the body politic in northern Greece / Jane K. Cowan.
        p.   cm.—(Princeton modern Greek studies)
    Includes bibliographical references.
    ISBN 0-691-09449-7 (alk. paper)—ISBN 0-691-02854-0
(pbk. : alk. paper)
        1. Dancing—Greece—Anthropological aspects.   2. Sexuality
in dance—Greece.   3. Greece—Social life and customs—
20th century. I. Title. II. Series.
    GV1588.6.C69   1990
    792.8'09495—dc20   90-30232

To Charlie, beloved mate

and in memory of
Ted Petrides and Athanassios Katsoufis,
esteemed teachers

CONTENTS

ILLUSTRATIONS

EVERY work bears the imprint of its author. This book explores issues that have become important to me over many years—the complex intertwining of power and pleasure in gender and sexual relations, the social shaping of the human body, the ambiguities of social experience—all examined in the context of an activity that I find fascinating: Greek dance.

This project had its genesis when, in 1975, I went to Greece for the first time. A college student, I was enrolled in an academic study-program in Athens where I hoped to study Greek culture and music. Under the tutelage of a talented teacher, Ted Petrides, I began to learn to dance—in the choreographic, if not the social, sense. Learning to dance required a particular coordination of mind and body: of simultaneously discerning often subtle rhythms and physically rendering them in the controlled movements and postures of my body. That fourth-floor classroom in the Hellenic-American Union in central Athens, Ted's tiny tape-recorder blaring out one exquisite tune after another, was the site where I first experienced the ordered sensuality of dancing. It was where I first recognized Greek dancing as embodied action (embodying skill, control and coordination) and as embodied experience (embodying my sense of my body and my bodily senses, my awareness of myself *as* a body and my awareness of others' awareness of me *as* an embodied female self). It was, as well, a first encounter with that paradoxically double sense of engrossment and reflexivity that characterize the experience of the dancer as much as that of the good ethnographer.

During that year I sought out many different kinds of social events in which dance was a central activity: Cretan village weddings, urban nightclubs, the formal dances of regional migrants' associations, regional taverns, and dancing in the streets during pre-Lenten Carnival in Macedonia. I slowly became aware that these events (dance-events, as I later learned to call them) were highly structured, complex yet also labile social situations. Indeed, I found them to bear only a tenuous relationship to the stereotypes through which such dancing is typically represented.

The words "Greek dance" conjure up a plethora of images. Sturdiest among them, no doubt, is the celluloid image of Anthony Quinn as Zorba the Greek dancing barefoot and solitary on a Cretan beach. That Zorba is dancing out his sorrow, not his joy, is a detail often forgotten,

and it is the simpler fantasy of Zorba as embodiment of earthy appe-
tites and unencumbered joie de vivre that is enlisted to sell everything
from "Opa!" restaurants to package holidays in Greece. The erasure of
complexity in Zorba's dance in favor of a more immediately comprehensible story is hugely telling. But the images proliferate. There is
Melina Mercouri, Greek actress and former Minister of Culture, in her
cinematic role as "hooker with the heart of gold" in *Never on Sunday*,
dancing lustily on the quay with a bevy of young soldiers, while the
Greek-American Homer, frozen in his arid intellectuality, looks on
helplessly. There are the images of remembered vacations—of an evening in an Athenian nightclub, perhaps, where a corpulent businessman in a three-piece suit, fingers studded with gold rings, hunches in
feigned concentration and circles around an imaginary point on the
floor as a bored waiter noisily smashes pile after pile of plates at his
feet. There are the fanciful literary images, authored by genteel nine-
teenth-century travelers, of rude peasants' "Dionysian revelry" and of
modest maidens dancing with downcast eyes. There are the carefully
crafted theatrical images of colorfully costumed dancers who perform
on stage: not just professional folk-dance troupes performing for tour-
ists in Athens but also, across the sea in America, children's dance
troupes performing for their non-Greek neighbors in countless Greek-
American community festivals.

   Foreigners' perceptions of dance in Greece—and, in complicated
ways, Greeks' perceptions of dance, as well—are inevitably mediated
by this shifting array of images. But if the joy and spontaneity those
dancing images carry are not exactly false, they are not the whole
story. I found that the tangible energy of the dance space often carried
a sharp edge of tension. Participants ate, drank, laughed, and danced
together, but they also scrutinized each other intensely. Exhilarated by
the dancing, I often returned home utterly drained, emotionally as well
as physically. Some of this, of course, was the anxiety of not knowing
the cultural rules. Being both foreign and female, and recognizing that
dancing was about sexuality—among other things—but in a highly
coded way that I did not yet understand, I worried that I might unwit-
tingly embarrass my hosts or even precipitate more serious misunderstandings. As time passed, though, I realized that the tensions I felt
were not *merely* those of a dislocated foreigner but were a common
feature of such events. Occasionally, quarrels erupted. I too learned to
watch closely. I learned that in a society where most people dance,
dancing is much more than knowing the steps; it involves both social
knowledge and social power. I noticed, too, that girls and boys,
women and men acted and reacted in dance-events in different ways.

   From the experiences of that year emerged certain hunches and questions about gendered selves, society, and dance that I returned to explore, six years later, in the Macedonian mountain town of Sohos. I had first visited this community in the spring of 1976, during the town's famous Carnival, and had returned for a few weeks in the summer of 1978. My third visit lasted for some sixteen months between February 1983 and February 1985.

Thus this book has involved many stages, and has been an (evolving) constant in an otherwise peripatetic life. It bears the traces of my moves from Greece to the American Midwest (where, among other things, I was part of a Balkan dance troupe before going to graduate school), back to Greece for fieldwork, and finally, after a brief return to Indiana, to Dylan Thomas' "ugly, lovely" hometown, the industrial port city of Swansea in South Wales where most of this text has been written. In each of these times and spaces there have been people who have helped and inspired me, many more than I can practicably name. I am grateful to them all, but here I would like to acknowledge especially the following institutions and individuals.

The field research on which this study is based was supported by a Fulbright-Hays Fellowship for Doctoral Dissertation Research Abroad. A National Science Foundation Dissertation Improvement Grant provided funds for videotaping equipment. Upon my return from the field, the Indiana University Department of Anthropology awarded me a Skomp Fellowship for a portion of the writing-up period.

For their warmth, hospitality, humor, and tolerance of the Amerikana who wanted to learn so much about them, my debt to the people of Sohos is enormous. The respect and affection I feel for many Sohoians and for many aspects of their way of life is profound. I want to express particularly warm thanks to the Bekiaris family, the Gaganelis family, Angeliki and Thanassis Iatrou, Chrysi and Angeliki Noïkou, and the late Athanassios Katsoufis. In the text all Sohoians appear under pseudonyms.

My parents, Dick and Norma Cowan, my sister Marcia, my brothers Richard and Robert, and my grandmother Marjorie Neill Dent have been loving and supportive through the long years of this project. The visits of several members of my family to Sohos in August 1983 made me more comprehensible to the townspeople by showing them that I belong to a family, too.

Marlene Arnold, Katharine Butterworth, and the late Ted Petrides first got me hooked on Greece, and Susan Auerbach and Ruth Mandel have shared with me the highs and lows of this addiction over many years. S. K. Frangos, with his insights into and passion for things Greek, contributed immeasurably to my understanding of myriad aspects of Greek society; he also collaborated in research in Sohos during the summer of 1983. Ivan Karp, Anya Peterson Royce, Tony Seeger, and Ruth Stone (all of whom read and commented on this text in its earlier guise as a doctoral dissertation), the late James Spradley, and the late Alan Merriam inspired and guided me. I am especially grateful to Michael Herzfeld, who read and reacted to many drafts, for his swift and generous feedback and for the pleasures of the lively argument it always contained. The pages that follow bear witness to the acuity, enthusiasm, and humanity of these gifted teachers. I will also never forget the camaraderie and intellectual stimulation I enjoyed with my cohorts at Indiana University, especially Martha Balshem, Lydie Brissonet, Carol Inman, Henry Kingsbury, and Sue Tuohy.

Many individuals helped make my time in Greece both productive and enjoyable. Richard Ammerman, director of the Fulbright office in Athens, and Harry Iseland, of the American Center in Thessaloniki, opened their offices to me whenever I was in town and also helped me cut through some nasty red tape. Gus Hadzidimitriou, the Fulbright representative for northern Greece, and his wife, Peggy, were an anchor of sanity in my first months. Alexandra Bakalaki, Nelly Goudeli, Janet Hart, Ariane Kotsis, Nelson Moe, Xanthippe Panayotidou, Nenny Panourgia and her family, Charles Stewart, Karen Van Dyck, and Eva Varellis-Kanellis offered me shelter, a patient ear, and the catharsis of laughter when I needed to get away and reflect. Conversations begun then have continued over the years, and this ongoing collective interpretive work has made possible a richer and more nuanced text than I could ever have achieved on my own. Nick Germanacos gave me the chance to put my fieldwork experiences into coherent form through teaching American students in Kalymnos and Nisyros. In turn, these students, especially the eight in my charge in Kalymnos in the fall of 1984, the other teachers, and the islanders taught me a great deal.

Many other friends, colleagues, and teachers have also discussed the ideas presented here with me, and some have read all or part of this book at one stage or another. I want to thank Ruth Behar, Diane Bennett, Mari Clark, Marcia Cowan, Loring Danforth, Catia Galatariotou, Gregory Jusdanis, Margaret Kenna, and Marianna Spanaki for their close readings and critical responses. Katie Lloyd and Sean Galvin gave unstintingly of their time and energy in the original production of this manuscript. At Princeton University Press, Elizabeth Gretz, Gail Ullman, and Wendy Wong cast an experienced editorial eye over the whole text and adroitly guided it to completion.

Finally, and most of all, Charles Gore's friendship, love, and unceasing encouragement sustained me during the long, rainy years of writing. In our countless Sunday walks by the sea, he quizzed and coaxed and prodded until my ideas began to take the shape of an argument. For his work as midwife of this extended labor, and for so much more, I am profoundly grateful.

DANCE AND THE BODY POLITIC
IN NORTHERN GREECE

Entering the Dance

> If you enter the dance, you must dance.
>
> —Greek proverb

FEBRUARY 1985. At half past midnight, in a chilly rented hall in a small town in the mountains of Macedonia, the Orpheus Association's annual dance is coming to a close. Although the musicians continue to play, the middle-aged couples who have dominated the event are gradually leaving for home. My video camera captures two images of a now-disorganized dance space.

In the background, at the top of the dance floor, a small, wiry youth is dancing a medium-tempo, rather acrobatic *zeibekiko*. The sleeves on his sweater are pushed up around his elbows with studied carelessness, a cigarette dangles from his lips, and the brim of his wool cap is pulled down over his eyes at an angle. His arms are raised and his back is slightly bent as he circles an imaginary point on the floor, then squats, spins, and slaps his heel. Seven young men, crouching on one knee and clapping to the moderate 9/4 beat, form a circle around him.

Simultaneously, in the foreground near the entrance, in a small space cleared by pushing aside several tables, Angelos, a boisterous and insistent sixteen-year-old from the association's folk-dance troupe, which performed earlier in the evening, has pulled Lakis, a young member of Sohos' entrepreneurial class and vice-president of the association, up to dance. Lakis, elegantly dressed, loosens his tie dramatically. With a cigarette pressed between his lips, his arms loosely raised, his shoulders hunched forward, and his gaze downward, he steps into the center. A small contingent from the dance troupe crouches around him in a circle, clapping, while off to one side, his wife and two of her female friends also watch and clap, leaning toward the circle from their chairs.

Feigning concentration and self-absorption, Lakis moves slowly; but when he reaches the three beats at the end of the slow 9/4 pattern, he performs three stylized stumbles, each deeper than the one before. Three times he catches himself at the last possible moment, his body balanced, motionless for the merest second. Then, to stress the first beat of the new pattern, he raises himself up in comic defiance. Those watching smile knowingly. Angelos stands in front of Lakis, very close, and shouts out the words of the song while marking the beats with his hand for emphasis. Moments later, Angelos rushes over to a nearby table where other teenagers in the dance troupe are sitting, and tries to grab a plate. One of the boys becomes irritated at Angelos' antics and restrains his hand, shouting at him not to be a "jerk-off" (*malakas*), to leave the plate alone. But a second boy, across the table, hands Angelos another plate, bits of cabbage and bread crumbs clinging to its greasy surface. Angelos carries this back to Lakis and smashes it on the floor near his feet. Fragments of cheap earthenware scatter everywhere. Lakis kneels down. Slowly, dreamily, with a sensuality that, even while mocking itself, retains a disquieting intensity, he rolls his eyes upward and gazes into the camera I am holding.[1]

THIS book is concerned with gender, dance, and the body, and with the ethnographic process through which these issues were explored in a town in northern Greece. I focus on the social construction of gender, examining this not so much within the everyday contexts of work, family life, and religious activity, as have previous studies of gender, but rather within the nonordinary context of what I call "dance-events."

Like other anthropologists who study "extraordinary" realms of social life, such as ritual, play, and the arts, I conceive the dance-event as a temporally, spatially, and conceptually "bounded" sphere of interaction. In the dance-event, individuals publicly present themselves in and through celebratory practices—eating, drinking, singing, and talking as well as dancing—and are evaluated by others.[2] I regard each dance-event as a site, both physical and conceptual, where celebrants perform in gendered ways and experience themselves as gendered subjects. I regard dancing in particular as an activity in which the body is both a site of experience (for the dancer) and a sign (for those who watch the dancer) in which sexuality—as a culturally specific complex of ideas, feelings, and practices—is deeply embedded. Examining both dancing and the dance-event as a whole, I explore how the gender ideas and relations of everyday life are actively embodied and explored in festive performance. And I consider how, in dance-events associated with pleasure, sensual intensity, and public sociability, gender inequalities and other social hierarchies are constituted and even celebrated.

Greece is in many ways an ideal location for such a study. Despite the massive social and demographic changes in Greek society since the 1940s, dance is still very much at the center of community life, in both rural and urban settings. Dance remains a central component of many celebrations—calendrical rituals (Carnival, Easter, religious feast

---

[1] This scene is briefly analyzed in Chapter 6.

[2] For theorizations on cultural performance, see Bateson 1972a; Goffman 1974; Simmel 1971a; Stone 1982.

days), rites of passage (particularly weddings), and the formal or informal gatherings of voluntary associations. The cultural emphasis throughout Greece on bodily presentation, moreover, and the association of this emphasis with issues of prestige, reputation, and sexuality lend special interest to the ways in which Greek men and women present themselves and evaluate each other's actions in the contexts of dance.

In Sohos,[3] the Greek Macedonian community on which this study is based, all dance-events share certain features. They are sensually intense, involving aural, visual, tactile, kinesthetic, and gustatory stimulation. They are also socially intense, involving interaction with an immediate group and with other, nonrelated celebrants. Dancing bodies are at the center of public scrutiny and, simultaneously, are the medium of experience (Royce 1977; Turner 1984). Dance-events are idealized as occasions of conviviality, pleasure, and release. Nevertheless, in a community that, like many in Greece, values sociability highly but is socially divided in a variety of ways, dance-events are often problematical and prone to breakdown. What makes the examination of gender and gendered sexuality in the dance-event interesting—but also complicated—is precisely its ambiguous status as a site of social action (Danforth 1978, 1979a) that is both set apart from and embedded in ordinary social relations and meanings.

Despite the importance of dance in Greece and the fact that so many issues coalesce at the dance site—notions and experiences of sexuality, gender, sociability, power—Greek dance has been neglected as a subject of serious ethnographic inquiry.[4] Greece, moreover, is only one ethnographic case in point of a legacy of anthropological inattention to dance more generally. This may be linked to a cultural bias in many anthropologists' societies of origin that sees dance as a kind of epiphenomenal icing on the cake of the "harder" structural realities of kinship, economics, and political organization (Kaeppler 1978). Equally important, however, have been the conceptual difficulties, including the issue of verbally analyzing the social and cultural meanings of a primarily nonverbal event.

In thinking about this problem and other conceptual aspects of this

[3] This community is best known within Greece for its unusual pre-Lenten Carnival celebrations, in which male, and nowadays some female, celebrants don a masked headdress, goatskin leggings and bodice, and a harness of five bells and feast, drink, and sing special songs in the local establishments. In earlier publications, I referred to the town under the pseudonym "Merio" (Cowan 1988a, 1988b) the old and seldom-heard Macedonian term for this masked figure, the *merio*, today usually called the *karnavali*.

[4] The work of Danforth (1978, 1979a) is an important exception, even though he restricts his examination of dance to the context of the Anastenaria ritual therapy. Other ethnographers have noted dancing in passing in their accounts and recognized its significance (for example, Campbell 1964:285, 287; Herzfeld 1985a:63, 65; Stewart n.d.). Their remarks have provided important hints, some of which I have pursued here.

project, I have drawn inspiration from a variety of intellectual sources. From the symbolic interactionists I have borrowed the evocative phrase "social construction"; the dual connotations of the term "construction," as both fictive and physical, are especially apposite here (Berger and Luckman 1967). The work of some in this tradition on "frames" and on the negotiation of meanings in everyday "performance" has influenced this study directly and also, through its effect on theorizations about cultural performance, indirectly.[5] Austin's (1975) work on "performative utterances" and performative conventions and the work of the post-structuralists, which has inspired a re-examination of the processes and politics of ethnographic text-making, have in their different ways been unexpectedly useful in this study of a largely nonverbal activity. They have helped me to think about dancing but also about words about dancing. Feminist scholarship, too, has over time sensitized me to the complex bonds, including the subtle expressions of power, between men and women at both inter-personal and collective levels.

I locate myself and my project in what Ortner (1984) has called "practice anthropology," and it is from this discourse that I draw my fundamental assumptions. I see gender in Greece (as elsewhere) as an asymmetrical social relation, and ask how gender is socially con-structed—expressed and experienced, produced and reproduced—in both bodily and verbal ways in the dance. The exploration of gender cross-culturally is not a new theme in anthropology, of course.[6] But until the advent of feminist anthropology, one of the major contexts in which a "practice anthropology" has been developing (Ortner 1984:145), it was often explored in functionalist or idealist terms or in terms of "meaning." I place the asymmetrical (rather than, say, the complementary) relations of gender at the analytical center. This, in turn, generates particular sorts of questions and implies particular sorts of theoretical models about consciousness, experience, and the rela-tions between social structure and human agency.

CONCEPTUALIZING GENDER

The historical elision of women from most ethnographic accounts, which concentrated on male-controlled activities and which assumed that men could unproblematically speak for men and women alike, has

[5] On everyday "performance," see Goffman 1959, 1974; Schutz 1970; Simmel 1971a. On cultural performance, see, for example, Bauman 1977; Geertz 1973a; Herzfeld 1985a; Stone 1982.

[6] For early explorations of gender, see, for example, Kaberry 1939; Mead 1949; Rich-ards 1956.

had important consequences for the development of gender studies. Once the elision was noticed as a "problem," proponents of the newly emerging feminist anthropology considered their first priority to be the recovery of women previously absent from the ethnographic record.[7] They began to investigate hitherto silent or invisible female worlds: women's accomplishments, words, experiences, goals, and strategies. It soon became clear that the process of investigating the lives of particular women in particular societies would have far-reaching repercussions, fundamentally altering not just ideas about men and women as social actors but conceptions of culture, society, and anthropological theory and method itself.[8]

Attending to women proved to be not merely an additive strategy but one that enabled the criticism and even, potentially, the transformation of existing paradigms. Yet this anthropological consciousness-raising has been a contradictory process.[9] One problem is that in too many ethnographic and subdisciplinary areas the study of gender has remained, as it necessarily began, conflated into and equated with the study of women. Within the overlapping areas of European, Balkan, and Mediterranean studies, for instance, the call to action from feminist anthropology has resulted in countless articles and books on women. These are only lightly (and lately) counterbalanced by a few works dealing explicitly—rather than implicitly, as before—with men, masculinity, or manhood.[10]

Still, the problem is not so much that women are overstudied and men understudied in gender studies. More studies that show masculinity to be as socially and conceptually problematical as feminists have shown femininity to be would indeed be welcome. But it remains true that in any consideration of gender too exclusive a focus on either sex can itself be misleading. The often highly segregated social worlds of men and women in Greece as in many parts of the world has no doubt exacerbated the tendency of anthropologists to write studies either of "manhood" *or* of "womanhood." Yet to the extent that either men or

---

[7] Ardener's seminal essay, "Belief and the Problem of Women" (1975, but written in 1967), echoed the chorus of female voices in the women's movement, in identifying the "muteness" of women as, at least in part, a consequence of the scientific community's "deafness." Early examples of feminist anthropological work on women include Reiter 1975; Rosaldo and Lamphere 1974.

[8] Such investigations include MacCormack and Strathern 1980; Ortner and Whitehead 1981.

[9] Strathern (1981, 1987a) has criticized in particularly provocative ways certain assumptions found among feminist anthropologists: for instance, the essentialist notion that one can already know what a "woman" is in a certain society. This she sees as the object—the end—of a gender analysis, not its pretext.

[10] On this subject see, for example, Brandes 1980; Herzfeld 1985a, Papataxiarchis 1986.

women are approached in isolation from the other gender, the dialectical energies of the original feminist impulse falter. It is only when gender is examined as a relational reality, when "being/becoming a woman" and "being/becoming a man" are recognized as mutually constitutive processes, that a feminist perspective generates its most powerful critical insights.

This is not a study about women; it is a study about gender.[11] It explores the relations not only of men with women but of men with men and women with women. For it is not only women who are, as Ardener (1975) quipped, "problematical." On the contrary, "from the perspective of social relations, men and women are both prisoners of gender, although in highly differentiated but interrelated ways" (Flax 1987:629).

To understand how this imprisoning occurs, one must examine both the ideational and the practical aspects of gender. As Flax has argued,

> The study of gender relations entails at least two levels of analysis: of gender as a thought construct or category that helps us to make sense out of particular social worlds and histories; and of gender as a social relation that enters into and partially constitutes all other social relations and activities. As a practical social relation, gender can be understood only by a close examination of the meanings of "male" and "female" and the consequences of being assigned to one or the other gender within concrete social practices. (1987:630)

Hence in the specific community of Sohos, as everywhere, gender relations exist in the dual dimensions of ideas and social relations, which, though I have at times analyzed them separately, are fused together in "concrete social practices" such as the dance.

Although it is intended to contribute to gender studies in a broad sense, this study has been deeply influenced by, and responds critically to, discussions of gender in the specific ethnographic context of Greece and the Balkans. Gender has long been an important theme in Greek ethnography, largely because it is so deeply implicated in the moral values of "honor and shame."[12] There has been a tendency, both in the

[11] I remain sympathetic to the need to study women's experience and do, in fact, take up such themes in this book, but I believe that these can only be made sense of in relation to men's experience. Moreover, though there may be some logic to studying "women" in the context of activities that are gender-segregated, this strategy quickly loses its usefulness in a dance situation, where men and women (and perhaps boys and girls) participate together.

[12] Gender has also been an important ethnographic theme elsewhere in the Mediterranean and Balkans; see, for example, Denich 1974; Pitt-Rivers 1961; Schneider 1971. On "honor and shame," the classic texts include Campbell 1964; du Boulay 1974; and Peristiany 1966. For a different emphasis on the question of gender, see Friedl 1967.

early studies and in the later work they inspired, to present gender as a set of essential and relatively fixed meanings, out of which a fairly rigid set of gender roles arises. This has been a logical consequence of the assumptions and concerns of two anthropological traditions that have dominated Greek studies: the implicit (and sometimes explicit; see du Boulay 1974:101–120) structuralism in the Oxford variety of British social anthropology and the cultural relativism and preoccupation with "meaning" of North American symbolic anthropology. Both traditions conceptualize society or culture as a Durkheimian totality, morally—if not socially or economically—bounded. Those trained in the British tradition have approached gender as an aspect of the various "parts" that fit together (hence the ongoing concern with the interrelationships among moral values, institutions, and roles). Those trained in the American tradition, with its more cultural emphasis, have approached gender in terms of the meanings that persons, spaces, and actions can have in a society organized in a certain way.[13]

In the two decades since the writing of the classic texts on gender in Greece that so deeply influenced scholars' analytical categories, massive social changes have taken place in Greek society. During the same period, the relevance of theoretical developments in feminism, Marxism, and linguistic and performance theories to gender issues has begun to be recognized. The widespread rethinking of gender among scholars of Greek society in recent years has been inspired by both of these trends: by empirical changes in gender practices and by conceptual reformulations (including those oriented toward traditional ethnographic concerns such as "moral values"; see Herzfeld 1980a) being worked through on the analytical level.[14]

Although as elsewhere, this rethinking of gender has by and large been conflated with the study of women, the varied approaches newly brought to bear upon the "problem of women" have revitalized debate nonetheless.[15] Some work has taken up Ardener's question of a specif-

[13] The works of Campbell (1964) and Peristiany (1966) are examples of this first tendency; those of Caraveli-Chaves (1980), Danforth (1982), and Hirschon (1978) are examples of the second.

[14] "Rethinking gender and kinship" was one of two major themes taken up at a symposium commemorating the founding of Greece's first department of social anthropology, at the University of the Aegean in Mytilene in September 1986 ("Symposium on Horizons of Current Anthropological Research in Greece and the Establishment of a Department of Social Anthropology at the University of the Aegean")—one indication of the centrality of the issue for anthropological studies of Greece at the time. The relationship between empirical changes in gender practices and conceptual reformulations of gender is, of course, complex. There is often a tendency to see them as alternative explanations when in fact both processes need to be taken into account.

[15] In a fairly recent edited volume on this subject, *Gender and Power in Rural Greece* (Dubisch 1986), all eight of the essays deal with women or "femaleness" and are concerned almost exclusively with rural, married women. Dubisch, however, does remark

ically female perspective. Many analysts have adopted an actor-centered approach and have turned their attentions to issues of women's strategies and powers. Others have emphasized situationally negotiable, rather than fixed, gender meanings or, more unusually, have examined "woman" as a contested category. Still others have approached gender issues from a Marxist or materialist perspective. The broader methodological and epistemological questions of gender bias on the part of the researcher and the effects of his or her gender on the research process are also increasingly addressed in such works.[16]

The value and contribution of the many voices of this debate must not be understated. A significant number of these authors, however, tend to describe gender roles and relations in Greece in terms of "complementarity." The notion clearly has descriptive validity. Many Greeks do seem to think of gender roles and relations in this way; indeed, the idea of complementarity is elaborated within Orthodox theological doctrine. But it is important to distinguish ideological claims of "complementarity" (whether they come from men, women, or institutional discourses) from sociological or anthropological evaluations of social relations and practices.

Unless explicitly qualified, "complementarity" implies separate and/or different but *equal*. I know of no Greek community that I would characterize as truly egalitarian, though admittedly the question of how equality between men and women is defined and how it may be realized is a contentious one (see, for example, Strathern 1987b). Taking sexual complementarity at face value is an inherent danger in analyses using the frameworks of functionalism, structuralism, and cultural relativism, all of which (though for different reasons, epistemological as well as moral) inhibit the analyst from taking a critical stance. Ironically, the same danger exists for those who are inspired by feminist anthropologists' challenge to ethnographers to take seriously previously neglected female worlds, powers, and strategies. In my

---

that discussions about gender need to be extended more explicitly to include males (ibid.:38). Herzfeld (1985a) and Papataxiarchis (1986) are examples of such work. This rethinking has also entailed a reconsideration of the established literature. Thus, though its implications were not really taken up within Greek studies for over a decade, Friedl's (1967) essay anticipated a major problematic in feminist anthropology, that of the relationship of the public/domestic distinction to gender (for an early and influential formulation, see Rosaldo 1974).

[16] On the question of a female perspective, see, especially, the papers in Dubisch 1986. For an actor-centered approach, see Danforth 1979b, 1983; Hirschon 1983. On situationally negotiable meanings, see, for example, Dubisch 1983, 1986; Herzfeld 1985a. On "woman" as a contested category, see Papagaroufali's (1986) study of Athenian women in feminist associations. For a Marxist or materialist perspective, see Bakalaki 1984; Cavounidis 1983; Dimen 1983; Handman 1983; Piault 1985; Skouteri-Didaskalou 1984; Sutton 1986. On gender bias, see especially Clark 1983 and Friedl 1970.

view, any sexual or gender complementarity—like women's powers generally—that may be observed in particular sites and moments must always be seen in the context of a broader asymmetry of male dominance and of the androcentric and patriarchal institutions through which it is manifested.

In this book I attempt to extend certain insights about gender ideas and relations introduced in the early ethnographies of Greece, as well as follow up certain questions raised by—and build on the theoretical trends exemplified in—more recent studies. The distinctive features of the approach to gender that I use coalesce around three themes: consciousness, power, and practices. These themes derive from, and enable an analysis in terms of, a particular conception of the relationship between structure and human agency.

Consciousness

It is common in anthropological discussions to talk in terms of *the* gender ideas of or within *a* culture, but such a formulation remains problematical. Although what culture is and how it works remain among the most vexed questions within anthropology, the concept of culture retains traces of its functionalist origins. It continues to be understood as the articulation of moral consensus and of shared symbols, beliefs, values, ideas. The problem is *not* that the claims are spurious and that nothing is shared. The problem, rather, is that when culture is defined as that which is shared, questions about this sharedness—*is* it actually shared? to what extent? by whom? how does it come to be shared?—disappear by definition. The conventions of talking about the gender ideas of the "X" exaggerate the impression of internal coherence within a society. They can also lead us to search for—and then, in our analyses, to privilege—an "indigenous" set of gender ideas that is deemed more authentic than those expressed by others in the same community or in the broader society.

My discomfort with the monolithic implications of such models of culture was heightened by the historical conditions of my fieldwork. I investigated gender in the heady atmosphere of the early 1980s in Greece when a newly elected socialist government, led by the Panhellenic Socialist Movement (PA.SO.K.), was promoting a platform of "Equality of Women." Feminism was then (as now) much in the air. As a result, gender was a more contentious subject than it had probably ever been in the past. At the same time a strong, if not wholly untroubled, conviction of the "naturalness" of the prevailing gender order still remained. Grappling with the problem of how best to represent the plural, sometime querulous, voices I heard raised on the subject of gender, I have found a consensual notion of culture unhelpful, even obtuse. Yet I have realized that an individualistic framework that would portray these voices as coexisting in democratically pluralist polyphony would be equally inaccurate. To make sense of the social relations between these multiple yet not equally powerful speakers, I have borrowed Gramsci's concept of "hegemony," which Gramsci originally developed to explore the question of class consciousness, and applied it to the sphere of gender.

Feminists have asked how and why women, far from passively submitting to patriarchal institutions, often play an active role in sustaining and reproducing them. Though Gramsci never really addressed the question of gender relations as such, his desire to understand why a revolutionary consciousness had not spontaneously developed in the working class and to explore the conditions under which such a consciousness might develop and the forms it might take seems to presage many feminist concerns.

How do those in power gain the consent of those over whom they have power? Gramsci's writings on hegemony are fragmentary and often vague, yet through this concept he opens up a way to understand the relations between consciousness and sociopolitical authority that differs from both the models of consensus and contract in classical political theory and the model of false consciousness in orthodox Marxism. Femia explains that according to Gramsci,

> The supremacy of a social group or class manifests itself in two different ways: "domination" [*dominio*] or coercion, and "intellectual and moral leadership" [*direzione intellettuale e morale*]. This latter type of supremacy constitutes hegemony. Social control, in other words, takes two basic forms: besides influencing behaviour and choice *externally*, through rewards and punishments, it also affects them internally, by moulding personal convictions into a replica of prevailing norms. Such "internal control" is based on hegemony, which refers to an order in which a common social-moral language is spoken, in which one concept of reality is dominant, informing with its spirit all modes of thought and behaviour. It follows that hegemony is the predominance obtained by *consent* rather than force of one class or group over other classes. And whereas "domination" is realised, essentially, through the coercive machinery of the state, "intellectual and moral leadership" is objectified in, and mainly exercised through, "civil society," the ensemble of educational, religious and associational institutions. Hegemony is attained through the myriad ways in which the institutions of civil society operate to shape, di-

rectly or indirectly, the cognitive and affective structures whereby men perceive and evaluate problematic social reality. (Femia 1981:24)

It should be noted that Gramsci did not conceptualize hegemony as a necessarily oppressive process. To the contrary, he saw the development of an alternative hegemony of the working class, under the leadership of those he referred to as "organic intellectuals," as a precondition of social revolution. He saw the establishment of this new proletarian hegemony—which, according to Femia, Gramsci envisioned as "open, expansive and critical" (1981:173–74)—as essential, moreover, in the formation of a just society. It is nonetheless telling that most of those who have borrowed Gramsci's notion have used it to help illuminate the more familiar situation of bourgeois hegemony; that is, how individuals in Western societies come to embrace, defend, and reproduce ideas and social relations that circumscribe their own life possibilities. It is this situation that seems most in need of explanation to Marxists and feminists alike.

Approaching the processes of gender construction in Sohos in terms of a notion of hegemony entails not a dismissal of "culture" but a reformulation of it. As Williams writes, "Hegemony is in the strongest sense a 'culture,' but a culture which has also to be seen as the lived dominance and subordination of particular classes" (1977:110). The analytical usefulness of the concept of hegemony, from the perspective of practice anthropology, is that rather than presupposing a moral consensus, it makes it problematical. The concept thus opens up the question of how members of different social groups—variously positioned—accept, manipulate, use, or contest hegemonic (that is, dominant) ideas. It also goes beyond some actor-centered approaches in analyzing this process in structural—rather than only in individualistic—terms.[17]

In the context of an examination of implicit and embodied meanings, hegemony has certain advantages over the notoriously difficult term "ideology" (see Bernstein 1976; Giddens 1979), even though the latter term may enable distinctions that are erased in the more globalizing concept of culture, which it sometimes replaces.[18] Definitions of ideology vary widely, but the term tends to imply a relatively formal-

[17] One problem with some actor-centered approaches (and according to Ortner [1984:155–57], much practice anthropology is vulnerable to the same criticism) is its incorporation of certain unexamined methodological individualist assumptions.

[18] Dubisch (1986), for example, uses the term "dominant ideology" in much the way that I use "hegemony." I will use "dominant ideology" in relation to sex and gender from time to time, especially when dealing with explicitly articulated meanings.

ized and articulated system of meanings, beliefs, and values (Williams 1977:109). Hegemony, in contrast, when defined as "a whole body of practices and expectations over the whole of living, the shaping perceptions of ourselves and our world" (ibid.:110), includes ideas that are known and felt but not articulated. As such, it encompasses what Giddens (1984) calls "practical consciousness." Although the notion of hegemony may appear just as totalizing as any concept of culture, it is best understood as a process that always entails the possibility of resistance as well as of accommodation. Hegemony powerfully penetrates individuals' senses and their senses of themselves, yet it is never total or totally determining:

> A lived hegemony is always a process. It is not, except analytically, a system or a structure. It is a realized complex of experiences, relationships, and activities, with specific and changing pressures and limits. In practice, that is, hegemony can never be singular. Its internal structures are highly complex. . . . Moreover, . . . it does not just passively exist as a form of dominance. It has continually to be renewed, recreated, defended and modified. It is also continually resisted, limited, altered, challenged by pressures not all its own. (Williams 1977:112)

In focusing upon gender, and in using hegemony as a conceptual framework for exploring the dynamics of consent and its ambiguities within gender relations, I do not systematically explore hegemony of other kinds: for instance, those of class or of state-local relations, which are themselves part of the multifaceted political, economic, and cultural hegemony of Western Europe and North America over Greece. I do, however, try to indicate the impact of such hegemonic relationships upon local social relations and ideas—including gender—in examining Sohos, particularly in my discussions of Sohoian "ethnic" identity, everyday sociability, and the formal dances of local civic associations.

Power

The concept of hegemony explicitly makes problematical the links between consciousness, sensory experience, and power in a way that the concept of culture, as a set of collectively shared symbols and meanings, does not. When we examine aspects of experience as intimate as those of gender and sexuality, the concept of hegemony helps alert us to the fact that the dynamics of power in the social relations of individuals who are acting and interacting as sexual beings can be extremely subtle and complex.

The fact that women in Greece sometimes withhold sex from their husbands in order to get their way has been cited, for example, as an exercise of power, albeit one that is looked upon with disfavor and culturally defined as illegitimate (Dubisch 1986:17). One might argue, however, that such an act is an exercise of power in only a very limited sense and, indeed, that it is not even fully illegitimate in the culture's terms. The phrase "to withhold sex" perfectly expresses a sexual ideology, familiar in Greece and elsewhere, that views sex as something that men obtain from women and implies that only men have real sexual needs and interests.[19] Although the first interpretation rings true ethnographically, it does not take account of either the possible physical and psychological consequences for a woman who in withholding sex from her husband also denies herself sex or the relevance of such consequences to the power that is being exercised. Thus one could interpret this ethnographic example differently, as indicating that for a woman in this society, power comes only at a price.

When a woman withholds sex from the one man who is thought to have a "right" to her body, she is doing something "wrong"; and inasmuch as control over a woman's sexuality is a sign of power, her action is not insignificant. Yet she is also, by showing herself to be chaste (that is, in control of her own sexual desires and submissive to injunctions of marital fidelity), doing something that is culturally "right." This is, at best, an ambiguous victory. In trying to get the better of a repressive system, a woman may in other ways be acquiescing to it.

This example points to the problem, noted by Dubisch (1986:19), inherent in treating power as something one "possesses" or as something that one exercises individually and intentionally over others, rather than as a process through which the contours of the "imaginable" or "realistic" come to be defined.[20] Foucault argues the point in this way:

Power is exercised, rather than possessed; it is not the "privilege," acquired or preserved, of the dominant class, but the overall effect of its strategic positions—an effect that is manifested and sometimes extended by the position of those who are dominated. (1979:16)

[19] It is echoed, for instance, in Hirschon's (1978) account of beliefs among Asia Minor refugees in urban Piraeus that men cannot physically control their sexual urges, while women can last "a thousand years."

[20] See also Bourdieu 1977:164; Giddens 1976:111–12; Lukes 1974. It is true that defining what is "imaginable" is not wholly under the control of female or male actors at the local level and is, to some extent, defined by institutions and processes outside the community (hence Herzfeld's [1985a] interest in the ways the construction of Cretan "manhood" is a response to state-local relations). To the extent that this is locally constructed, however, women suffer distinct disadvantages.

Acquiescence and resistance may be complexly intertwined, for subordinate groups are bound by the hegemony even though they may
resist it.[21] Foucault continues:

> Furthermore, this power is not exercised simply as an obligation or
> a prohibition on those who "do not have it"; it invests them, is trans-
> mitted by them and through them; it exerts pressure upon them, just
> as they themselves, in their struggle against it, resist the grip it has
> on them. (1979:16–17)

In Foucault's words, one is always "inside" the power (1978:95).

It is not only in situations of conflict that power is expressed (Giddens 1976:112). As Foucault's work on sexuality (1978) and much feminist work (see Vance 1984, for example) suggests, relations of domination can be expressed in the midst of pleasurable activities, with the
apparent consent of the dominated. The concept of hegemony compels us to recognize this consent but also to question it: What needs
and interests motivate this acquiescence? Is consent unstable? Does it
constitute a defense? A ploy? An anticipatory surrender?

These are difficult issues. But I would argue that if one wants to
explore how power is transmitted by those who do not themselves
have power, one ought to consider "practices."

Practices

Rather than look at gender "roles," I focus my attention on "practices,"
especially "sociable" social practices. Gender ideas and gender relations, which are always also power relations, are embedded in and
structure these practices.[22] Practices are the means through and the site
in which gender ideas and relations are *realized*—that is, comprehended and made real. In certain respects, this perspective resonates
with Herzfeld's (1985a) discussion of the poetics of manhood, where
the construction of manhood is shown to be an active, creative, and
reflexive process; and inasmuch as "poetics" is about "doing" and
"making" oneself (in the case of Herzfeld's study, making oneself "as
a man"), it echoes my concern with the "doing" rather than the
"thinking" of gender. Both emphases reiterate Marx's insight that in
making the world, we make ourselves (Marx 1977 [1844]: 125–48; see
also Ollman 1971:73–126). Herzfeld's depiction of "doing," however,

[21] Haug et al. offer an excellent examination of this process, though they criticize
Foucault's pessimism about the possibilities of resistance, an attitude they believe stems
from his tendency to see human beings too much as "effects of the structure" rather than
agents (Haug et al. 1987:185–230 and passim).

[22] As Flax notes, "we live in a world in which gender is a constituting social relation
and in which gender is also a relation of domination" (1987:637).

portrays it as a more entrepreneurial and innovative process than I would wish to.[23] I believe we must also keep in view the constrained nature and unchosen conditions of human beings' "making" and "doing." This is all the more important given that the social practices in the sorts of situations I examine here—*sociable* social practices, such as coffee drinking, celebrating, and dancing—are surprisingly conventionalized, even though they also, for Sohoians, connote spontaneity and freedom.

Indeed, what I find especially striking about the bodily and social practices of these contexts of sociability is the compulsory quality they often have. Because the practices of pleasure and conviviality are also the practices of reciprocal social exchange, it is difficult to opt out of them without being seen as arrogant, odd, or unsociable. In any case, opting out is not always an option. When Sohoians (and other Greeks) say "That's how we do it [*etsi to kanume*]," they admit that they are both enabled and constrained by their social forms—in this instance, by their own celebratory practices.[24] My task here is to show the ways power, submission, and pleasure come together—or come apart—in the process.

CONCEPTUALIZING THE DANCE

The growing body of anthropological work on dance in recent years constitutes an implicit grounding for this study.[25] Many of those involved in this research have argued that dance is not a self-evident universal category, but is rather a term that glosses bodily activities whose forms and meanings vary widely from one society to the next. Their efforts as ethnographers to understand dancing in relation to its specific social and cultural context have provided impetus and tools for delving beyond the seemingly obvious meanings of Greek dancing.

This study, however, unlike many of its predecessors, is relatively

---

[23] This may reflect differences in our respective fieldwork situations: he, after all, deals mostly with Cretan men, who are *given* "meaning" (that is, significance) by their fellows to the extent that they can *invent* it. Sohoian men, too, have more latitude for innovation than do Sohoian women, but they tend to express things much more conventionally, I suspect, than Glendiot men, where *hui*—personal eccentricity—is valued unusually highly (see Herzfeld 1980a). Yet I am left wondering whether Glendiot women have such scope for innovation, for creating meaning. Indeed, is this difference one of gender (of the anthropologist and/or of the anthropologists' subjects)? Of place? Or of the interpreter's interpretation and theoretical inclinations?

[24] Though this phrasing comes from Giddens (1979), whose discussion on the dual nature of social structure as enabling and constraining is abstract and morally neutral, Sohoians would recognize Simmel's more tragic vision of this duality, as I discuss below.

[25] See, for example, Blacking and Kealiinohomoku 1979; Hanna 1979, 1988; Kaeppler 1967; Lange 1975; Lomax 1968; Royce 1977; Spencer 1985.

unconcerned with defining what, as Spencer expresses it (1985:ix), "dance itself" is or does. Likewise, it is relatively unconcerned with delineating the structural or morphological features of particular dance forms or of dance more generally or with issues of classification.[26] It is concerned, rather, with dance as a medium and as a context of social action. Indeed, in its concern with the social aspects of performance, it is closer in spirit to studies of other sorts of cultural performances than to some studies of dance.[27]

I am primarily concerned with dance "as event," that is, as a "dance-event" (Kealiinohomoku 1973; Royce 1977:12; Stone 1982:1–34). This unit, the dance-event, has conceptual validity for the Sohoians, because the Greek word for "dance" (horos), like the English word, can mean a particular kind of dance, a particular instance (performance) of that kind of dance, or the event as a whole. Though it is impossible to understand Sohoian dance-events without knowing something about the forms and the social and historical connotations of particular dances, the analytical level here is that of the event. I focus therefore on performances of dances within the larger framework of the dance-event. The descriptions that I give about each dance are oriented toward the goal of providing sufficient information on the forms and connotations of the dances so that their (sometimes renegotiated) meanings in performance can be understood. Detailed descriptions or analysis of steps, body movements, or the structural aspects of individual dances are, for the most part, not directly relevant to the basic questions explored here.

I take the dance-event as a sphere of interaction that is bounded in several senses (Stone 1982:2). It is temporally and spatially bounded, to be sure; but this tells us fairly little, for all action happens somewhere and sometime. More important, the dance-event is conceptually set apart from the activities of everyday life: it is "framed."

The sense in which I use "frame" is drawn primarily from Bateson's

---

[26] On features of particular dance forms, see Lomax 1968; Singer 1974. On dance more generally, see Williams 1978. A substantial literature exists on Greek dancing, in both Greek and English, oriented to both scholarly audiences and the general public. Much of this work is concerned with the description and classification of Greek dances, though writers use a variety of criteria for these tasks (including place of origin, topological characteristics of place of origin—"mountain dances," "island dances"—morphological characteristics, and structural characteristics of dance). Some books combine description with instructions on dance steps. Examples of this literature include Crosfield 1948; Holden and Vouras 1965; Petrides 1975; Romaios 1973; Stratou 1966. In the past few years, several dance analysts have published research that attends in much more detail to issues of the social and cultural contexts of dance performance (Loutzaki 1979–80, 1985; Makreas 1979; Raftis 1985).

[27] Abu-Lughod (1986), Ortner (1978), and Schieffelin (1976) are examples of studies of other kinds of cultural performance whose concerns and approach are similar to mine.

discussion (1972a:177–93).[28] Bateson uses the term in a psychological sense, to speak of the premises that organize how communication within a particular context (temporally and spatially bounded) is to be understood.[29] The frame is metacommunicative: it communicates about communication (for example, "this is play," "this is dance"). Bateson makes a number of intriguing points about frames: that they are established and broken through both verbal and nonverbal cuing; that they are often implicit, and may be more or less conscious; and that they are labile, constantly renegotiated, and easily break down.

My understanding of the framed quality of dance also draws on the work of Simmel. His (1971a) essay, "Sociability," anticipates certain features of Bateson's formulation. But if Bateson's notion of frame is formal yet morally neutral, directed to exploring logical paradoxes of communication ("the playful nip that is not a bite"), Simmel's sociological formalism includes a poignant recognition of the tragic aspects of human interaction. Simmel proposes that sociability can be seen as the "play-form of association" in which everyday life is bracketed. As long as participants abide by the etiquette of sociability, the play frame—with its playful, exploratory, inconsequential pleasures—can be sustained. Simmel sees sociability as an almost ideal form of social life, democratic and mutually enhancing, providing for its participants a vision of what collective life could be. Yet he admits that this frame is fragile, always liable to break down in the face of cross-purposes and conflicts.

That the dance-event in Greece is a similarly ambiguous locus of social action is suggested by the discourse about dance in everyday life. Danforth, for example, in his work on dance in the Anastenaria ritual in a northern Greek community (1978), describes the contradictory associations surrounding dance among the Kostilides. Dance is "associated with happiness, joy and release," yet Kostılıdes also associate it "with suffering, punishment, and obligatory, controlled or forced action" (ibid.: 291–95 and passim). To support his claims, he cites various metaphorical meanings of "I dance" (horevo). When used transitively, it conveys control and manipulation of another: "She dances him any way she pleases [ton horevi opos theli ekini]" means "she has him at her beck and call, she has him in the palm of her hand"

[28] The idea of "frame" is used in different ways in social scientific discourse: Giddens, for example, talks about a "frame of meaning" much as Kuhn speaks of a "paradigm," or Wittgenstein a "language-game," and he describes how the hermeneutic process always involves the mediation of one frame by another (Giddens 1976:78–79 and passim).
[29] Similar notions of set-apart spheres, involving a different set of assumptions about action and meaning from that of everyday life, have been developed by others: see, for example, Boon's "privileged operational zones of a culture" (1973) and Schutz's "finite spheres" (Schutz and Luckman 1973).

(ibid.:293). It can convey suffering: "I did it and I danced [*to ekana ke horepsa*]" means "I did it and I paid the penalty" (ibid.:294). In Sohos I found similar associations and many of the same metaphorical usages, some of which may be common throughout Greece.

Other Sohoian expressions use the metaphor of dance to recall the ambiguities of collective participation. This usage emerges from the fact that dance, in Sohos as throughout Greece, has long been at the literal center of communal social life as a central activity within ritual and secular celebrations. Thus, when a young man, embroiled in a political quarrel on account of a somewhat provocative article he and his friends had printed in the local newspaper, remarked ruefully, "We entered the dance, and now we're dancing [*bikame sto horo ke tora hore-vume*]!" he was stressing that active engagement in the central affairs of communal life entails obligations that one can neither fully anticipate nor fully control. Similarly, when Sohoians proverbially counsel, "If you enter the dance, you must dance [*ama bis sto horo, prepi na horep-sis*]" or, with the wisdom of experience, "If you enter the dance, you will dance [*ama bis sto horo tha horepsis*]," they are asserting that once you enter into an activity, you may find yourself compelled or obliged to follow it through, even against your will (see also Danforth 1978:294).

Alternatively, the dance metaphor can evoke the wholly positive aspects of belonging to a collectivity. To be a participant in the dance is to be in (and with) the group; it is also to be in the thick of the meanings created. When, during discussions, people saw that I grasped what they considered a uniquely Sohoian turn of phrase or some aspect of their experience they considered knowable only by insiders, they would say, "You're inside of everything [*s'ola ise mesa*]" or "You quickly come inside the dance [*benis mani-mani sto horo*]." The dance, graphically suggesting a collectivity bound by shared knowledge, skill, and physical connection, is considered an apt metaphor for the community itself.

"Entering the dance," therefore, whether metaphorically or literally, is an inherently ambiguous experience, one that promises both pleasures and problems. Just as dance is used metaphorically to talk about the ambiguities of social action and experience in everyday life, so is talk about actual dancing preoccupied with these same ambiguities. Dance is associated with control by others ("being danced") but also with freedom; suffering but also release; sociability but also competition; display but also exposure; sensuality but also the potential for loss of status; power but also vulnerability; expressions of individuality but also of social accountability. And the dance-event itself—that is, the ensemble of practices that compose it, including feasting, talking, singing, and dancing—is a place where these themes are expressed and explored.

Although it is essential to take account of the associations surrounding "dance" as a cultural category (as a "frame" in its broadest sense), very different kinds of dance-events do exist, and each constitutes a different frame or set of premises. Sohoians distinguish between "formal exhibitions" (*sovares ekdhilosis*, such as certain moments in the wedding celebrations) and dancing as a kind of "entertainment" (*dhiaskedhasi*). Sohoians dance in a variety of contexts, only some of which I examine in this book: at weddings, during Carnival (both in the street and in local restaurants), during the summer celebration (*paniyiri*) of the feast day of the town's patron saints, at formal dances sponsored by local civic associations, and occasionally—spontaneously—at picnics, nameday celebrations (of younger people), excursions to a restaurant, and so forth. Though each type of dance-event may have specific rules and ideas associated with it, there is a great deal of overlap; dancing at even the most informal occasion, for example, involves a kind of etiquette. Nevertheless, despite the very real differences in ambience that these conventionalized categories of frame ("serious" dance versus "entertainment") usually imply, they cannot be said to determine either what happens, or how it gets interpreted (Moore 1976).

Finally, dance-events can involve frames within frames. A person who performs a dance within a dance-event that is considered inappropriate for that kind of dance-event can attempt to transform the meaning of his or her act by reframing it. Lakis, the man described at the beginning of this chapter, who performs a *zeibekiko* (a dance for "tough guys") at a formal dance, defuses it through parody. He makes a communication ("I'm being ironic") about a communication ("I'm showing I'm a tough guy"). Yet, as I will show in Chapter 6, whether he is "understood" or "misunderstood" is by no means *simply* a matter of communication.

CONCEPTUALIZING THE BODY

I see the human body not merely as a natural object but as one socially and historically constituted. This idea animates most recent work on the body, however theoretically divergent it otherwise appears.[30] Recognizing that it was only by attending to human engagement in "sensuous practical activity" that he could hope to understand "real, corporeal man," Marx was the first to suggest and to theorize a dialectical

[30] Recent theoretical work on the body includes Bourdieu 1977; Douglas 1973; Foucault 1978, 1979; Gallagher and Laqueur 1987; Haug et al. 1987; Jackson 1983; Martin 1987; Scarry 1985; Turner 1984.

relationship between the body and the social and natural worlds; to insist, in other words, that the body acting upon the world is, in turn, acted upon by the world the body has helped to create.[31]

Marx himself saw this dialectic mediated most fundamentally by human labor. Subsequent writers, however, have explored this dialectic in terms of a much broader compass. Foucault and those taking up lines of inquiry he initiated trace "the history of the body" by investigating the historical development of discourses and institutions as seemingly disparate as sexuality, psychoanalysis, medicine, and prisons. Feminists look at the representations of bodies, particularly women's bodies, within myriad discourses—art, advertising, and popular romances, to name just a few—and ask how these shape both how women experience their bodies and how others treat them as embodied beings. These writers insist that discourses and institutions impinge as powerfully as does the labor process upon how the body is *lived*. But the common ground shared by Marx and many of these writers is a dual concern with the ideological and the material aspects or, in Foucaultian terms, the discourses and the techniques of the lived body.

Rich and provocative as this work is, the body it investigates is almost always (and often implicitly) the "Western" body. Yet the problem of the body has been pondered by anthropologists, too. Probably the earliest meditation on the ways each society literally shapes the human body is Mauss' 1935 essay, "Techniques of the Body." Cataloguing the startling cross-cultural variations in the bodily techniques for all manner of activities from swimming to sex, Mauss emphasizes how powerfully each society inscribes itself on the body of each of its members, and how resistant the body can be to altering the techniques it "knows." These techniques are not necessarily consciously taught; rather, they are shaped by and express the "habitus," a notion Mauss invents but does not really develop.

The notion of habitus is central to Bourdieu's *Outline of a Theory of Practice*. Much more than an ethnographic study of the Kabyle of Algeria, the book is a polemical disquisition on the question of human agency, addressed as much to Continental philosophers as to anthropologists. Bourdieu is not renowned for succinct clarity, but it is worth struggling through at least one of his labyrinthine definitions of "habitus" to get a sense of what he means by the term. Habitus, he tells us, are:

> systems of durable, transposable *dispositions*, structured structures predisposed to function as structuring structures, that is, as princi-

[31] Scarry (1985) brilliantly elucidates the implications of this philosophical position.

ples of the generation and structuring of practices and representations which can be objectively "regulated" and "regular" without in
any way being the product of obedience to rules . . . (1977:72)

The term "disposition" signals the special place the body occupies in
Bourdieu's elaboration of habitus.[32] Dispositions are "cultivated"
through interaction with "a whole symbolically structured environment," and these "cultivated dispositions" become "inscribed in the
body schema and in schemes of thought" (ibid.:15). Bourdieu cites the
Kabyle "sense of 'honour,' " a phrase that nicely emphasizes the dual
location of honor in the mind and in the flesh. In Bourdieu's conception, mastery of the body is essentially the successful in-corporation
(literally, the taking into the body) of particular social meanings, inculcated through various bodily disciplines oriented to such mundane
practices as "standing, sitting, looking, speaking, walking" (ibid.). It
also involves the seemingly trivial mastery of details of dress, bearing,
and manners. Mastering his or her body, the child develops the skills
to act in and on the world, a dialectical process that Bourdieu calls "the
appropriating by the world of a body thus enabled to appropriate the
world" (ibid.:89). Bourdieu recognizes that this is a gendered process
or, phrased differently, a process of gendering, as well.

  Bourdieu's habitus entails a theory of embodiment. He argues that
the way the body is conceived, used, and experienced necessarily reflects the practical and symbolic structures of the outside (natural, social, and political) environment. An example from closer to home may
clarify this formulation. As I was completing this book, I had a discussion with my aunt, a sociologist and dean of nursing, in which I tried
to explain the idea of embodiment I was using. "You mean, like my
'Methodist feet'?" she asked. She had been raised a strict Methodist in
a small town in rural Ohio: dancing, like drinking, was regarded by
her parents and the church community as a sinful activity. Her older
brother broke this prohibition when he returned home from his first
year at a Methodist college having learned how to dance the jitterbug.
Her parents never objected to dancing after that: if Bob was doing it,
and had learned it *there*, maybe it wasn't really so bad. But though she
has always loved music, my aunt has never been able to overcome the
prohibitions so thoroughly drummed into her during her childhood.
Her spirit is willing but her flesh is not: her clumsy "Methodist feet"
just won't dance.

[32] As he explains in a footnote, "disposition" can designate "the *result of an organizing
action*; . . . it also designates *a way of being*, a *habitual state* (especially of the body), and in
particular, a *predisposition, tendency, propensity* or *inclination*" (Bourdieu 1977:214; emphasis in original).

In arguing that the ideas and relations of the world "outside" the body permeate our senses and generate "a certain subjective experience" (1977:87), Bourdieu's ideas of habitus and embodiment share much with Williams' (1977) description of hegemony as "the shaping perceptions of ourselves and our world." They also bear many similarities to Giddens' (1979) idea of "practical consciousness." "Ideology" or "culture," such writers stress, is not only in our heads; it is—and perhaps more profoundly—in our bodies too.

Here the problem of reflexivity arises: can human beings become aware of the social construction of their bodies? Bourdieu suggests that they cannot. For him, the significance of the human body in the reproduction of habitus is precisely this: that its sociality is masked. The endless techniques of the body, practically mastered and mutely enacted, are rarely objects of verbal elaboration. Rather, the principles thus embodied are placed "beyond the grasp of consciousness and hence, cannot be touched by voluntary, deliberate transformation, cannot even be made explicit" (1977:94).

I would agree that individuals cannot become fully aware of the social and historical contingency of their bodies and selves; but I would also argue that there are certain contexts in which individuals may become more reflexively conscious than usual of their bodies. The stereotypical, and often self-consciously and playfully exaggerated, postures of power, submission, and pleasure that celebrants assume in dance-events are evidence of this kind of reflexivity. Probably more than in everyday life, the celebrant in the dance-event is acutely aware of the dual aspects of embodiment: that she or he "has" a body, and that she or he "is" a body (Turner 1984:1). This is why it is necessary to approach dancing not only as a "spectacle" in which dancing bodies are "read" as "signs" but also as a process of intersubjectivity. Dance must be considered from the actor's point of view, as both performance and experience.

Yet if we wish to understand how these often stylized postures that celebrants assume help to sustain (though also, occasionally, to challenge) particular gender ideas and relations, we may need to look beyond intellectual or cognitive processes. Ritualized embodiments may have powerful effects for the individual not so much because they enable reflexivity but because they are engrossing. Although assuming certain postures may be for some participants humiliating or painful, since the social relations they embody are hierarchical or oppressive, they are often at the same time associated with events that are sensorially and socially intense and symbolically valued.

DECIPHERING BODIES

How does one get at the meanings of nonverbal forms, especially bodily forms? This is a problem familiar to anthropologists and others concerned with nonverbal forms of action or with implicit meanings in any kind of human activity. It is, moreover, a problem partially created by the very logocentricity of Western discourse. Yet until scholars are able to musick about music and dance about dance as convincingly as they talk about talk, they will find themselves compelled to convey through words what they believe their anthropological subjects are expressing, verbally and nonverbally.

In formulating my analysis, I watched, listened, and joined in the dance. In this text, I have focused especially on the conventionalized social and bodily practices of various dance-events and on conventionalized poses, postures, and gestures. I have tried to discover indigenous codes for reading the body, while acknowledging that meaning does not lie *in* the body. I have looked for patterns of form and interaction, noted typifications, made inferences. My interpretations of these poses and practices are grounded in my knowledge of Sohoian everyday life.

Yet this text is also an interpretation of Sohoian interpretations, that is, of Sohoian verbal accounts. I did not initially anticipate the importance that words about dancing would have in my analysis. I expected both more and less talk than I actually got. I expected more in the sense that I initially imagined that every dance-event would include a running commentary among the spectators on the performances as they were occurring and an abundance of narratives (in the form of gossip) afterward. In fact, collecting such commentary *during* the event was extremely difficult, if largely for physical and logistical reasons: the deafening reverberations of amplified musical instruments and the constant murmur of the crowd of excited celebrants deterred eavesdropping. I could see people watching dancers, but I could seldom hear their comments. After an event I could elicit commentary mostly when something rather exceptional had occurred. Sohoians preferred dancing to talking about dancing; and from the perspective of that vivid moment when we were "in the dance" together, talk did seem superfluous. I struggled for a long time to figure out ways to ask questions about dancing that were not banal or obvious.

But if the Sohoians did not always give me words in the way I expected, their words said a great deal more than I initially imagined they could. The verbal accounts I gathered about dancing, which provide much of my evidence for interpreting it, include everything from paralinguistic utterances ("*A pa pa!*") to long narratives. Language is used to construct meanings about dance in many ways: in this book I look at grammatical constructions, metaphors, verbs, adjectives, paralinguistic retorts, and a variety of types of narratives. The narratives include descriptions of rules and ideals, gossip, plausible explanations, and longer stories: idealized accounts of custom, specific dancing incidents or events remembered from the past, and personalized reflections about dancing.

In using these accounts of meaning, I have become aware of the importance of keeping in mind the questions, Meaning *for* whom? *About* whom? When a person dances, he or she can try to negotiate the dance's meanings, but there are limits to what can be negotiated. The negotiation of meaning is ultimately about power. Multiple voices certainly exist, but these voices, since they belong to differently positioned individuals, do not all have equal power to define what embodied actions publicly mean. In a number of places in the text I have used a dialogical mode to indicate the plurality of voices that argue with each other. Such a format allows me to stress the social bases of interpretation, and the repercussions for both the authors and objects of such interpretations; " 'untrue' interpretations may become true by virtue of their consequences" (Karp and Kendall 1982:265).

The analysis begins with Sohoian actions and Sohoian accounts of what they and others do and feel when they dance. For as Karp and Kendall insist,

> The first datum of the field anthropologist is the expressed consciousness of the members of a society. Only by understanding the accounts people give of themselves can an anthropologist follow through and show them to be "false," "inadequate," or "incomplete" in some way. The notion of false consciousness, which we think stands at the very center of anthropological analyses of behavior, depends upon prior discovery of forms of consciousness that exist in a given social formation. The lessons that should be drawn from this are obvious. First, if social analysts take seriously native accounts and try to reconcile them with higher-order explanations, they must also surely have to come to grips with the shifting sand beneath their own feet—i.e., they have to face the very real possibility that the meanings they assign to others' behaviors are influenced by factors outside their *own* consciousness. (1982:268)

I argue that in dancing and in the discourse which surrounds it, Sohoians express important social identities and relationships; they also explore many of the ambiguities and tensions in them, though not always through words. This study portrays Sohoian acts and intepretations as they are mediated by my own anthropologically rooted understandings: one frame of meaning is mediated by another (Giddens 1976). Like the Sohoians' understandings, mine are also contingent, interested, and historically grounded.

THOUGH an obviously ethnographic endeavor, this book does not pretend to be a comprehensive ethnography in the traditional sense. Rather, it explores issues of gendered action and engendered experience by focusing on one circumscribed, if complex, type of context: the dance-event. The social construction through which one becomes a gendered, sexualized person occurs, nonetheless, in its trivial and dramatic ways, *someplace, at some time*. My discussion, therefore, begins "here," *in* and *with* Sohos, a community located in space, time, and various discourses, which I came to know at a particular moment.

CHAPTER ONE

Place, Distinctions, Identities

> The radical challenge for interpretive ethnography [is] how to represent the embedding of richly described local cultural worlds in larger impersonal systems of political economy. This would not be such a problem if the local cultural unit was portrayed, as it usually has been in ethnography, as an isolate with outside forces of market and state impinging upon it. What makes representation challenging and a focus of experimentation is the perception that the "outside forces" are an integral part of the construction and constitution of the "inside," the cultural unit itself, and must be so registered, even at the most intimate levels of cultural process.
>
> —George Marcus and Michael Fischer,
> *Anthropology as Cultural Critique*

THE JOURNEY from Thessaloniki, Greece's northern capital, to Sohos begins from one of the cavernous one-room bus depots scattered about the city. The depot for Sohos borders on the ruins of Byzantine ramparts near Vardari. There are few places to sit, and unless it is raining most people stand outside, leaning against the glass window panes, a day's worth of shopping in plastic bags at their feet, waiting anxiously for their bus to be called. Everyone listens carefully; whoever misses the garbled shout is pushed aside by a stampede of passengers rushing to get to the bus first and find a seat. Any unfortunate stragglers have to stand up, holding on for dear life to the leather straps suspended from the ceiling. Almost forty miles away, Sohos is the end of the line.

Upon leaving the station, the bus turns onto a main northbound road, lined with garages and auto-parts warehouses, passes through the working-class suburbs in the industrial outskirts (where many Sohoians who have migrated now live), and gradually climbs a low hill. Once over it, the bus descends into a wide plain, eventually reaching the first large plains town. Here many people get off, and a few get on. The bus continues, hurtling across the plain until, abruptly, gears shift noisily and the bus begins a steep climb.

Very quickly, you lose sight of the plains, finding yourself sucked into endless folds of a rising plateau that is cratered, rocky, creviced, and eerily desolate, without a sign of life. Only dusty green scrub, wild herbs, and a few forlorn trees grow on this land. Occasionally, you catch sight of an enormous concrete house, a half-built villa, standing far across an empty valley. As the bus nears the top of the plateau the road becomes more level, and villages, small clusters of white set against the dark curves of the wooded mountains, can be seen in the distance.

After a while, having passed through fields of tobacco, the bus reaches some of these small villages. They bear idyllic names like "Five Fountains" (*Pende Vrises*), "Little Hill" (*Lofiskos*) and "Virtue" (*Areti*), but they are muddy and far from picturesque. They appear to be in mid-construction. Tiny bungalows whose front gardens brim with tobacco seedlings draped in plastic are bordered by square, half-finished concrete buildings; on the road in front sit mud-splattered tractors. Many of these villages are, in fact, relatively new. They were built for Greek-speaking refugees (*prosfiyes*) from Asia Minor, victims of the Lausanne and Sèvres treaties that ended years of war between Greece and Turkey and marked the final demise of the Ottoman Empire (Stavrianos 1958:589–92). The refugees, many of them penniless and landless, arrived in Macedonia from 1923 onward and were resettled on lands either completely virgin or near to the hamlets and cultivated fields left behind by Muslims, then considered to be "Turks," who were themselves being "repatriated." Except for the proprietors' surnames painted on the windows of the few shops in each village, there is no obvious sign that one village is composed totally of Pontii (from the Black Sea region), a second totally of Thracians, and a third, half of Pontii and half of Sarakatsani shepherds who have left their former transhumant way of life (see Campbell 1964). Nor, in villages that predated the refugees' arrival, is there any sign of the old Turkish names— such as Rendina and Besikia—that are still heard in Sohoian conversations. The past has been erased from the visible landscape.

As the bus finally approaches Sohos, its difference from the villages that precede it is striking. The bus whizzes past more fields of tobacco, then fruit orchards, close on either side—cherries, apricots, peaches, apples, pears—and then on the right is a large well-laid field where the Soccer Association plays its matches. Just further on is a tiny manicured park with a marble war memorial standing tall amid the greenery; across the road (marking the boundary between the town and the wild) is a shrine to Saint Christopher, patron of travelers, taxi-drivers, and truckers. Next comes a huge Alpine-style house with gingerbread shutters. This is bordered by a concrete two-story building, whose first floor is the town's newest restaurant (*kendro*), sometimes rented for large celebrations. Past another *kendro*, the Vendetta, and more concrete structures, to the right and shaded by one large tree, is a vast, open tank of water. It is usually visited by housewives doing chores and horses who are thirsty, but on January 6, the day of Epiphany, it is surrounded by children who jump in, hoping to retrieve the crucifix that the town's priest has cast in the water. Townspeople call this dusty and nearly treeless bit of road the Eksohika, the countryside, and on winter Sundays, and almost daily in summer, teenagers and couples walk up and down it for an evening stroll, or *volta*.[1]

Beyond, to the left, a gasoline pump announces a small garage, and after that the road forks. The right-hand fork descends southeastward, out of town, skirting just above a bleak and windowless ladies' garment factory, the major employer of local women and girls, and just below an equally austere high school. The left-hand fork—the main road—drops, then rises. As the bus climbs steadily upward, passing muddy tractors parked here and there, each with a string of blue-beads draped across the front fender to protect it from the evil eye, it passes a tiny playground, houses, and metal-welders' workshops. You may glimpse, tucked amid the concrete, a fence made of tall, thickly set wooden stakes encircling a courtyard, but all that can be seen of this old-style house are the cantilevered wooden beams holding up the ceiling of the open, second-story veranda. Beyond are a small corner grocery, more half-finished concrete buildings, and a pharmacy. Here, near the center, if the weather is decent and it is not afternoon siesta time (*mesimeri*), townspeople in the streets turn to watch the oncoming bus.[2] Neatly dressed housewives rest their overflowing plastic bags on the roadside, white-aproned proprietors look out of their shops, and dark-kerchiefed old women—the ones Sohoians wryly dub "the dresses" (*i fustanuses*), after the high-waisted, ankle-length smocks they always wear—lean out from their doorways. They search swiftly for a relative or friend returning home from "below," and they wave with delight when the person is spotted. The bus passes through another crossroads, whose right fork (the one not taken) leads into the old market—its tiny wooden stalls with corrugated iron roofs perched precariously on the sloping road—and reaches a short block in which the ubiquitous nondescript concrete buildings flank prettier wood-and-plaster structures of the 1930s. Going past Varvara's Boutique, a butcher shop, and a coffeehouse, the bus finally pulls into the central square and parks at the edge of its wide paved surface in front of a majestic white church.

[1] Until the 1950s, no houses were built beyond the plane tree by the tank; the Eksohika was flanked only by gardens, fields, and the small park and war memorial.
[2] *Mesimeri* is a midday lunch and subsequent rest period between 1:30 and 5:00 P.M.

Making a Living

Unlike many Greek communities studied by anthropologists, Sohos is neither tiny nor remote.[3] With a year-round population of about 3,500, it dwarfs the much smaller villages that form a necklace around it.[4] And at least six times a day, the nearly forty miles separating Sohos from the city below is traversed by public buses and group taxis in little more than an hour.

In part because of these reasons, Sohos does not fit neatly into the familiar rural/urban dichotomy. It seems an awkward size: too large to call a village, too small to call a city. And like many Greek communities, even more so since the devastation caused by a major earthquake in 1978 and subsequent rebuilding, its architectural landscape is a bewildering hodge-podge of old and new. The busy market is cluttered by tractors yet intermittently edged by three-story blocks of flats.

The town's position as a commercial and administrative center within the region is a legacy of Ottoman rule. From a surviving Ottoman legal document dated 1695, we know that Sohos was a large estate (*timar*) "belonging" to a Muslim living in Constantinople.[5] Its inhabitants, mostly Christian tenant farmer-laborers (*dhuli*), made a meager living cultivating grain and vineyards and raising livestock. It was probably around this time that a handful of the local inhabitants, along with some adventurous souls who migrated from Epirus and Halkidiki, began to seek their fortunes as traveling merchants and caravanners (*kiradjidhes*), transporting merchandise on pack animals— mules, horses, oxen, even camels—across the paths that criss-crossed

[3] Anthropologists studying Greek society have generally chosen to work in very small villages. The fieldsites of du Boulay (1974), Friedl (1962), Herzfeld (1980a), and Kenna (1976) all had fewer than 400 inhabitants, and many other examples could be cited. Sometimes a community was selected specifically for its remoteness (see, for example, du Boulay 1974:4). The selection of small, remote villages—a choice that continued even after the majority of Greece's population had migrated to the cities and abroad—seems to have expressed both theoretical priorities (the desire to record "traditional" or "dying" ways of life) and methodological proclivities (toward holistic studies of face-to-face communities using participant-observation) characteristic of anthropology as a discipline.

[4] Approximately 1,500 Sohoians now live and work in Thessaloniki. These individuals usually retain their property in Sohos, including houses, which remain locked up and may be used only during brief visits, typically in the summer and during Carnival, and fields, which are rented out to resident farmers. Townspeople often refer to an individual who has left the town and lives in Thessaloniki as a *ksenos*, or "outsider." The populations of surrounding communities range from 100 to 2,000, but most are around 300–600.

[5] Strictly speaking, land could belong only to the Sultan, Allah's representative on earth. However, the Sultan customarily awarded parcels of land—that is, the right to enjoy its "fruits"—to men who had served the Ottoman Empire in some way, usually militarily.

Macedonia, connecting Constantinople with Central Europe (Stoi-anovich 1960). Not all were successful, but out of these trading activities an indigenous Christian merchant class gradually emerged, and Sohos became a thriving market town (Cousinery 1831; Leake 1835).

By the latter part of the nineteenth century, this local merchant elite controlled virtually all local commerce and a good deal of the local agricultural land. Members of this elite group, along with the much smaller number of Ottoman landowners, were known as the *kojabad-jidhes*, the elders or the influential men, or the *arhondes*, the local notables. Cultivating a strong, Western-oriented Greek identity, the Christian elites sent their sons to be educated in Constantinople and Thessaloniki, and sometimes even further afield, to Alexandria and Odessa, for business. From their ranks were drawn the *kapnomesites* (tobacco middlemen), who from the latter part of the century to the Second World War controlled the town's highly lucrative tobacco trade.

Since the devastations of the 1940s, the postwar migration of a third of the town's population to Thessaloniki, Germany, Sweden and America, and the gradual rising of a new middle class, the identity of those in the marketplace has changed. The sons of wealthy merchants can still be found, but others have joined them. Nowadays about 120 households are involved in commerce.[6] This category includes everyone from small artisans, such as the welders, tailors, and the badly crippled cobbler, to modestly successful grocers, butchers, bakers, and barbers, to skilled workers, such as the electricians and plumbers, to the entrepreneur who owns the Alpine villa, the gasoline station, and a number of other business ventures.

Others engaged in nonentrepreneurial pursuits work in the marketplace as well. A small but significant number work as professionals (a dentist, solicitor, doctor, magistrate, and several social workers), as low-level civil servants or clerks (in the post office, town hall, police station, tax offices, public utilities offices, and the local branch of the Agricultural Bank), and as teachers in Sohos' primary and secondary schools. This group comprises educated Sohoians, outsiders who have married native Sohoians, and young professionals obliged to work several years in the provinces before they can be considered for coveted urban posts. The Socialist government's efforts to decentralize social services will no doubt strengthen the town's role as a regional center in the future: during the period of my fieldwork, a day center for the elderly (see figure 1) and a newly built nursery school opened, and a

---

[6] According to rough figures provided by the town hall secretary in 1984. All information rendered in the present tense refers to the situation during the period of my fieldwork between 1983 and 1985, unless otherwise stated.

1. A group of Sohoian women, most of them dressed in the distinctive ankle-length smock (*fustan*), pose for a photograph in the town's new day center for the elderly.

center for adult education (Laiki Epimorfosi, literally, "People's Education") was reopened. When I visited the town in August 1989, a small hospital and a day-care center had been completed, as well.

Although the marketplace gives Sohos its distinctively Balkan atmosphere, the majority of its inhabitants have always worked the land. Approximately 400 of the 850 working households make their living primarily from farming: 170 of these grow mainly tobacco and some wheat and barley, and the remaining 230 concentrate on wheat and barley. Nearly all of these families cultivate a collection of small, scattered plots, some inherited from the smallholdings of the husband's (and occasionally, the wife's) parents, some acquired in the land redistribution schemes of the 1930s, and some rented (or sometimes bought) from Sohoians who have left the town for Thessaloniki or abroad. About 100 families are said to live primarily off the cultivation of their fruit orchards (apples, peaches, pears, apricots, cherries, quinces) and nut trees (walnuts, almonds, chestnuts), which flourish in the cool mountainous climate. Another 100 families are involved in the raising of livestock. About half of these raise dairy cattle in barns at the bottom of town, where the mountain slope begins to ease into a gently rolling plateau, and the other half herd sheep and goats that graze on the steep mountainsides above the town. The densely wooded mountains also provide a livelihood for about eighty men employed by the Forestry Cooperative. They cut and transport the wood that fuels the woodstoves most Sohoian households use to cook on and to keep at least one room warm in the cold Macedonian winters. In addition, there are a dozen or so fishermen and fishmongers, who catch fish in the two nearby lakes and sell them to both local and Thessaloniki markets. Finally, nearly forty families are supported by men involved in construction work, a number made possible by the enormous amount of rebuilding required after the 1978 earthquake.

What an individual (or more precisely, a household) does for a living is not the only basis upon which Sohoian distinctions rest, but it is an important one. Certainly the fundamental distinction in this complex communal division of labor is that between the *epanghelmaties*, the businesspeople and professionals—or, more colloquially, "the people of the market" (*tis aghoras*)—and those who make a living from the land, the *agrotes* (farmers) and *voski* (shepherds). These are regarded as class distinctions by many Sohoians, for though all businesspeople are by no means rich and not all farmers are poor, it is nonetheless true that the wealthiest Sohoian families are the merchants, the entrepreneurs running small productive enterprises, and those involved in truck transport and that the members of the poorest families typically combine family farming on smallholdings and rented fields with working for wages. Although the system of political clientelism, among other things, makes it impossible to correlate class position with political affiliation, it is true that those "of the market" tend, as a group, to support the Right, and that those identified as "the powerful" (*i meghali*) tend to belong to the commercial class.

These rough statistics are useful in suggesting both the diversity of the local economy and the emphasis on particular occupations. But they are in another sense misleading. One major problem is that a household is categorized on the basis of the husband's occupation alone. Although this is consistent with the way Sohoians regard male and female labor, it obscures the considerable involvement of girls and women, both historically and as a consequence of so-called modernization, in waged work outside the house.

Like their brothers, who worked not only the family fields but also, if they could be spared, made charcoal or cultivated other people's fields in other villages, the daughters of peasant-laborer households have for generations worked for wages before marriage. Until the 1950s a girl often left school (when it was available and could be afforded) after one or two years, and became a full-time worker from the age of seven or eight. She continued working, usually in a work group composed, for propriety's sake, entirely of girls and young women, until her engagement or, at the latest, her marriage, when she left in order to "look after her house." Sohoians generally concur that it was then considered highly inappropriate for a married woman to work for wages, and a sign of greatest poverty. The wages she earned were used both to support her natal family and to enable her to purchase items for her trousseau.[7] Until the 1940s most Sohoian girls found employment sorting and threading tobacco leaves in one of the town's half-dozen tobacco workshop-warehouses (*kapnomaghaza*). Some also left home for several months every autumn to work in small, all-female work groups (*parees*, or "companies"), always accompanied by a male chaperone, picking and sorting tobacco on the agricultural estates one to two days' journey to the east.

With the demise of the *kapnomaghaza* during the war and the postwar introduction of tractors and combines, the cultivation, processing, and sale of tobacco increasingly became the concern of individual households. Though households related by kinship might reciprocally help each other (as had been the custom among households growing small amounts of tobacco in the past), they rarely hired extra laborers. Sohoian girls from poor families were forced to seek other kinds of waged employment to supplement family earnings. Many took domestic work as housekeepers and nannies, a few working for the wealthier Sohoian families but most for the swelling ranks of the urban middle class in Thessaloniki and Athens. Other girls left for the cities to take whatever they could find: usually production-line jobs in the nascent manufacturing sector, or janitorial or menial work. The dearth of jobs within the community for unmarried girls profoundly troubled the townspeople. Many were jubilant when, soon after the fall of the military dictatorship in 1974, their mayor, Grekos, managed to persuade a large ladies' garment-production operation to locate in the town. Like virtually all garment-production operations in the area, its work force is all female. Owned by a German firm, it is known in Sohos simply as "the German [factory]" (To Yermaniko).

Nowadays it is not only unmarried girls who work for wages. With rising inflation and ever higher material expectations for their children, and with their generally reduced role in agricultural production, an increasing number of married women work for wages as well. Some married women describe themselves as temporary workers, working just long enough to earn the money for a particular purchase: a wash-

[7] In the past, a girl would have used some of her wages to buy primarily raw materials, such as fabric and thread, which she then transformed by weaving, crocheting, and sewing; today, working girls often buy items that other women have woven, crocheted, or sewn.

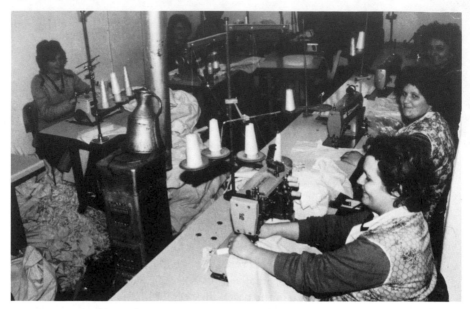

2. A family-run ladies' garment workshop, in which two married sisters, their brother's wife, a second brother, and his wife and two daughters work together sewing ladies' trousers for a contractor in Thessaloniki. The four siblings and their spouses and children also work cooperatively in raising tobacco and dairy cows.

ing machine, perhaps, or English lessons for a child. But others have been working for many years.

The majority of the town's female wage earners work in garment production—cutting, sewing, and ironing clothing destined for sale in the northern parts of Europe—in workshops in Sohos and in surrounding villages (see figure 2). The size of the Yermaniko's work force fluctuated during the period of my fieldwork from 70 to 150; an additional handful of small workshops, some of them allegedly operating outside, or just barely within, the margins of the law, employed from 5 to 20 female workers each. The working conditions in many of these operations, particularly the Yermaniko, are reputed to be extremely stressful. But after a short-lived strike for better pay and conditions at that operation was brusquely put down in 1980–81, female workers had become reluctant to voice their complaints publicly.

The remainder of those involved in garment production work at home. These are primarily young women caring for small children or, occasionally, an elderly parent. They sew at their own machines in their "spare time" and are paid by the piece. This kind of contractual work is notoriously insecure, poorly paid, and usually lacks any pen-sion or insurance benefits, but women who want or need the income have few alternatives. Outside of this kind of sewing work, or perhaps crocheting or weaving items for other women's houses and trousseaus as a good number of older housewives do, only a few other sources of (nonprofessional) waged employment for female workers exist. These jobs are generally occasional or seasonal—for instance, shelling walnuts and almonds, packing fish and frog's legs, or picking fruit.

The implications and social meanings of these and other female labors will be explored in the next chapter. But the invisibility of these labors in the public reckoning of what people do for a living also figures in a second source of statistical distortion: the fact that Sohoian households are frequently engaged in several kinds of productive activity simultaneously. However categorical the distinction between those "of the market" and those who work the land as a basis of social identities, the distinction in practice is more difficult to sustain. As was remarked in an article in the local monthly newspaper, with perhaps only slight hyperbole: "The almost nonexistent economy of Sohos has transformed all Sohoians into petty traders."

The case of the Serrenidhis household (as it was in 1984) illustrates the point. Serafim and Litsa live in a neighborhood on the northeastern edge of town, in a narrow and strangely trapezoidal two-story house. The first floor was inherited from Serafim's parents, and the second consists of two tiny apartments (sharing a single bathroom), built by the couple for their two sons, Petros and Pavlos, and the sons' future brides. Serafim and Litsa come from poor families who had smallholdings on which they cultivated tobacco and wheat. Since their marriage, they have worked together raising tobacco (see figure 3). Some of their fields belong to them, but most are rented from other Sohoians who no longer farm. For most of the year they live on money borrowed from the Agricultural Bank. They sell their produce to the Tobacco Cooperative at a price fixed by the government.

Tobacco work begins with the early spring planting and lasts until the early winter, when the dried leaves are bundled. The most exhausting period is the summer cultivation. In addition to working in the fields, Litsa does all the housework, including baking homemade bread twice a week. In the winter, she supplements the family purse by joining a small work group of neighborhood women who meet occasionally to shell walnuts or almonds. A long afternoon's work brings in about 500 drachmas (in 1984, about four dollars).

Although the two sons "grew up with the tobacco," for several years they lived for long periods with Serafim's relatives in Thessaloniki, working as manual laborers in the construction boom after the 1978 earthquake. Petros finished his military service in 1982 and, now back

3. The ethnographer pays a visit to a farming family relaxing after a morning of labor in their tobacco fields.

in Sohos, helps his parents with the tobacco whenever he can. He also spends a good deal of time setting up the furniture-finishing work-shop, located in the marketplace, that his parents recently bought for him and his brother.

Petros is engaged to Ellie, who works in the Yermaniko and who plans to continue working there after their marriage until their first child is born. Pavlos, now in the middle of his military service, became engaged to Mara, then seventeen, on Christmas Day, 1983. Pavlos had been involved with another girl, but Litsa disapproved: "She was just 'for the house.' She doesn't know tobacco, she goes to high school, she wants everything ready-made. She wasn't for us. I told my son I can't do the tobacco all by myself." Litsa is pleased with Pavlos' final choice: "She knows tobacco, she's from a good family, and she's never been mixed up with any other man." Mara comes from an unusually tight-knit extended family. Her father is one of five brothers and sisters who, with their families, continue to share the work of tobacco cultivation, raise dairy cattle, and cooperatively run a small ladies' garment work-shop in the basement of the patrimonial home (shown in figure 2, above). Mara works there as a seamstress.

Serafim and Litsa hope that they and the two young couples will continue to work together to survive economically. Serafim favors keeping strict separate accounts for each family's expenses, but he believes, too, that they should "help each other," with Ellie continuing her factory job, Mara helping Litsa with the tobacco, and the men working together in the fields and the workshop. "A little from here, a little from there," Litsa says, "and we'll manage. The main thing is to be loving and to help each other."

SOHOS IN THE MACEDONIAN CONTEXT

The Sohoians' complex identity as a community, as well as the ethnic and political distinctions that divide them, are consequences of Sohos' position in Macedonia and all that this has meant historically. From the fifteenth century until 1913 Macedonia was part of the Ottoman Empire, and it was only after a bitter and protracted struggle that this part of Macedonia was subsequently annexed to Greece. Under Ottoman rule Sohos was predominantly an Orthodox Christian community, yet at the time of the compulsory "exchange of populations" between Greece and Turkey in 1923 over a hundred families, about a fifth of the population, were forced to give up their homes and lands and "repatriate" to a Turkish "homeland" they had never seen.

The Christian inhabitants who remained behind, and their descendants, are today both numerically and culturally dominant in Sohos. They call themselves *dopii*, "people of this place." They say that they are "Macedonians" (Makedhones) or sometimes, more pointedly, "Greek-Macedonians" (Ellinomakedhones). Despite the fact that many of the older people know both Vulgarika—the local term for Macedonian, which is a Slavic language—and Turkika, they distinguish themselves from what they call the "Turkish-speaking" (Turkofoni) and "Bulgarian-speaking" (Vulgarofoni) refugees resettled after 1923 in the surrounding villages.[8] And they vigorously contest the intimation that they are anything but Greek.

The vehemence of this claim is striking, especially when juxtaposed to the polyglot and often syncretic character of local tradition, and underlines the success of the Greek authorities since annexation in establishing Greek linguistic and cultural hegemony in the town. The defensive tone with which I usually heard the claim made, moreover, is a reminder of the continuing political sensitivity of the issue and the importance placed on making sure that potentially powerful outsiders do not get the "wrong" impression. But the claim is also, in a certain sense, "true." Its paradoxical truth is the trace of an even older hege-

---

[8] Sohoians distinguish Vulgarika from the language that Bulgarians speak.

mony, and a reflection of the changing meanings of ethnic labels from Ottoman times to the present.

Until the end of the eighteenth century, linguistic distinctions were much less relevant than those of religion and wealth. According to the Ottoman *milyet* system, the Sultan's subjects were divided into religious communities—Muslims, Christians, Jews—and though non-Muslims faced certain disadvantages, each *milyet* was permitted to administer its own internal affairs (Vacalopoulos 1973). Sohos' Christians were under the jurisdiction of the Greek Patriarchal authorities in Constantinople. In such a context, the fact that the Sohoian peasant-laborers who constituted the majority of the community's Orthodox Christians spoke mainly the Slavic language of Macedonian had little significance. In fact, according to Dakin (1966:11), the word Vulgarika was in Ottoman times *not* associated with Bulgaria (an as yet unimagined nation-state) but was simply an adjective for anything associated with, as he terms it, "low peasant culture." Much more significant was the Sohoians' identity as Christians, which in the eyes of many made them "Greeks," the two terms in this era often being used interchangeably.

In the final two centuries of Ottoman rule, the merchant-landowning elite (*arhondes*) were the leaders of Sohos' Christian community and worked closely with the Church for mutual advantage. In 1770, for example, the wealthy thread merchant Hadzihariskos (who, as the prefix to his name announces, had demonstrated his piety by making a pilgrimage to Jerusalem) master-minded and financed the secret construction of the town's main church. To ensure that it was not subsequently pulled down, he made a number of generous gifts to well-placed Ottoman officials. This act was undoubtedly an assertion not only of his religious devotion and patriotism, which Sohoians today invariably stress, but of his own wealth and influence. The interests of the elite and the Church were not incompatible, however. The men of substance supported the Church financially and the Church used its ecclesiastical authority to protect that group's economic interests. The close ties between the two also had cultural consequences. Whether they were originally Greek-speaking or Vlachs who had become Hellenized, members of the elite cultivated a Greek identity. They took charge of the running of the local church and learned Greek literature and history in the Greek language at the church-organized schools that only they could afford.[9]

[9] S. Papadopoulos, cited in Kutsimanis (1974:44), reports the existence of both a girls' and a boys' school, with a total of one hundred pupils, in 1871–72, as well as a third school with 180 pupils at the beginning of the next century. This last school was prob-

Though divisions between the town's Muslim and Christian communities were in certain ways absolute (for example, intermarriage was prohibited, and various privileges and obligations non-negotiable), economic distinctions between Sohoian inhabitants were more visible than were religious differences. According to elderly Sohoians' descriptions of the early twentieth-century social landscape, the wealthier Greek families had cordial relations with both the Turkish landowners and the Ottoman officials posted to the town. Likewise, the impoverished farmer-laborers and artisans who constituted the majority of the population were composed of two groups: the mostly Macedonian-speaking Christians and the "Turks" (that is, Muslims, predominantly Yuruk shepherds who had migrated to the town from the surrounding hamlets).[10] The two groups lived generally in separate neighborhoods but sometimes side by side in a mixed neighborhood (*mahala*), the men patronizing the same coffeehouses, the women exchanging labor and utensils, and each group attending the other's (gender-segregated) celebrations.

With the decline of the Ottoman Empire and the rise of the Balkan nationalist movements in the late nineteenth century, Macedonia became contested territory. Its strategic position linking the Balkans with the Aegean and Central Europe to Asia, its fertile farmlands in a predominantly mountainous region, and its dynamic port city of Thessaloniki made it attractive both to the fledgling Balkan nationalists and to the Great Powers, who had long been involved in the area. Macedonia's "ethnic mosaic," the coexistence within multiethnic towns and cities and monoethnic villages of distinct communities of Greeks, Turks, Slavs, Jews, Gypsies, Kutsovlachs, became problematical (Jelavich and Jelavich 1977). Using churches and schools more than bullets as weapons of propaganda, and competing as much against each other as against the Ottomans, four distinct groups of nationalists—Greeks, Serbs, Bulgarians, and Macedonians—now claimed Macedonia as rightfully theirs, each hoping to annex it to its own (actual or envisaged) territorially defined nation-state.

From the 1870s until the close of the first World War, Sohoians, too, experienced the propaganda campaigns of the various nationalist

---

ably established as part of the Greek campaign for Sohoian hearts and minds during the Balkan nationalist struggles.

[10] Many Macedonian-speaking Christians knew some Greek as well, especially those who were artisans, small traders, and laborers for the wealthier Greek-speaking families, but Sohoians generally admit that at that time, Macedonian was the language of families at home. I knew a few old women born in Sohos who had never learned Greek. The fact that these Christians also knew a fair amount of Turkish was sometimes cited by Sohoians as an indication of Christian cunning and superiority over the Ottoman authorities, who seldom knew Greek or Macedonian.

groups. The question that no doubt worried the local notables (who considered themselves Greek) was the extent to which the Macedonian-speaking peasant-laborers were likely to identify with and support either the Macedonian or the Bulgarian nationalists and their cause.[11] The virulently partisan tenor of accounts of this period, particularly of the Macedonian Struggles of 1903–1908,[12] and the fact that Sohoians describe the past from the vantage point of their present situation, make it very difficult to know what really happened and how the Macedonian-speaking majority responded. But one can surmise two possible responses. On the one hand, the longtime affiliation of the poor peasant-laborers with a Greek-controlled Orthodox Church, whose hegemony in the area around Thessaloniki was never seriously threatened, and their acquiescence to the moral and practical authority of the local notables may have inhibited the development of a sense of distinct "Macedonianness" or—more precisely—of a Macedonian national consciousness, as certainly developed among less socially and economically stratified villages further west. Even at that time, in other words, they may have considered themselves in a religious and national sense as truly "Greek."[13] If this were the case they would have reacted with some alarm to Macedonian and Bulgarian nationalist propaganda. On the other hand, this propaganda may have received a more sympathetic hearing than present histories imply (see, for example, Stavrianos 1958:517–21). Whether or not such propaganda appealed to an other-than-Greek (that is, Bulgarian or Macedonian) national identity, it may have spoken to as yet unarticulated class antagonisms that the Greek religious, cultural, and economic hegemony, and the patriotic propaganda that the Greek nationalists now promoted with equal intensity, otherwise masked.

There are hints in elderly Sohoians' stories of the period that some of their compatriots did, indeed, find the Macedonian or Bulgarian propaganda persuasive. Because the cause they espoused would have had little chance of success given the superior power, prestige, and resources of the notables, however, such sympathizers mainly emigrated

[11] Many Greek historians do not distinguish between Macedonian and Bulgarian nationalist movements (for example, Martis 1984:98–99). They refer to their members simply as "Bulgarians" or as "apostates" (Orthodox Christians loyal to the Bulgarian Exarchate, which was established in 1870). Sohoians, too, rarely make this distinction. However, though the two major nationalist revolutionary organizations, established in 1893 and 1895, respectively, had strong Bulgarian links, the Internal Macedonian Revolutionary Organization (IMRO) favored a separate "Macedonia for the Macedonians," while the External Organization wanted Macedonia for Bulgaria (Stavrianos 1958:519–20).

[12] See, for example, Martis 1984 and Zotiades 1961.

[13] This is a position supported by many Greek scholars, for example, Kofos (1964:13, 23) and Martis (1984).

north. They would not have been treated kindly at home, in any case. During the period of the Macedonian Struggles, the notables organized a local militia to defend Sohos as a "bulwark of Macedonian Hellenism" against other nationalist movements. Armed Sohoians periodically clashed with Turkish soldiers and bands of Macedonian nationalists, the so-called *komitadzidhes*, in Sohos and the surrounding countryside (Anestopoulos, cited in Kutsimanis 1977:116–22). It was only in late 1913, when Sohos came definitively under the jurisdiction of the Greek state, that open skirmishes finally ceased.

What is implied, socially and politically, when Sohoians speak Macedonian (Vulgarika), and Turkish, too, has changed over time. The speaking of these non-Greek tongues, unproblematical in the early Ottoman period, became problematical during the rise of Balkan nationalism and has made state authorities extremely nervous ever since. In a political context in which the language people speak is generally seen as the definitive factor in determining their national identity, Greek officialdom has been uneasy about communities that profess loyalty to the Greek state while continuing to speak something other than Greek. Greek policy over the years has thus been to eradicate these other languages by education, persuasion, or force. A schoolteacher from Epirus who had fought in the Macedonian Struggles was subsequently sent to Sohos to teach Greek to the inhabitants. In the 1930s, considering the presence of speakers of Macedonian in Greece's newly acquired Macedonian territory to be politically embarrassing and potentially dangerous, the dictator Ioannis Metaxas instigated a harsh campaign throughout the region to suppress all languages except Greek. Townspeople remember being fed castor oil and locked up in the local jail for speaking Vulgarika in public.

The officials' negative attitude toward the language continues to this day. But the status of Vulgarika for the *dopii* is more ambiguous. It is duly denigrated whenever a representative of officialdom is within earshot, but it surfaces fragmentarily in certain phrases, jokes, insults, and nicknames. It provides a coarse, intimate idiom for self-reflexive, often self-mocking humor. Turkish, too, is sometimes heard, and its connotations are even more positive. Some of the grandest and most beautiful elements of the local tradition—the distinctive *zurna* and *dauli* instrumental ensemble and its songs, for instance—are identified, particularly by the older *dopii*, as "Turkish things" (*ta Turkika*), probably because they were inspired by or actually imitate the remembered practices of the wealthy local Turks. Ironically, it is this amalgam of Greek, Turkish and Macedonian elements that now signals a uniquely local historical experience that only "insiders" can properly understand—an experience that is Balkan and Macedonian as much as Greek.

Although the *dopii* are by far the largest group, comprising probably 85 percent of the local population, two other nonindigenous groups also live in Sohos, and this, too, is a consequence of the town's position in Macedonia. After the "repatriation" of Sohos' "Turks" in 1923, 100 to 150 refugee families from Asia Minor were resettled in the town by the Greek authorities. They were given abandoned Turkish houses to live in and Turkish fields to cultivate. The settlement of these refugees of largely urban origin in a predominantly agricultural community in Macedonia arguably had more to do with the Greek government's nationalist goals than with the refugees' needs. Before the exchange, most had been petty traders and craftsmen; a few had been professionals (a doctor, a jeweler). They knew little about farming, and those unable to master the unfamiliar skills soon migrated to Thessaloniki where they hoped opportunities would be better.

From the start, cultural, social, linguistic, and class differences, as well as resentment among the *dopii*, who felt that the refugees were receiving an inordinate share of the property left behind by the Turks, exacerbated hostilities between the two groups. The *dopii* called the refugees *mazir* and *kaparilazai* ("degenerate Laz").[14] They were scandalized by the refugees' European ways and dress, particularly the women's bare arms, which the *dopii* considered a sign of immorality. For their part, the refugees mocked the *dopii*, whom they called Vulgari, for their social conservatism, their "heavy-sounding" Macedonian tongue, their unsophisticated manners, and their traditional dress (wide wool pants for men and long dresses and billowing bloomers for women).

The third group in Sohos today is made up of about thirty families of Vlachs, or Vlahi (as they are called and call themselves). They are probably Kutsovlachs, and most of them originate from the western Macedonian village of Blatsi. For as long as both they and the *dopii* can remember, these families used to bring their herds of sheep and goats to the mountains above Sohos every summer, setting up temporary shelters, and grazing their animals.

Despite the regularity of their migrations to Sohos, they maintained an assiduously separate identity from the locals throughout the Ottoman period and well beyond. *Dopii* insist that it was the Vlach families, more than they themselves, who resisted intermarriage, refusing to "give their daughters" to the despised sedentary Greeks. Indeed, *dopii* frequently "quote" the defiant Vlach assertion: "We'll turn Turkish

---

[14] *Mazir* (from the Turkish, *mazi*) means "bygone, of the past." Its connotation here is unclear. The term "Laz" properly refers to those from the Black Sea region in Turkey, but here it is used as a general term for Asia Minor Greeks.

[that is, convert to Islam], but we won't turn Greek [*Turkevume, dhen Grekevume*]!" It was only in the 1940s, when the movements of the Vlahi were severely restricted by the authorities during the Second World War and the Civil War, that this way of life began to come to an end. Vlach families were forced by circumstances to settle in the town in requisitioned, and later rented, quarters. For many this temporary resettlement became permanent. These Vlachs are now sedentary, and though they have also become involved in other enterprises (notably, a successful cheese-making operation), many continue to raise herds that they graze, as before, on the mountainsides.

Intermarriage has begun to blur these intracommunal distinctions. Such marriages, practically unthinkable before 1950, were becoming increasingly common by the mid-1970's, a generation later. The ethnic "origins" of individuals and families are still known within the community, but these distinctions have increasingly fewer and weaker repercussions for the ways everyday life is organized. It is now explicitly political, rather than ethnic, affiliations that most visibly matter in the ways individuals and groups organize for collective action.

POLITICAL DISTINCTIONS

Since the re-legalization of formerly banned political parties in 1974 and the institution of free elections, parties of the extreme Left and Right can always count on a small percentage of Sohoian votes. But in the years between 1983 and 1985, most Sohoians (in roughly equal numbers) supported one of the two major national parties, either the ruling PA.SO.K. (Panhellenic Socialist Movement) or the opposition New Democracy party. The swelled ranks of PA.SO.K. in a community whose indigenous Left was largely decimated by the Civil War are partially explained by the defection of former supporters of the Right, who either were disgusted with that party's political record (especially the military dictatorship of 1967–1974) or foresaw the changing political winds and wanted to be on the winning side when the votes were counted. This "distortion" notwithstanding, the current division between the two parties reflects a more long-standing rift within the community. Though the roots of this division reach even deeper into the past, both sides take as their major point of reference the years of the Civil War, between 1946 and 1949.

The decade of the 1940s has contributed importantly to the Sohoians' sense of themselves as a community, in a tragic way. Unlike the resistances against the Turks and the "Bulgarians," which can be remembered as collective struggles, this period of war wrenched the community apart. Deeply partisan positions and an extraordinarily complex political situation meant that individuals' experiences of the war and its meaning were and are not just unique but fundamentally polarized.[15] A brief outline of the events of this period must suffice here to convey what for Sohoians is one of the most important experiences (or legacies, passed down by their parents) of their lives.[16]

With the Axis occupation of Greece in 1941, Sohoians became involved in resistance activities organized by the coalition organization, EAM (National Liberation Front), and its military wing, ELAS. Some left to live in small bands in the surrounding mountains and wage a guerrilla war against the Germans. Others who remained in town supported the Resistance by providing, collecting, and distributing supplies (food, clothes, bandages) to the EAM-ELAS partisans or by passing messages. But as early as 1943, Sohos saw clashes between rival Resistance factions, the left-wing EAM-ELAS and the right-wing PAO (Kutsimanis 1974:28). In the same year the Security Battalions, a vehemently anti-communist collaborationist force, also occupied the town and skirmished with EAM-ELAS partisans (Kortsidhas 1980a, 1980b; Svoronos 1986:140). The fact that Sohos and surrounding communities were at this time beginning to implement EAM's scheme for popular self-government (Laiki Aftodhikisi), which would have involved such reforms as universal franchise, people's courts, land reforms, and new schools and cultural institutions, is some indication of the support enjoyed by EAM among people in the area, despite the attacks by right-wing forces (Kortsidhas 1980a:65).

By December 1944 it was clear that, given Allied uneasiness about EAM's left-wing leadership and social agenda, EAM's role in the new government would be extremely minimal despite its wide-spread popular support. In February 1945, at Varkiza, EAM nonetheless agreed to disarm. Sohoian EAM-ELAS partisans reluctantly turned in their weapons to police headquarters in a nearby town. A regiment of the National Guard was installed in a building in the center of Sohos, the same building where the Sohos EAM offices had been. Guardsmen sought the names of EAM-ELAS partisans, now under suspicion as "Communists." Reprisals began: arrests, beatings, imprisonments, and at least one murder.

Sohoian partisans, who felt their cause had been betrayed, left for the mountains to fight the right-wing government they considered il-

[15] Two who have written about the events during Civil War in the region around Sohos, for example, describe the period in such radically different terms that it is hard to believe they are writing about the same place. Kortsidhas (1980a, 1980b) fought as a partisan of EAM-ELAS, the major resistance organization. His first-hand account is written from a left-wing perspective. Kutsimanis (1974:28–30, 188–95), though he did not personally participate in the fighting, describes events from a right-wing perspective.

[16] For a more in-depth examination of the Civil War, see Eudes 1972 and Stavrianos 1958:785–837.

legitimate. Between August 1946 and August 1949 these partisans clashed continually with the government police (*horofilakes*) stationed in Sohos and the government's armed civilian units. Families from surrounding villages, particularly those villages suspected of being sympathetic to the partisan cause, were evacuated and relocated in Sohos. Though these relocations were justified by the authorities as necessary for villagers' safety, they also ensured that pro-EAM-ELAS villagers, on whom a close watch was kept, could not easily assist the partisans. Many Sohoians describe being caught in the middle between right-wing bands, who ransacked the houses of those they suspected of supporting the EAM-ELAS partisans, and these partisans, who pressured civilians for supplies. By the time EAM finally surrendered in 1949, most Sohoian partisans either had been killed or had fled across the border, usually to Bulgaria. Those who had assisted their organization faced harassment and sometimes house arrest.

The decade of war both reordered and polarized social relations and social groups in Sohos. The traditional authority of the local notables, already much diminished, could never again be resurrected. The once clear social distinctions between the small merchant elite and the peasant-laborer-artisan majority, and among the different "ethnic" groups, began to blur; new, differently constituted distinctions were to follow. Stances taken by individuals in wartime were motivated in some cases by deeply held political or class convictions but in other cases by personal and contingent factors. Those related by kinship or marriage—cousins, affines, and even members of nuclear families—often found themselves divided.[17] New political allegiances and alliances were forged.

The war also brought economic upheaval. Individual fortunes were made (some reputedly in the black market) and also lost. Though a few of the traditionally powerful notable families were economically destroyed, it was those on the losing side—the Left—who were, collectively, hit hardest. Sohoian EAM–ELAS partisans, particularly, when they fled across the border, left behind not only their property but their parents, siblings, wives, and children.

The postwar period was one of major restructuring in Greek society generally. At the political level, leftist organizations were banned. Individual leftists, especially those who had been involved in EAM, were politically repressed and made ineligible for public jobs, and the Right emerged much more powerful than before. In Sohos a slightly new collection of powerful families (including many members of the tra-

---

[17] In some cases, the divisions remain today; in others, though wartime opponents have apparently reconciled, rifts can be reopened by a careless remark at a *kafenio* or at a wedding celebration.

ditional elite, but also some others who had benefited economically from the war or its immediate aftermath) began to consolidate its position, allying with the ruling Right. Those from economically weaker families, too, acting variably out of fear, self-interest, necessity, or political conviction, also cast their lot with the Right.

Within this general framework of postwar right-wing dominance in Sohos, those in the center and on the left have not remained entirely silent. Right-wing political dominance was briefly eclipsed when the son of a highly respected Sohoian family, Yannis Grekos, was elected mayor as a Center party candidate in 1964. Grekos was removed from office after the right-wing military coup in 1967. After the military dictatorship finally collapsed in 1974 and left-wing parties were legalized, however, Grekos was reelected and retained his position until 1981, when he stood for election to parliament as a PA.SO.K. candidate and won. In local elections in October 1982 Stellios Evangelidhis, a lawyer born in Sohos but raised in Thessaloniki and something of a dark-horse candidate, ran for mayor as an "independent" and—to the surprise of many—won. Officially neutral, he has tried to mediate between Left and Right, but his attempts have for various reasons merely exacerbated tensions between the two groups.[18]

Indeed, the political animosities between Left and Right are as vivid and volatile as ever, and the Civil War, which each side interprets very differently, remains a symbol of that rift. Though never forgotten, the war was for forty years a taboo subject; PA.SO.K.'s insistence, since coming to power in 1981, on the public airing of this painful era is as resented by the Right (who accuse PA.SO.K. of divisiveness) as it is welcomed by the long-silenced Left. PA.SO.K. argues, with reason, that without a public reexamination of this historical period the wounds of the Civil War will never heal. But this healing still seems a long way off. The ideological divisions between Right and Left, the memories of particular attacks and retaliations, the feeling of having been betrayed by fellow townspeople (and, for the Left, by their previous allies, Britain and America), and the postwar reprisals, especially by the Right against the Left, all continue to fuel the political passions and antagonisms that animate everyday life in Sohos, that unite one group against another, and that break through even into celebratory contexts.

---

[18] The most important reason for this is that Evangelidhis had originally been associated with PA.SO.K., and had—with Grekos' support—been selected as its candidate for mayor in the 1982 local elections. Evangelidhis and Grekos, however, at a crucial moment in this process, had a "falling out" (no one in Sohos that I spoke to seemed to know exactly what it was about); an alternative candidate was put forward, and Evangelidhis left the party to run as an "independent." After Evangelidhis' election, his relationship with Grekos continued to deteriorate. Grekos' supporters could never, therefore, accept the legitimacy of his role as mediator; they accused him of being a closet "rightist."

CHAPTER TWO

Gender, Household, and Community

> Hegemony is . . . not only the articulate upper level of "ide-
> ology," nor are its forms of control only those ordinarily seen
> as "manipulation" and "indoctrination." It is a whole body of
> practices and expectations, over the whole of living: our sense
> and assignments of energy, our shaping perceptions of our-
> selves and our world. It is a lived system of meanings and val-
> ues—constitutive and constituting—which as they are experi-
> enced as practices appear as reciprocally confirming.
>
> —Raymond Williams, *Marxism and Literature*

THE IDEAS about gender currently hegemonic in Sohos bear the
imprint of local circumstances and histories: the patterns of the sexual division of labor within the peasant-laborer household, the relations between the different social and ethnic groups, and the shared
Orthodox religious culture. But they are also affected by extralocal
processes. In Sohos as elsewhere, changing notions about men
and women, and especially about women's roles, and the changing
material conditions of men and women's lives need to be seen in the
broader national context of growing middle-class aspirations, conservative (until recently) political control, and long-term economic
underdevelopment. If the end of the decade of war and a postwar
period of "modernization" heralded profound changes in the everyday lives of Greek men and women, such changes have been a mixed
blessing. Processes and ideologies of modernization, so often thought
to challenge traditional gender roles and relations and, in particular,
to benefit women, have just as often reinforced the "traditional"
sexual division of labor (see Mouzelis 1978; Stamiris 1986; Sutton
1986).

Though this investigation focuses on expressions of gender ideas
and relations outside the household sphere, it must nonetheless begin
inside it. For, however diverse or creative their productive strategies,
Sohoian households tend to organize their activities in terms of a fairly
strict sexual division of labor. This division of labor is understood in
terms of and helps to reproduce a particular set of ideas about males
and females.

THE DOMESTIC ORGANIZATION OF
GENDER AND SEXUALITY

Though the importance of marriage in the achievement of full social adulthood is stressed for both males and females in Sohos, gender categories reveal that this is even more important for women than for men. As is the case in virtually all previously described Greek communities, a Sohoian woman tends to be identified with reference to a man. Female gender categories, and the way they are used in everyday life, indicate both relationship to a man and the state of the female individual's sexuality (see also Hirschon 1978). A "girl" (*koritsi*) is identified in relation to her father. Girls of adolescent years or younger with whom I was keeping company, if encountered by an adult who did not know them, were often asked not "Who are you [*pya ise*]?" but "Whose girl are you [*pyanu koritsi ise*]?" Though young boys might be asked this question, adolescent males never were.[1] The term *koritsi* is actually less a category of age than of social status.[2] It is only through marriage that a *koritsi*, whatever her age, becomes a *yineka*, a "woman."[3] *Koritsi*, grammatically neuter, can also in local discourse mean "virgin," because betrothal is the moment when active female sexuality is collectively acknowledged to exist. Similarly, *yineka*, a grammatically feminine term, also means "wife."

Although many parents want their daughters to obtain some kind of vocational training, such as secretarial, bookkeeping, or hairdressing instruction, after secondary school (see Bakalaki 1984), and bright girls are encouraged to take the entrance examinations for university, those girls who do not continue their education face incredible pressures to marry.[4] A girl who reaches her mid-twenties without marrying risks being labeled an "old maid" (*yerondokori*, literally, "old girl/daughter"). Parents feel obliged to "marry off" their daughters, and the inability to do so may be seen as a kind of moral or social failure. Girls who remain unmarried encounter not only concern and pity

---

[1] The appropriate answer is to say "[I am the daughter/son] of so-and-so," giving the father's name (see also Hirschon 1978).

[2] "Little girl" is indicated by adding the diminutive: hence, *koritsaki* or *kortsudha*. Throughout the book, I use the term "girl," my translation of *koritsi*, in this strict categorical sense of unmarried female. The term has sexist overtones, of course, when used of mature young women, but I use it both because it is the most accurate translation ethnographically and because it reminds the reader, with every use, of the patriarchal character of the world I am describing.

[3] Actually, an older unmarried female tends to be referred to as a *kopella* rather than as a *koritsi*. *Kopella* is more ambiguous in its connotations: it is never used of pre-adolescent girls, but it may be used of youthful yet married women (under thirty-five years or so in age) in wholly positive—admiring, affectionate—ways. To call a fifty-year-old unmarried female a *kopella*, however, has inescapably negative overtones.

[4] This pressure is merely postponed for girls who continue their studies.

from kin and neighbors but anger, as well. Unless she leaves Sohos for work or studies, a girl resides with her natal family until marriage.

Once married, a woman is expected to direct her energies primarily toward her husband and children. Whether or not she works outside the house (and a significant number of women do), she remains domestically defined. She is considered responsible for virtually all domestic work, labeled here—as in the West—"women's work" (*yinekies dhulies*). She is also expected, by virtue of her "natural" maternal sensitivities, to keep family relationships harmonious. Married women assert that the management of family relationships requires a combination of deference, self-abnegation, and manipulation; they also know what awaits them if they fail. "People say that 'it's the woman's fault,'" they often assured me with grim certainty (see also Danforth 1983:207). In addition to her emotional labor, the wife assumes responsibility for the spiritual well-being of the family. She represents the family in church, keeping the Lenten fasts, observing memorial days for family deaths, and so forth.[5]

If, with the recent reform of archaic divorce laws, divorce is becoming more common in Greek society generally, in Sohos it is still extremely rare. However miserable their marital or family lives, few women separate from or divorce their husbands. A woman who does so is severely stigmatized; she is called a "living widow" (*zontohira*).[6] The analogous term, "living widower" (*zontohiros*), is never heard.

Marriage is important for men, but as du Boulay (1974:121) has remarked, it is not important in the same way. For a youth (*neos*), often called a *pedhi*,[7] military service marks the transition to social adulthood, the point at which people begin calling him a "man" (*andras*). Marriage merely completes the process, enabling him to set up his own household. Marriage never precedes military service, and usually follows it, but a man may delay marrying until well into his thirties without incurring criticism if he is seen to be establishing himself economically in preparation for eventual marriage. Failure to marry may be excused on other grounds, as well: the bachelor status of the dy-

[5] See also Caraveli-Chaves 1980; Danforth 1982; Dubisch 1986; Hirschon 1983; Kenna 1976.

[6] During my fieldwork, though I heard about several cases of informal separation, I encountered only one divorced woman: a young woman who had married impulsively at sixteen and whose marriage had ended after a very short period. This young woman, who remained in school (and eventually went on to a university), suffered much unpleasant gossip and harassment from peers and other townspeople alike.

[7] *Pedhi* is a complex term. It can mean "child" (gender unspecified), but in everyday usage it often means "male child" or "male youth." (The gender-specific terms for "boy," *aghori*, or "little boy," *aghoraki*, are used less often, generally when the child's maleness is being stressed.) Though *pedhi* connotes the absence of full social adulthood, it does not necessarily imply the state of sexual innocence (as does the term *koritsi*).

namic and mid-fortyish political leader Yannis Grekos was justified by his supporters with the argument that the heavy commitments of his political work left little time for family life.[8]

Like his female counterpart, an unmarried man remains in his natal home until marriage, and under his father's authority. Practically speaking, however, he has a great deal of freedom, and he spends the greater part of his leisure time with other bachelors his own age. Once he marries, he transfers his energies to his own new household; yet it is the economic dimension of his household responsibilities that is defined as primary. The exclusive quality of a woman's social, emotional, and sexual orientation to husband and family is not demanded in the case of a man. He is considered responsible for his family's material well-being, but the degree and nature of his involvement in the social, emotional, and sexual aspects of "private" family life may vary widely.

HOUSEHOLD LABOR

According to Sohoian accounts, marriage was until the postwar period largely village endogamous. At marriage, the bride came to live with her husband in his parents' house. In those days it was not uncommon for several brothers to live together in a single house with their wives, children, and parents. In the past, the bride's major contribution to the new household was usually her trousseau—that is, linens, blankets, rugs, clothing, cooking pots and utensils. Daughters of wealthier families, of course, might also bring substantial amounts of cash and, occasionally, fields or animals. Though today the trousseau remains the symbolic focus of the Sohoian bride's contribution, she and her parents are now expected to contribute a great deal more: electrical appliances, furniture, perhaps even a shop in Sohos or an apartment in Thessaloniki.

Households with two or more married brothers and their families are now hard to find. Even the pattern of patrilocal postmarital residence, still evident but waning, is generally explained as a consequence of the "poverty" of the past. The autonomous nuclear-family household is held to be ideal. Until recently lack of financial means often made this impossible, but after the 1978 earthquake, many of the town's houses were rebuilt with two or even three self-contained apartments. Usually the husband's (or more rarely, the wife's) parents

[8] He did eventually marry in the autumn of 1984, when it was widely rumored that the woman with whom he had long been involved had become pregnant. The Sohoian grandmother who told me this voiced hearty and admiring approval of this woman's cleverness in getting her reluctant lover to marry her.

live on the ground floor, and the young couple above.[9] Though there is a good deal of mutual help between them, these households usually remain separate economic units.

Typically, then, a Sohoian household includes only the nuclear family: a married couple and their children. A number of three-generation households also exist, however. Since the youngest son customarily inherits his parents' house, his household usually includes his mother and/or father. In the rarer cases of the "housegroom" (*spitogambros*), the new couple shares the house with the wife's mother and/or father.

Ideally, each household has a common purse to which all members contribute any regular wages and from which they draw spending money (*hardziliki*).[10] In some cases, the household is also a productive unit. Before the introduction of mechanized farm equipment in the 1950s, this was even more true for most Sohoians, who survived by working the land. Then, in addition to caring for the house, the wife worked side by side with her husband and children in the fields and vineyards and with the animals. Today, as new farming methods and machinery have altered farming practices, women's role in agricultural production has been relatively marginalized. Nonetheless, women and children still participate in agricultural tasks, particularly in peak periods and in tasks that must be done by hand: the first planting, harvesting and processing of tobacco; the harvesting of fruit and nuts; and the care of animals.

Likewise, in what is a familiar Greek pattern, workshops and the many shops and restaurants in the marketplace are often family-run enterprises. A husband and wife, and the occasional child and grandparent, may work together in such an enterprise. Alternatively, the two adults may work in shifts. A third arrangement, in which women run these shops independently while their husbands are involved in some other work, is also not at all rare. A Sohoian woman is sometimes given a small business (a hairdressing salon, a boutique) by her parents before she marries, which she continues to run after marriage. Or the wife may hold title to a family business acquired after several years of marriage, primarily for legal or financial reasons. In both cases, the woman can easily become the one who is in charge practically as well as technically.

Despite the fact that women both work in and even occasionally

[9] Consequently, mother-in-law and daughter-in-law no longer share one kitchen, a traditional locus of conflicts among women over who holds the power in the household (see Danforth 1978; Hirschon 1981).

[10] Unmarried daughters who work for wages are generally excepted from this. They are expected to keep some or all of their wages to purchase items for their trousseau or other items for their own future households. Unmarried sons who work seasonally or occasionally, too, are expected to keep their wages as spending money.

own such businesses, however, I found that Sohoians overwhelmingly described men as the ones who bear the burdens of economic responsibility for the family. When, pointing to her mother's long days doing all and sundry at the family bakery, I used the expression, "She works," thirty-four-year-old Panayota dissented. "My mother doesn't work. She helps." A friend sitting with us elaborated on the point. "It's the man who has the responsibilities."[11]

The hegemonic ideology of gender, which associates women with domesticity and men with economic responsibility, has practical consequences for all Sohoian women. Whatever waged work a woman takes on, and whatever unremunerated "help" she offers to a family enterprise, is in addition to her domestic duties and responsibilities to care for her children. Men are generally thought to be unwilling or unable to do these tasks; the occasional helpful husband, I was told, has to sweep or tidy "in secret" in order to avoid the mockery of male peers. Though the support of a mother or a mother-in-law can sometimes be enlisted to enable a woman to work outside her home, and though limited public child-care facilities do exist, a woman often copes with the competing demands of work and household by taking on part-time, seasonal or periodic waged work or by working at home in her "spare time."

A woman's particular socioeconomic and personal circumstances make a difference, of course. Although on the whole women's jobs in Sohos tend to be insecure and poorly paid in comparison with men's, there are variations. In a practical sense, it makes a great deal of difference whether a woman sews ladies' blouses for a Salonikan[12] manufacturer on her sewing machine at home in her spare time, or works planting and weeding tobacco, or is an accountant in the tax office, or runs a small boutique. But the fact of working, in itself, does not undermine the association of females with the domestic sphere. Rather, as has been noted elsewhere in Greece and in other parts of southern Europe (see Bakalaki 1984; Giovannini 1985; Hirschon 1989; Lambiri 1968), the wide and varied participation of girls and women in the public world of work continues to coexist with, rather than to challenge, powerful assumptions about a woman's proper place, the nature of her contributions, and her position as dependent on men.

FIELDWORK

As a young, foreign, solitary woman coming to stay in a town where I had neither relatives nor even compatriots, I must have seemed to

---

[11] For the dual meanings of women's "work," see Sutton 1986.
[12] *Salonikan* is the adjectival form of *Thessaloniki*.

most Sohoians tremendously out of place. Yet fortunately I was not a total stranger. My arrival in the town in early spring 1983 was already, in some sense, a return. Though the combined length of my two previous visits totaled less than three weeks, I had already established a strong friendship with the family that had hosted me in 1978 and was acquainted with a handful of other townspeople, as well. This host family insisted I stay with them until I (actually, they) could find a suitable place to rent. Within a fortnight the women of the house—the spry septugenarian Irini and her daughter-in-law, Katina—had negotiated an arrangement with a neighbor, Vangelio, a cantankerous elderly widow who lived alone and had two empty rooms (a bedroom and a kitchen, though bereft of appliances) on the second floor. It was an old house with a small courtyard, in the town center, barely fifty yards from the central square yet, in its position on a side street, very peaceful.

I lived happily in this house for six months. But when for various reasons it became necessary to leave it, I found a small second-floor apartment in a new concrete building, built after the earthquake by a Sohoian who had moved to Thessaloniki. It was only two blocks away from my first house, and in the heart of the market. Though more modern in its amenities, it was damp and slightly claustrophobic. These drawbacks were outweighed, though, by the fact that it overlooked the market and gave me a wonderful bird's eye view of Sohoian public life. Irini and Katina envied me for my location "in the center" and I, too, soon recognized the advantages of this for my fieldwork. Wedding processions, for instance, always made a circuit through the market; from my balcony, the clamorous instrumental ensemble (*daulia*) could be heard a good half mile away, time enough for me to gather up my camera, tape recorder, and notebook and even to set up my video equipment before the procession passed by on the street below.

That November, Artemis, a young Salonikan woman about my age, also a "foreigner" (*kseni*) from the townspeople's perspective, moved in with me. She taught English to classes of local children Tuesday through Friday, and usually spent weekends at her parents' house in Thessaloniki. My acquisition of a flatmate reassured the townspeople, who considered my "aloneness" troubling. For me, Artemis was not only a fine companion but a source of information about, and insight into, Sohoian life. I lived in this tiny apartment until I left the town in March 1985.

My relations with the Sohoians were, as they are for most fieldworkers, extremely complex, a story in itself. I had different kinds of relationships—some emotionally intense, some jovial and superficial, some polite but wary—with different individuals. These relationships also developed and changed over time. Although the fieldworker's personality, temperament, and a whole gamut of intangible, contingent factors inevitably affect the fieldwork process and the social relations it entails (see especially Karp and Kendall 1982), I will focus here on the ways the townspeople made sense of me as a scholar (my professional identity) and as a female (my gender identity).

Most Sohoians knew me either as "Yanna" (the informal version of Ioanna, the Greek form of my name) or merely as "the Amerikana." They learned—at least, I often felt I had explained this (and much more) to each of the town's 3,500 inhabitants—that I was a student from America, doing research for a doctorate.[13] Most assumed I was researching Carnival, for it was the town's unusual ritual figure, the goatskin-clad and bell-toting *karnavali* that had put Sohos on the map and brought it both prestige and resources, generally in the form of funds from government ministries, for Carnival and folkloric activities (see figure 4). They were accustomed to the visits and questions of researchers, both foreign and Greek, about the *karnavali*. My arrival in the town the week before Clean Monday, the climax of the Carnival period and the first day of Lent, could only have reinforced their perception that I would do the same. But when Carnival ended and I stayed, their confident assumptions turned to puzzlement. "You're still here?" they queried as they passed me in the street.

My persistent residence caused many to realize that my interests were not wholly confined to Carnival. I became known as a *laoghrafos*, a folklorist. Given that my interests—Carnival, dancing, music, ritual, "tradition"—fell easily within the provenance of the Greek *laoghrafos*, the title was apt. It was no doubt the closest Greek equivalent that Sohoians knew to "anthropologist," as I discovered when I experimented with other titles. *Anthropologhos* evoked puzzled murmurs about bones and medical doctors, *kinoniologhos* (sociologist) prompted stories of questionnaires and television interviews by intellectuals about the problems of contemporary Greek life, and *ethnologhos* drew only blank stares. I did try, somewhat awkwardly, to revise this title— "I'm something like a *laoghrafos-kinoniologhos*" or "I'm not just interested in the past, I want to know about the present," I'd lamely explain—but *laoghrafos* was the title that stuck.

Being known as a *laoghrafos* gave me a fairly wide latitude for working. Sohoians were only too happy to answer my questions about their history, customs, rituals, and kinship system—many of the areas, in

---

[13] Being a "student" was not—as, for example, Herzfeld describes was the case in Rhodes (1983a:154)—as much a negative category as an unfinished one. The fact that I had not completed my studies, and that I needed their help in order to do so, enabled the townspeople to define me as dependent on them, even though I was, at certain times, called upon as an "authority" (Cowan 1988b).

4. A *karnavali*, grasping a
decorated wooden sword in
one hand and bottles of ouzo
and liqueur in the other, greets
a couple at a celebration on the
eve of Clean Monday.

fact, about which I wanted to learn. The title allowed me to speak
freely to all categories of people, including men, and to ask questions
frankly and openly, a practice that, had I lacked some comprehensible
scholarly label, might have created many problems. It legitimated my
attendance at a variety of ritual and public events, particularly if the
townspeople could define them as somehow "traditional," even when
I did not personally know the principals involved. The title did not
wholly dispel anxiety in a society where, as a Greek proverb warns,
"Things written cannot be unwritten," over the fact that I was "always
writing." Yet it did help to explain my ubiquitous notepad and my
often-produced camera, tape recorder, and video equipment in terms
that people not only understood, but that some also quite appreciated.
It enabled me to accept invitations to attend certain all-male celebrations from which women are normally excluded involving singing and
dancing, without creating misunderstandings. It gave the townspeople
opportunities to help me in my work.

There were certain drawbacks to this title, however. It was hard to escape the impression that my work concerned old things, old customs, old people, the past, a time when life itself was "purer" and more folklorically authentic: "You should have been here forty years ago!" Sohoians often quipped, half-apologetically. "Now, we've become 'modern'!" These attitudes hint at some of the local repercussions of the complex historical relationship between Greek folklore as an institution and discourse, along with the domain it studies—"traditional" peasant life—and national identity (see Cowan 1988b; Herzfeld 1982; Kyriakidhu-Nestoros 1978). The *laoghrafos* identity carries with it a whole set of associations and proclivities, one of which is a persistent orientation to an authenticating and legitimating past.[14] As a result of their Carnival's fame, the Sohoians have become caught up in these issues perhaps more than many Greek villagers. They have encountered folklorists and folklore (*laoghrafia*) both indirectly, through radio and television programs, school lessons, and books, and directly, especially during Carnival (see Ekaterinidhis 1979).

Sohoians not only tended to tell me what they thought I wanted to know (or what they thought I *should* want to know); they also could become suspicious or surprised when I wanted to know something that fell outside the category of the "traditional" (*ta paradhosiaka*) or "folklorically interesting."[15] My interest in politics (for, if nothing else, "traditional" features of Sohoian life were permeated with politics) prompted frequent speculation about which Greek political party I supported—whether, in terms of local factions, I was "ours" (*dhikia mas*) or "theirs" (literally, "not ours," *dhen ine dhikia mas*). It even gave rise to playful accusations that I was an American spy, though these had less drastic consequences than those suffered by a few of my predecessors (see Campbell 1964:vii; Herzfeld 1983a). My constant efforts to obtain accounts of specific incidents (including situations of conflict and breakdown) rather than idealized descriptions were also perplexing, and at times disconcerting, for informants, who expected to discuss the impersonal, public aspects of collective rites. As did Danforth (1978:2), I encountered some resistance when asking questions of a psychological, sociological, or anthropological nature. I did, of course, learn much about the ins and outs of love affairs, neighborly relations, political vendettas, and what happened at last night's dance, and I was able to elicit individual Sohoians' personal reactions to various things. But I suspect that much of this sort of information was told

[14] Danforth 1984; see also Fabian 1983 for an exploration of analogous themes in the institutional history of anthropology.

[15] Danforth, working in another "studied" community, encountered similar reactions (1978:2).

to me not in my seemingly "official" capacity as *laoghrafos*, but rather
in my identity as Yanna, the *kseni* who, like Simmel's "stranger," was
simultaneously near to and far from the raw immediacy of their daily
experience (see Karp and Kendall 1982; Simmel 1971b:143–49).

Townspeople's perceptions of my gender identity gave me insights
into their own perceptions of gender more generally, and especially
helped me to see that even in everyday life gender identity is *performed*,
not simply taken for granted. I was married when I arrived in Sohos
(though my husband did not accompany me, except for a few months
my first summer there), but although I always told people this—in
response to the question about my marital status they never failed to
ask—they seemed to find my answer hard to grasp. When a middle-
aged man I knew rather well asked me, eight months into my fieldwork, "Now, Yanna, are you married [*pandremeni*]? Or are you engaged [*arravoniasmeni*]?" it dawned on me that the problem was not one
of language. My reply had always been consistent, but my actions
were confusing. I had no husband present on a day-to-day basis and
no children, I was still a student, and I lived in a rented apartment not
only in their town (where my furnishings were "make-do" or *prohira*,
as were most students' rooms) but in America.[16] In addition, I looked
much younger than twenty-nine year-old Sohoian women and did not
dress or carry myself like a married woman, much less a "professional"
laoghrafos. Indeed, a few weeks after I arrived, at the first Sohoian wake
I attended, a woman across the room (but not out of earshot) leaned
over to her neighbor and commented, "She's a high-school student
[*mathitria*]. I can tell from her shoes!"[17]

I thus fell somewhere between the categories of *koritsi* and *yineka*,
depending on the situation, and the ambiguity turned out to be very
helpful for my work (see Clark 1983; Dubisch 1986; Golde 1986). I got
to know a few married women quite well, though I did find that it was
from certain individuals of this group that I experienced the most (usually veiled) antagonism. Given the social construction of wifehood,
my apparent evasion of wifely duties may have been particularly upsetting to them. I found, too, that though I was married, I did not
share many of married women's daily concerns with husband, children, and household work. As it happened, I spent a lot of time in the
company of *koritsia* (girls), a category of persons within the community that I found to be quite fascinating. To a few, I became a symbol

[16] From the Sohoians' perspective, though my husband visited, he could very well
have been my fiancé, since in this town and much of northern Greece it is fairly common
for engaged couples to cohabit before marriage.

[17] They were handmade, thick-heeled flat shoes, not the pumps that married women
wear for any public occasion (see also Friedl 1962:5).

of liberated womanhood, a foil allowing them to reflect on their life "here"—"good to think with." They were, also, good for me to think with; for it was certainly my experiences with girls and young women that convinced me that it was necessary to question anthropological assumptions about consensus in gender ideas and relations.

Though I knew, as Sohoians say, "many houses" and many individuals, there was one particular group that I came to think of as my "*parea*," my "company" of friends. This was a group made up predominantly of girls who, though unmarried, were not particularly young; they ranged in age from about twenty to thirty-two. In fact, it was as a *laoghrafos* that I was first introduced to thirty-two-year-old Dimitra, the shrewd and dynamic president of the Sohos Youth Association (a folklore association) and a central personality in this *parea*. Spending time with Dimitra and the mostly unmarried girls who were active in this association was not only personally congenial but theoretically fascinating. In this context my interests in gender and in questions of tradition came together. I saw, at close hand, the inner workings of a folklore association, one whose leadership was female (which in itself was very unusual). I also became very close to some of these girls, as we shared and explored details of our lives and relationships over time, a process that taught me a great deal about this variety of female experience.

My identities as *laoghrafos* and as *koritsi / yineka* thus had both productive and problematical consequences for me. Although I could sometimes slightly renegotiate their meanings, I could never fully control them. It was largely through these identities that I encountered the people of Sohos, and they me; and the ethnographic "data" generated in the process are profoundly marked by them.

SHIFTING IMAGES OF PLACE

As both village and town, farming community and market center, Sohos resists easy categorization in social scientific terms. This ambiguity is something that Sohoians also recognize. Initially I found their variable, situationally shifting ways of describing their community frustrating. In a letter I wrote home in late 1983, I lamented, "I can't figure out this town. On the one hand, they're always boasting that they're an old village, which makes them 'better' than the refugee villages. On the other, they've abandoned so much in favor of being 'modern.' They point this out themselves. It's like a contradiction rooted in their own self-perception." Much later I came to understand that it is only by talking in these seemingly contradictory ways that Sohoians can make sense of their complicated historical experience and express the multiple aspects of their complex contemporary identity.

Sohoians like to portray their community as a bit of a bustling metropolis, a *komopoli*, in relation to the smaller, newer, ostensibly sleepy and wholly agricultural villages that surround them. They take the thriving marketplace as a sign of Sohos' precedence—in age and in importance—over these smaller places. Throughout the year, men and women, young and old, crowd the market during shopping hours, that is, every morning except Sunday and four evenings a week.[18] On the other evenings, men still gather in its coffeehouses (*kafenia*) and restaurants, which are generally open all day, every day.

Clearly the marketplace is the town's center not only geographically but ethically and socially. The phrase "man of the market" epitomizes the properly "social" or "public-spirited" person (*kinonikos anthropos*). The market, a place for getting and spending, is equally a social meeting place. Women take off their head scarves, put on a clean sweater and skirt, and exchange slippers for shoes before setting off on their morning shopping expeditions, child in tow. Returning from the fields in the evenings, men replace their muddy overalls with slacks and a frayed but presentable wool jacket and tie and climb back onto their tractors, off to the *kafenio* in the center. Coming to the market, seeing others and being seen, is a way that Sohoians show their membership in the community (see also Errington 1984:56).

Paradoxically, though the market is very old, it has for Sohoians come to symbolize the degree to which they are becoming (or have become) "modern" (*modherni*). It is in part through the consumption and display of manufactured and mass-produced, rather than homemade or even locally made, objects that townspeople show that they are not just "country bumpkins" (*horiates*). In the late Ottoman period, the wealthiest local merchants expressed their identification with European culture in various ways: they spoke Greek rather than Macedonian, they sent their sons to western Europe to be educated, and some of the men (but not the women) adopted European garb. Now, though it is not only members of the commercial middle class who have embraced "European" ways, it is they who are affluent enough, and sufficiently removed from the vicissitudes of farm work, to embody this identification most visibly through their clothes, speech, and "clean" ways of making a living.

Some Sohoians see living in a *komopoli* as a mark of their collective superiority over residents of other communities. At the same time this

---

[18] A widow, however, who is expected to withdraw from active social life, will go very early in the morning, before it becomes crowded, or will avoid the market altogether, sending a relative to shop for her.

unifying sentiment vis-à-vis outsiders is opposed by the awareness that a *komopoli*, by definition, is a place where intracommunal distinctions—of wealth, class, prestige—exist. As a woman farmer, equating "villageness" with lack of differentiation, explained to me, "Sohos isn't a village, it's a *komopoli*: we have social classes [*dhen ine horio, ine komopoli, ehume taksis*]!"

Most of the time, however, when a comparison with these smaller villages is not being explicitly made, Sohoians refer to their community as "the village" (*to horio*). The implicit contrast is with Thessaloniki, "the city," but this is not merely a distinction of size. The term *horio* has multiple connotations, evoking Sohos' rural character, its supposed backwardness, and its introverted social relations: that is, the proximity of kin but also of enemies, the ubiquity of gossip, the familiarity that promises both security and boredom. The term has an intimate feel to it: one can speak of "my *horio*," but one would never say "my *komopoli*," for the latter has a technical and formal connotation. Yet it must be stressed that the Sohoians' perception of their community as a *horio* does not emerge wholly out of their experience within it. It is in part the interest of important urban outsiders (Greek and foreign scholars, government officials, television crews) that inspires the Sohoians' sense of pride in their "traditional village" (*paradhosiako horio*). Indeed, as epitomized in the fascination outsiders show for its traditional *karnavalia*, Sohos derives prestige, not scorn, for its un-citified qualities.

Consequently Sohoians sometimes deride the niceties of civilized living and prefer instead to emphasize their identity as "mountain people" (*vunisii*). I was present one afternoon in the boisterous atmosphere of a classroom of teenagers assembled for an English lesson, when Artemis, their teacher, asked one of the youngest, a twelve-year-old boy, to adjust the venetian blinds against the glaring sun. The boy pulled himself upright, threw back his shoulders exaggeratedly, and affected a thick "local" accent. "We're mountain people!" he roared, to the delighted squeals of his classmates, "What do we want with venetian blinds?" The defiance and rough manners he wryly and lovingly parodied are echoed in many contexts of male sociability: in the rowdy camaraderie of the wedding procession, in the alternately pensive and jubilant moments when men sing Carnival songs together, even in the ways men call out to each other on the street in everyday life. What young teachers and civil servants from the cities on two-year posts, and even some local young people, decry as the uncouth manners of backward yokels (*kathisterimeni*) is for other Sohoians, at least some of the time, a way of being to revel in.

Negotiating Place and Placement

The particularities of place are not merely a background in front of which the dramas of the dance occur. They are also constitutive of them. It is the specificity of the Sohoians' personal and collective experience that is always drawn upon, incorporated and represented in these events.

Yet Sohos is also, as it has always been, enmeshed in social, economic, political, and ideological processes and histories that range far beyond its boundaries. This placement has both material and ideological ramifications. It is registered in the concrete details of daily living, and it also situates the very ways Sohoians imagine themselves as a community (Anderson 1983). Thus many of the terms that figure importantly in the local discourse about "what kind of people we are in this place" derive from more encompassing discourses: notably, those of folklore scholarship and of modernization theory, themselves products of an evolutionary perspective on human history that still informs the dominant economic, political, and philosophical discourses of the West.

In discussions of everything from jellied fruit to gender, Sohoians are prone to muse: "Are we backward or civilized? Traditional or modern? Farmers and mountain people or cosmopolitan townspeople?" It is largely on these terms, whose moral overtones are hardly unambiguous, that Sohoians draw as they construct stories, verbal and embodied, about their experiences "here."

CHAPTER THREE

Everyday Sociability as Gendered Practice

> What are little girls made of?
> Sugar and spice
> and all things nice.
> That's what little girls are made of.
>
> —English nursery rhyme

BECAUSE the gendered practices of dance-events both draw upon and transform those of everyday life, it is useful to examine the ways Sohoians learn to be male and female within the practices of everyday sociability. Coffee drinking, for example, is a gendered practice: the different ways and places that male and female Sohoians drink coffee both express and reproduce the gendered ordering of their world. Moreover, as a seemingly trivial pursuit in which gender is symbolically and practically realized (both comprehended and made real) with much pleasure and little ado, coffee drinking exemplifies the hegemonic process that gendering involves in this community.

Though convivial and pleasurable, coffee drinking is neither free nor formless. This sociable practice is also a social obligation. After sharing endless cups of coffee with my Sohoian friends I too came to feel enmeshed in its meanings and reciprocities. Indeed, the power relations animating these apparently consensual forms of sociability which are especially worthy of attention. The very triviality and taken-for-granted quality of these routine encounters over the coffee cup are a significant part of their power. For, as Bourdieu argues, it is over trivial matters of form and formality that those in power "extort the essential while seeming to demand the insignificant" (1977:95).

FOOD, SPIRITS, AND ENGENDERING PERSONHOOD

A centrally important context within contemporary Greek society for expressions of personhood (both as ideally conceived and as practically negotiated) is that of commensality, the sociable sharing of food and drink. It is through the idiom of feeding that Sohoians assert the exemplary moral worth of their town. Comparing themselves collectively to other communities in the area, they would insist to me that Sohos was more honorable and worthy (*pio filotimo*). Since being *filotimo* is a term of moral value whose specific meaning varies according to situation and across communities (see Herzfeld 1980a), I pressed them to explain what this meant. They frequently answered: "If you were a stranger to the village and I saw you on the street, I would take you home to my wife, who'd give you something to eat." Many people, in fact, considered *filotimia* to be essentially synonymous, in this context, with *filoksenia* (literally, "love of the stranger"), the word most often glossed as "hospitality." In offering such translations, they were stressing the extent to which being proper human beings requires generosity: it requires those who are *filotimi* to "feed"—rather than "eat" (that is, betray or steal from)—others.

The conventional practices of eating and drinking in Sohos give this emphasis meaning. Uncooked foods (salads, raw vegetables, breads, sweets) and tidbits are not even considered "food" (*fai*); and these are usually eaten away from home, in restaurants, in the streets, or when visiting. By contrast, proper food, in the form of meals, is prepared by the mother or daughter-in-law to be eaten only by members of the family and any houseguests, who are temporarily reidentified as honorary family members. It is rare to invite a fellow villager over for dinner casually. Dinner parties as a purely social event are not a part of local practice. The fact that sharing food within the house is so strongly associated with everyday familial conviviality is an important aspect of the meaning of ritual occasions when this convention is broken.

Everyday exchanges among individuals of separate households involve not "food," in local terms, but special, abbreviated forms of it (sweets and tidbits) and also drink. The form of the exchanges typically reflects the pervasive reality of a gender-segregated spatial world: women and men eat separately. Gender difference is also codified through the foods and drinks that appear in these everyday exchanges. The association of men with pungent and salty substances and women with sweet substances is pervasive.

This is clearly exemplified in the formal *kerasma*, the customary offering of hospitality. When I visited women in their homes for the first time, I received this *kerasma* in its most elaborate form. The first item offered by the woman of the house (or sometimes a daughter) is a tiny glass of a syrupy, usually fruit-flavored liqueur called, revealingly enough, "the womanly [drink]" (*to yinekio*). It is always served in a richly adorned thin-stemmed glass, silver or crystal, from a tray held by the hostess, who stands in front of the seated guest. Many women make their own liqueur from local fruits.

The second item offered is a chocolate candy wrapped in shiny me-
tallic paper. Such was the conformity among households on the details
of this procedure that nearly every Sohoian hostess served me the same
brand of chocolate, a cube with a hazelnut center, wrapped in shiny
green foil.[1]

The third item, and the symbolic focus, is a piece of home-made
jellied fruit, bathed in sugary syrup. This jellied fruit, called a *ghliko*
(sweet), may be prepared from a dizzying variety of fruits and nuts,
including cherries, figs, quinces, eggplants, tomatoes, and walnuts,
often grown on the household's lands. Making this sweet is a hot,
time-consuming, and not inexpensive project, and for local women
the gluey but perfectly preserved fruit constitutes an emblem of the
housewife's artistry and skill.

Finally, I would be offered a glass of cold water, to be drunk not at
my leisure but instead, after a conventionalized toast to the hostess and
her family, downed in a few gulps. After all of these sweet things had
been eaten, I was often offered coffee, with the perfunctory query,
"You drink it sweet, don't you?"

This *kerasma* was virtually identical in every house I visited for the
first time. It is customarily offered to any stranger, male or female, on
his or her initial visit. Though it is not mandatory for subsequent visits, I noticed that many women liked to serve this to me and to each
other during even impromptu everyday visits. Since a typical afternoon's round of visiting could, for me, easily include two or three
houses, I sometimes found Sohoian housewives' famous generosity
something of an ordeal. My attempts to refuse the afternoon's third
ghliko, in a cultural context where refusing offers of food and drink is
always problematical (for example, see Kenna n.d.), were likely to be
greeted with dismay and surprise. After all, women "liked" sweets![2]

In this community, sweet substances are the medium of everyday
female exchanges. Ingesting sweets, these girls and women literally
produce themselves as properly feminine persons; they do what they
"should" (observe the etiquette of guest–host relations) as well as what
they "want" (since they "naturally" desire sweets). The conflation of
moral propriety and desire tends to obscure the socially constructed
nature and coercive dimension of this pleasure. Rather, the association

---

[1] Other brands of chocolate were available, but this was considered the best.

[2] The way in which a woman's culturally formulated "desire" becomes an injunction,
especially when located in sociable practices, was further revealed in a discussion I had
with a young unmarried friend, Miranda (see Chapter 7), about "being polite." Sym-
pathizing with my plight at having to eat all those sweets, she remarked on the difficulty
of refusing, "But if you refuse a sweet, the woman will say [to others], 'she doesn't
condescend to eat our sweet!' "

of femininity and sweetness becomes naturalized as it is encoded in both practices and substances.

Women and girls eating at a celebration or in a tavern, for example, conventionally mark their avoidance of too much or too strong liquor by diluting and sweetening their wine with soda pop, usually a cola variety. This gendered practice is echoed both in the local terminology about types of wine and in assumptions about wine consumption. A local shopkeeper, describing to me the wines he had available, characterized the sharper, drier, and stronger red wine, the *brusko*, as "harsh and manly" (*skliro, andriko*). The *imighliko*, a sweeter and milder variety, which he thought would most interest me, he described as softer (*pio malako*) and "more womanly" (*pio yinekio*).

Similarly, the symbolic association of maleness with pungent and salty substances emerges in everyday exchanges among men. *Kafenia*, where men gather, do not serve sweets and pastries at all. Exchanges typically center around coffee (prepared according to each man's taste but tending to be less sweet than women's) and ouzo, a clear, distilled anisette-flavored brandy. Ouzo, in particular, is of key importance in the contexts and practices of male conviviality. It is the central object of reciprocal, and sometimes competitive, hospitality in the *kafenia*. Its potency is recognized as a force that suspends inhibitions between men, facilitating sociability yet also at times causing them to forget their manners and lose control. Ouzo is always eaten with tidbits (*mezelikia*) to counteract its corrosive effect on the stomach and to soften the intoxication it produces. These customarily include bits of sausage and cheese, olives, smoked fish, raw vegetables such as tomatoes and cucumbers, and bread. It is not merely its alcoholic potency that renders ouzo a "male" drink, however. Like wine, which is distinguished according to sweetness into manly and womanly varieties, ouzo is conceptually opposed to "the womanly [drink]," that category of syrupy sweet fruit and mint-flavored liqueurs.

COFFEE, LOVE, AND PASSING THE TIME

In the symbolic universe of commensality, coffee is an element used by both men and women. This simplest and most commonly shared beverage is the obligatory offering among women when visiting each other's houses, and among men congregating in the *kafenia*. It is clearly a quintessential symbol of everyday sociability. For female Sohoians, the act of drinking coffee is rich with morally ambiguous connotations, which can be unraveled by looking, first, at the dominant mode of coffee drinking among women and the sorts of associations surrounding it.

Married women who live in close proximity frequently gather in each other's houses for coffee. Informal visiting may occur during the late morning (after the morning chores have been completed and the midday meal is on the stove), after lunch during the midday rest period (particularly if the men of the house do not return home for lunch), and in the evening. These breaks from the daily routine provide women a chance to relax, to commiserate, and to exchange news. In the mornings such breaks may be brief, because there is housework to complete, but midday breaks may last an hour or two, and evening visiting—particularly among neighbors and relatives—even longer.

During these visits, women pass the time in each other's company. Being with others is valued for itself. Sohoians use a Turkish word, which they perceive as a local usage not found in surrounding villages or Thessaloniki, to highlight the pleasurable and comfortable intimacy of this sort of talk. They say, "We are making *muhabet* [*kanume muhabet*]."

In a community where competition among families for prestige and wealth is taken for granted, however, this talk is, in fact, often focused on the exploits and misfortunes of others. Significantly, many Sohoians identify malicious and mocking talk as an activity to which women are especially prone. Thus it is frequently said—by both men and women—that women get together in their neighborhood "to drink coffee and gossip." The coffee-drinking event, an emblem of intimate sociability, is in such moments redefined as an index of women's easy life and idle talk. People attribute women's proclivity to gossip both to envy (*zilia*) and to their need to find release from the boredom of a routinized and restricted existence. Many women accept this definition of themselves as "gossipers" (*kotsomboles*), at least to an extent. And though some women view men's propensity to spend long hours and often considerable amounts of cash in the *kafenio* as a vice equal to their own, most tend to accept this as an inevitable aspect of male privilege.

One of the ways coffee is used among girls and women, but almost never among men, is for divination. Strictly speaking, reading coffee grounds is forbidden by the Greek Orthodox Church as a pagan form of magic seeking to unravel a future that only God may know. Though pious Sohoians strongly disapprove, most people—male and female alike—regard "saying the cup" as recreational. They may also feel the practice is slightly shameful, though more for its connotations of superstition than of sin. It is viewed as a way in which silly women pass the time. The technique is simple: Greek coffee, a finely pulverized coffee boiled with sugar and water, is served in demitasse cups, and the grounds are allowed to settle, making a thick mud on the bottom. If one turns the cup over, rolling it as one allows the slightly moist grounds to run out into the saucer, the sediment that clings to the sides of the cup forms patterns of light and dark spaces and vaguely shaped objects. There is a restricted vocabulary of symbols that can be discerned, and depending on their location in the cup, they can be "placed" in time and in social space (that is, near or away from the "house"), and their significance guessed.

Participants do not necessarily agree on the reliability of the ritual. Many young women can relate stories of unlikely romantic predictions suggested by the cup that miraculously came true, but others are more skeptical, joining in eagerly "just for a laugh." Regardless of the degree to which girls and women believe in or deny the coffee cup's power as a tool to divine the future, however, the coffee cup is compelling because it concretizes a language of emotions and relationships that configure the female world.[3] As such, it is also a center for this sort of talk and may, indeed, be its excuse.

A good deal of my experience in observing coffee-cup readings was in the company of my *parea*. Though their homes were far apart in town, they managed to meet nearly every afternoon for coffee, and saying the cup was a crucial part of this daily ritual. The diviner of the cup might be a mother or another older female relative, a neighbor, or one of the group of contemporaries, but the themes of the cup hardly changed from one day to the next. Readers often saw rings or a table filled with people (signifying engagements), male figures of various proportion and coloring or letters of the alphabet (references to a prospective suitor), and, more vaguely auspicious, crosses and coins (indicating good news or good fortune). There were also signs for news or letters from afar (white or black birds) and for money (a pattern of bubbles at the top of the cup). "Roads" (understood in the widest metaphorical sense) might be "open" or "blocked." More generally, the reader interpreted the emotional state of the cup's owner, both present and future, by the overall shade of the grounds: "light" or "open" cups indicated joy and "dark" or "closed" cups indicated anxiety or sorrow.

The crowning moment occurred at the end, when the reader asked the owner of the cup to impress the bottom of the cup lightly with her finger while silently making a wish. The bottom interior of the cup is believed to be the "heart." The pattern left by the finger was then interpreted by the reader, who usually saw a letter, face, or figure, and this was customarily attributed to a romantic interest, whether nearby

---

[3] Coffee-cup reading, as an intimate context where female emotions and relationships are explored, seems analogous in some ways to the informal recitations of personal love poetry among Bedouin women, analyzed in Abu-Lughod (1986).

or remote. Since the reader often knew many personal details about the young woman whose cup she was reading, she would in her interpretations allude vaguely to these. She frequently asked the young woman to concur or elaborate upon her interpretations. If the reader was not well acquainted with the owner of the cup, she often asked leading questions in an attempt to feel out the situation and garner information.

I always asked for my cup to be read, and I noticed that this was a forum in which various female acquaintances tried to find out information about my marriage, my feelings about my husband and our physical separation, and my general emotional response to being so far away from home. In responding, I often felt the same ambivalence about volunteering detailed personal information that I noticed in my friends. For though it was a situation of great intimacy, it was also one of vulnerability and danger. To readers they did not fully know or trust, my friends gave vague, cryptic answers with as little detail as possible, though all the time hanging on every word of exegesis. With readers they trusted, interpretation was often a dynamic, shared project.

Coffee drinking among Sohoian females, then, is a focus for passing the time and it resonates with a certain moral ambiguity. It is associated with pleasurable sociability, but also with idle and malicious gossip. And it is a context for—and the coffee cup a symbolic focus of—the exploration of emotions girls and women experience toward individuals loved or desired.[4] That is, it elicits talk, sometimes clothed in highly metaphoric or elliptical language, of love, sexuality, and the directions of female destiny—talk that reiterates traditional notions of the contours and limits of female experience.

In truth, this is not quite all. There is at least one more meaning to coffee drinking. Jokes, stories, and expressions full of innuendo note in the cups of coffee shared by a man and a woman flirtation and the pursuit of sex. But this part of the picture cannot be explored until the place where such sharing occurs is described.

THE MORAL GEOGRAPHY OF PUBLIC LEISURE SPACE

The dominant gender ideology in Sohos is powerfully manifested in the symbolic and practical organization of space. This association of

---

[4] I am indebted to conversations with Alexandra Bakalaki, who has also written about Greek women's coffee-cup readings, for the insight that stories created from the cup refer not to the future but to women's and girls' *present* experience. In this respect, Sohoian coffee-cup readings bear similarities with scapulomancy, observed and analyzed in Crete by Herzfeld (1985a:247–58).

5. Three men pass the time playing cards in Sofulis's *kafenio*.

gender and space is a familiar theme in anthropological studies of Greece and, indeed, of the Mediterranean and southern Europe generally. Although to say that rural Greek communities are divided into male and female spaces seems accurate, at least as a rough approximation, to even the most casual of foreign observers, anthropologists have for years vigorously debated the situational nuances and regional variations of this all-too-neat dichotomy. I limit my task here to an examination of how the dominant gender ideology organizes public leisure space in Sohos—specifically, in three institutionalized leisure spaces: the *kafenio*, the *zaharoplastio*, and the *kafeteria*.

The quintessential institution of male social life in Greece, as in most Balkan societies, is the coffeehouse, or *kafenio* (see figure 5). It is here that manhood is expressed, reputations are negotiated, and social relationships are enlivened through endless card playing, political debate, competitive talk, and reciprocal hospitality (see Campbell 1964; Herzfeld 1985a, 152–55 and passim). The ambience and social meanings of the *kafenio* space can vary from one region, or even one community, to the next. In Sohos the identity of the *kafenio* as a male space was, on the level of everyday use, nearly inviolable. As an ethnographer and visiting American, I was given the courtesy of limited access to these sites. I even frequented on a fairly regular basis one *kafenio* renowned for its singers and storytellers, where I gradually came to be regarded as a sort of adopted daughter to the predominantly elderly clientele. I never saw a Sohoian girl or woman enter a local *kafenio* as a

casual customer, however. Most avoided entering at all, preferring—
on occasions when it was necessary to fetch a male relative—to stand
outside an open door or a window and attempt to gain his attention by
gesturing or hissing in a stage whisper. Girls and women often insisted
to me that they could not imagine going into the *kafenio*. They stressed
that even the souvlaki grills (*suvladzidhika*), which are less definitively
"male" spaces, though still dominated by male customers, and which
girls sometimes enter to order sandwiches to take out, made them
acutely uncomfortable. "*Drepome*," they explained, using the verb that
conveys the speaker's sentiment of both embarrassment and shame.
They described feeling intimidated by the stares of the men and uneasy
about talk that might ensue among the men after the girls had left. As
the girls' remarks underline, the boundaries of the *kafenio* as a male
space, though largely implicit, were absolute and almost sensually per-
ceptible. With rare exceptions, the girls I queried expressed little desire
to intrude. Nevertheless, they saw the *kafenio* as a symbol of men's
freedom to gather together and move freely within public space, a
freedom they themselves lacked.[5]

Kafenia tend to be simple and functional. Wooden or metal tables
and hard, wooden straight-backed chairs stand on a gritty floor cov-
ered with cigarette butts and mud from the street. The walls are often
painted a nondescript chartreuse, a color those familiar with Greece
recognize as "*kafenio* green." With their friendly splashes of color and
archaic posters on the wall, the older *kafenia* are cozier than the newer
cavernous, concrete-walled versions. In winter, with heating ineffi-
cient or too expensive to use freely, they can be uncomfortably chilly.
Yet the dearth of creature comforts actually highlights the *kafenio*'s human focus: it is a bare and unpretentious setting for the serious business
of male sociability.

Although women's coffee drinking occurs primarily on an everyday
basis within the house and neighborhood, women may, on occasion,
go out to establishments in the community. Most married women rely
upon their husbands to "take them out" now and then, and sensitive
husbands feel an obligation to do so (see Hirschon 1978). Throughout
Greece, the site of such an outing, often a Sunday afternoon event, has
typically been the "sweet shop" (*zaharoplastio*).

Though they coexist in public space, the *zaharoplastio* stands in conceptual opposition to the *kafenio*, according to the symbolic association
of women (and here, also children) with sweetness and men with pungent and salty tastes. On a more practical level, too, gender difference
is apparent in patterns of use. One rarely observes men who do not

[5] An awareness of the symbolism of the *kafenio* in Greek society also animated the
decision by Athenian feminists to establish a "Women's Kafenio" in central Athens in
the early 1980s.

have their wives with them spending time in a *zaharoplastio* except, perhaps, to keep company with the owner. Both men and women may enter its doors as customers, to buy chocolates, rich and elaborate tortes, or bottles of liqueur to take as gifts when visiting.

The one Sohoian establishment that explicitly identified itself as a *zaharoplastio* did an excellent trade in selling sweets, but I rarely saw more than four or five people seated at its surfeit of tables. The contrasts it provided with the local *kafenia* were remarkable, though this must in part be attributed to the unusual artistic sensitivity of the proprietor. Located slightly up the hill from the central square, the *zaharoplastio* consisted of one large and airy room, whose windows overflowed with large, luxuriant plants. Sunny and spotless, it featured a massive color television hung high from the wall.[6] I came here several times with my *parea* to share a local specialty (*tulumbes*), sausage-shaped and fluted pieces of fried batter soaked in sugar syrup, a delicacy whose shape evoked a slew of bawdy remarks and off-color jokes. These visits notwithstanding, I noticed the shop was usually empty, used by families and groups of young women only occasionally. In the cities, the contrast between the *zaharoplastio* and the *kafenio* is even greater, but it is clear enough in Sohos. Always pleasant, sometimes elegant, the *zaharoplastio* provides an airy, refined, respectable contrast to the smoky, noisy, and often volatile *kafenio*.

Sometime between my second visit in the summer of 1978 and my return for extended fieldwork almost five years later, a new kind of establishment appeared in Sohos. The evening of my arrival in February 1983, I was taken by my host, Mihalis, and his first cousin Yannis, on a walk up the hill to the town center to see "how things had changed." Aching with cold and tired from my journey as well as from our trek up the icy road, I followed them across the central square and down a steep, snow-packed side street. We opened a door to what I had remembered as the so-called German garment factory. Inside, hidden behind cheap velour curtains that hung unevenly across the window panes, was a large interior, wood paneled and hung with scenic posters of forests and rivers. Wide plush chairs were set around low metal tables, and in the center an enormous spot-lit fountain sprayed tiny blue jets of water. Far against the back wall was a cocktail bar, above which hung a television equipped with video. We sat down, I—as the only female in sight—rather self-consciously, and ordered not Greek coffee, which was not on the menu, but Nescafé® with milk. This, I learned, was the *kafeteria*, the largest and most popular of three now operating in Sohos.

The *kafeteria* is a hybrid establishment combining aspects of a bar

---

[6] During the period of my fieldwork, none of the *kafenia* had televisions.

and a *zaharoplastio*. Inspired by the Italian *cafeteria*, which it imitates in both name and style, the *kafeteria* was originally an urban phenomenon. I noticed them first in 1975 in areas near the university in central Athens, where they catered to student tastes, exuding an ambience both "European" and "sophisticated." They tended to serve tea (a beverage rarely encountered in a Greek household) and coffee (but only Nescafé®, occasionally espresso, and almost never the heady brew known as either Turkish or Greek coffee); "European" apertifs such as whiskey, vermouth, cognac, and only sometimes ouzo;[7] canned juices (sweetened, yet a noticeable innovation from the carbonated soft drinks of the *zaharoplastia*); and *tost*, a grilled sandwich of cheese or salami that was just emerging as competition to the traditional and still popular cheese and spinach pies (*tiropites* and *spanakopites*). Architectural space reiterated the symbolic detachment from demotic culture. Unlike *kafenia*, which are nearly always situated at street level, whose doors and windows perpetually open out to the street, and whose tables may even spill onto the sidewalk, *kafeteries* were often at basement level or occasionally upstairs. At the very least, they were closed off from the street by heavy curtains. The ethos of *kafenio* sociability—a constant awareness of and intermittent engagement in the street life that bounds it—was here replaced by a withdrawal into a dark interior haven. Absent was the *kafenio*'s characteristic harshness, its bare, glaring lightbulb hanging on a wire from the ceiling. The *kafeteria* was softly lit, and sometimes featured jazz playing quietly in the background. It was, in the Athenian context, a place for students to spend long hours in conversation. With its connotations of cultural sophistication, political activity, and sexual freedom, it seemed a Greek analogue of not only its Italian counterpart but also, perhaps, the Parisien café of the late 1960s.

In the late 1970s *kafeteries* gradually began to appear in other provincial cities and in the countryside. Most attempted to replicate an atmosphere of urban, European sophistication. In the cities the *kafeteria* has become a new haven, along with the bar, for working-class youths, for whom *kafenia* hold little interest. In the countryside the responses have been curious and mixed.

WHEN WOMEN DRINK COFFEE IN THE KAFETERIA

One of Sohos' three *kafeteries* is patronized almost exclusively by the high-school crowd, and though this space is male territory during cer-

[7] Distilled alcoholic drinks imported from Western Europe are sometimes referred to as "European drinks" (*evropaïka pota*).

tain times of the day, groups of girls often congregate here after school. They socialize both among themselves and with their male classmates. The dominant clientele of the other two *kafeteries* is youths and men in their prime.[8] Scattered among this dominant group on any weekday afternoon, however, are one or two clusters of girls. They are almost without exception unmarried. They buy juice, a soft drink, or a Nescafé® and talk for a while, joking and laughing among themselves and with other acquaintances they may see in the *kafeteria*. Yet they always appear conscious of the eyes of the men around them. They arrive and leave in groups of two or more, never alone.

As an establishment that does not fit neatly into the familiar classification of gender and space, the *kafeteria* is a topic of discussion among Sohoians. Such discourse ostensibly concerns the moral tone of the place, but its subtext revolves around the nature and moral capacities of the categories "man" and, more especially, "woman." "Is it a good thing, or not, for girls to pass their time in the *kafeteria*?" Sohoians disagree. Amid the polyphony of opinion is the ideological struggle to define gender. As I listened and sought to analyze what I heard, five voices, each of which articulated a distinct position on women and the *kafeteria*, stood out.[9] Three upheld the dominant gender ideology, though for different reasons. The remaining two challenged it—one begrudgingly, the final one with conviction.

Katina

The first voice belongs to Katina, wife of Mihalis and my initial host in Sohos. Although Mihalis first introduced me to the *kafeteria*, Katina never goes. One day I was discussing with Katina and her elderly mother-in-law, Irini, the vicissitudes of life for girls in Sohos, and the conversation turned to the perils of narcotics. "Things are very difficult for young girls," Irini lamented. "They go into the *kafeteries*, and in the cigarettes they are offered, or even right into their sodas, men slip in drugs." In emphatic agreement, Katina told me a story: A teenage girl of a good family commuted daily from a neighboring village to attend the local high school. One afternoon she left her group of girlfriends on the pretext of buying a pastry, and in the *kafeteria* she briefly entered she was approached by a man. Every morning thereafter, instead of going to school, she met him there. When one of the

---

[8] Elderly men remain attached to the *kafenia*, though they may patronize *kafeteries* occasionally.

[9] I use the term "voice" somewhat loosely to refer to a verbally articulated position on the subject of gender. Three of the voices belong to individuals, speaking alone; two draw on utterances of more than one individual.

teachers noticed her extended absences, and ascertained her where-
abouts, he informed her grandfather (who was at that time acting as
her guardian because her parents were guest workers in Germany).
Horrified at this news, the old man vowed to catch her in the act of
leaving and drag her away by the hair. The teacher calmed the old man,
and together they apprehended her.

Katina ended her tale of woe this way:

> They got hold of her, and she confessed [pause] that in that place
> where they were going, in the *kafeteria*, they had found drugs. And
> in this way, they had corrupted the girls. And it wasn't only her,
> there were six other girls, too. . . . They put drugs right in the or-
> ange soda, or perhaps in the glasses they offered the girls. They can
> put in anything they want, are *you* going to realize what they're
> opening up and putting in?

The way Katina used the word "confess" surprised me. Given the way
the story was unfolding, I expected the girl to "confess" to her illicit
relationship with the man. Instead, Katina portrayed her as confessing
to being victimized. The couple's sexual involvement is taken for
granted, but the girl, in Katina's portrayal, had defined her role as passive. If she were involved in indecencies, they were "being done to
her," presumably while she was in a drugged stupor.

Katina tells us of girls who are vulnerable, not treacherous. Under
the circumstances, such an attribution seems remarkable. But it is
likely that this perception of the female condition predates the story.
Married women, particularly mothers of teenage girls, constantly fret
over their daughters' vulnerability. "Girls are a worry," mothers would
often lament. One woman, remarking that "a girl is dangerous,"
clearly did not have in mind an image of Eve-like sexual destructive-
ness, because she paraphrased this statement by listing everything that
could be done to a girl. Women who stress girls' vulnerability perceive
their entrance into the dangerous and unsupervised space of the *kafeteria* as threatening not to men or to the "moral order" in the abstract
but to the girls themselves. In this explanation, the implicit source of
danger is the voracious and predatory sexuality of men.

Yet if this proclaimed "fear" acknowledges the very real dangers a
girl faces, to her reputation and to her person, in a patriarchal society,
it does little to challenge that society's dominant assumptions. Indeed,
the fear expressed by girls—many, echoing their mothers, laughingly
confess to fearing "being watched," "wolves," "the dark," "everything!"—can be seen as a claim of virtue (see Abu-Lughod 1986:158).
Linking vulnerability with virtue, a girl's claim to being afraid articulates her dependence and calls forth a protective response. Whether

made by or on behalf of girls, such utterances do acknowledge girls' vulnerable social position. But inasmuch as they suggest that the solution lies in increased protection of girls, rather than in challenging the aggressive behavior of men, even these sympathetic speakers uphold the banishment of girls to domestic or female-dominated space.

Stellios

The second voice is less ambiguous and certainly less ambivalent. It belongs to Stellios, a farmer in his early fifties. Stellios was one of the participants in a conversation in the *kafeteria* about the *kafeteria*. The discussion occurred just after an afternoon speech in honor of International Women's Day in March 1984. The speaker, a young woman belonging to the PA.SO.K.-affiliated Union of Greek Women, had been invited by a town official and spoke on why the townswomen ought to organize as women and what the present government was doing to improve women's working and living conditions and to further their interests. The speech was poorly attended, and the few women and girls who came felt that the absence of more women had much to do with the location of the event in the *kafeteria*. After the speech finished, I struck up a conversation with several of these women and girls, hoping to find out what they felt about various women's issues. I asked two girls, Amalia, aged seventeen and Soula, aged twenty, to discuss with me (as I tape-recorded them) their experience as girls in Sohos.

As this conversation proceeded, Stellios listened from the next table. Initially amused and skeptical, he gradually grew uneasy with the girls' assertive rhetoric. He began to protest with his own stories. In one, he told of a woman who was uncontrollable despite her husband's constant and severe beatings. She left the house unattended, ran around with other men, and eventually drove her husband to his death from shame and defeat. Stellios portrayed this woman, allowed to pursue her own whims and desires outside the controls of society (especially as expressed in the husband's authority), as thoroughly incorrigible and treacherous. And when we began to explore the specific issue of married women drinking coffee in the *kafeteria*, he became adamant:

> Do you know where all this leads to, everybody? It leads to filling up the orphanages, the homes for abandoned babies, that's where it leads to, all this kind of thing. Because today we start coming here, tomorrow we come again, we start talking. . . . Either because I'm good at talking, or maybe I find that she speaks attractively, now, day after day, surely some kind of flirtation, some kind of love will

start up. Once two people fall in love, what happens? The kids are left out in the street. You mark my word!

Stellios' remarks as a whole portray woman as naturally treacherous. Ironically, they also identify her as the guardian of moral order. She is the one who should not enter the *kafeteria*, lest flirtation ensue. It is a characteristic contradiction of this ideology that though women are held to be guilty for luring men into sex (their "temptress" quality), they are also responsible for keeping men out of trouble (their rational and tempering influence). By no means unique to the Sohoian and Greek ideologies of gender, this contradiction is at the heart of Western liberal conceptions of woman.[10]

The Wife of Stellios

Stellios believes that a woman would wish to go to the *kafeteria* for one reason only: to pursue a sexual adventure. (Note his explicit reference to a married woman, reinforced in his reference to the fate of children.) Stellios believes that this compelling attraction cannot be resisted. In his view, women demonstrate that they are good by repudiating such a place, indeed, by not wanting to be there at all, as he indicated in telling us about his wife's reaction:

> *Jane*: Tell me, did your wife come to the speech?
> *Stellios*: No, she heard about it—I was sleeping—and she told me about it. So I say, "Why don't you go with the neighborhood women?" She laughs. "To do what?"
> *Jane*: Why didn't she want to come?
> *Stellios*: "To do what?" she says. I say to her, "Maybe you have some kind of complaint about the situation at home?"
> *Amalia*: Ah, bravo! Why do you think that just to come listen means she must have some complaint?

His wife, Stellios tells us, ridicules not only the *kafeteria* and the speech on women's issues, but indeed, the entire implication that she is dissatisfied with her personal situation at all.

---

[10] This contradiction, rather than merely articulating the Orthodox devil/Virgin Mary dichotomy, can probably also be traced to the influence of Enlightenment views of women on Greek thought since the eighteenth century. Kitromilides (1983) argues persuasively that Enlightenment philosophers (especially Rousseau), though critical of the appalling social condition of women, were reluctant to recognize women's rights to full equality with men. These thinkers put forward an alternative view of womanhood, in which through moral training and social discipline a woman sublimated her female nature to become "the subordinate complement of the perfect male nature." Chaste, self-abnegating, submissive, the woman was supposed to use her "Minerva-like prudence" to temper male excesses (Mably, cited in Kitromilides 1983:50).

This is the third voice. In some sense it is fitting that though the voice is that of a woman, a wife, it is uttered by a man, for a married woman's voice is the feminine voice most invested in male discourse and most tongue-tied and ambivalent (see Irigaray 1974). Although we must not forget that this third voice is a quotation (presented by her husband) of a woman who is not present, the attitude her words convey is not unfamiliar. A married woman—when speaking to her husband or to other women—may well deny any interest in going to a woman's meeting or in going out for coffee. She may even mock those who do. Indeed, this is precisely what Anna, herself married, who had attended the Women's Day discussion and who joined our conversation briefly, described as befalling her and the woman, also married, with whom she came:

> We were walking down the road, on our way here, and some women asked us, "Where are you going?" We were afraid to answer. "We're going to the gathering," we called out to them, "Come on with us!" But as soon as we said this, they started to make fun of us, saying: "What's so wrong with things that you want to go to this meeting? What will the men say?" Yet, in fact, when we were talking at home, our husbands had themselves said, "Go, listen, see what happens."

To which Amalia replied:

> It is the *women* who say, "What are you going to do?" Many women are like this. They think that a woman who comes here to listen is not acting right. That she wants to go against her husband. That she is stupid.

Stellios' wife, the townswomen Anna encountered, and Amalia's "many women," all invoked through quotation rather than present to speak for themselves, seem to say something similar: that the desire to go out to the *kafeteria*, whether to attend a speech or to drink a cup of coffee, is illegitimate. It challenges the implicit contract in which the married woman exchanges her good behavior for her husband's protection and respect.

Yet is repudiation of an interest in going out (a moral act) equivalent to a lack of desire? Younger married women often complained to me that they felt bored and restricted and that they wished there were places a woman could go to get out of the house. They admitted that there was now much greater freedom to go out with their husbands to clubs or to attend the formal dances sponsored by local civic associations. Indeed, they knew that their expectations for entertainment were comparatively greater than were their mothers' and grandmothers'. Yet they felt that in terms of everyday socializing, their right to enjoy certain small pleasures was not acknowledged. Such women often disparagingly noted the taboos against their movement in public as indicative of the community's grinding conservatism. "In other places," they remarked, "married women can go out for a cup of coffee, but here? *Po po po!*"[11] They thus indicated—but with some contempt—the disapproval that would greet them were they to act out this desire. In so doing, they marked the quality of the desire as unrealizable, fantastic, in relation to the world they inhabited.

Such a confession of interest to me, the ethnographer, and sometimes also to her peers, is not consistent with the married woman's public proclamation of disinterest articulated in this third voice. Why should this be so? In part it reflects her accurate sense of the politics of interpretation. One of the ways that those with conservative interests use a social definition of space (in this case, a space organized by gender) as a system of control is by controlling meaning.

In Greek popular discourse, when a man shares a cup of coffee with a woman the act has—at least potentially—sexual connotations. It is the first moment in many courtships, and both male and female actors know the rules of the game. A woman who accepts a cup of coffee from a man is thought to be looking, at the very least, for a game of flirtation. It may (and perhaps usually does) remain at this level, but people believe that sharing coffee can lead to seduction and illicit affairs.

Although a woman may have her own reasons for wishing to drink coffee in the *kafeteria* (say, to visit with her friends, to assert that she is independent, to get out of the house, to relax over a cup of coffee in a pleasant place "like a human being," or even to flirt), her own reasons are not recognized. Her act has a public meaning, indeed, a predetermined meaning, the only meaning allowed plausibility. The "triviality" of her desire, moreover, especially when she acts upon it, makes its predetermined meaning even more difficult to challenge. It is not as if a married woman must go into the *kafeteria* to do anything serious, such as earning a living or accomplishing important work for the family.

The emphasis upon this issue of meaning and interpretation is indicative in the use of the word *pareksigo*. It is usually glossed, "I misunderstand." But rendering it in a slightly clumsier but more literal way, we might read it as "I mis-explain." Consider Soula's story, as she ex-

---

[11] *Po po po!* is an expression of dismay, disbelief, or disapproval of something. In this context, one might gloss this as, "For shame!"

plains how people view older women who go out to a *kafeteria* together:

> *Soula*: In Potamia women go out regularly, that is, as men do. Yet
> here, I don't know why men have got it in their heads this way,
> they think the woman should be in the house. They've twisted
> things. I have a sister married in a village near Drama, and
> there, women—thirty, forty, fifty years old—they'll go out to
> a *kafeteria* alone and drink coffee.
>
> *Jane*: Alone? [I ask because the meaning of this word is ambiguous:
> it can mean "a woman by herself" or "women without a man
> or men."]
>
> *Soula*: In a group, only women. Here, for a woman over twenty-
> five—I'm not putting the age even lower, as I might—to go out
> with her friend, they'll "mis-explain" her [*tha tin pareksighisun*].

Creating a meaning out of a woman's coffee drinking is an active
process, an assertion. Mis-explaining is not merely befuddlement. If it
were, the woman could presumably state her case and clear up the
problem. In fact, mis-explaining her coffee drinking is an accusation,
though one that is hardly ever directly made; the criticism is perfectly
effective when it exists only as innuendo. Indeed, in the cloudy world
of what is implicitly understood, it seems almost superfluous to name.
Our conversation continued:

> *Jane*: What would they say of such a woman?
>
> *Soula*: A thousand and two things. [pause] What can I tell you now?
> [embarrassed laughter]
>
> *Amalia*: I already told you [earlier she had told me they see this
> woman "as a whore"].
>
> *Jane*: That she's, shall we say, "of the road"?
>
> *Soula*: Ah, bravo. They say, "How does her husband allow her to go
> out?"

Soula and Amalia are well aware of the terms of the moral framework in which the married woman's action will be explained. They
also recognize the possibility of the gap between what she wants when
she goes to the *kafeteria* and what the community says that she wants.
Married women are aware of it, as well.

The third voice, then, is one that states publicly that a "good"
woman does not refrain from going to the *kafeteria* because she is pre-
vented; rather, it asserts that she does not wish to go. It is a proclamation of virtue. The virtuous woman—it is claimed—is in perfect
harmony with her husband (who is always presumed to disapprove of

her entry into the *kafeteria*) and has no desire to jeopardize domestic harmony and her family's well-being for some trivial desire.

Married women bear a particular burden with respect to both the reality and the public image of family unity. To the extent that a woman's identity is domestically defined, her sense of competence, self-worth, and satisfaction may be strongly tied to how well she carries out her domestic responsibilities, including the emotional labor of managing familial relationships. At the same time, the public perception of her family's situation may be as important to such a woman as her own assessment and experience of it. Married women have very real interests in preserving the image of a harmonious family, for inasmuch as the woman is perceived as responsible for the house, any family and marital problems reflect negatively on her. This can be a cause for real suffering. As women often repeated to me, "People will say that 'the woman is to blame.'" Consequently, though some women may genuinely have no desire to go to the *kafeteria*, such a statement cannot necessarily be taken at face value. The denial of interest articulated in the third voice is contradicted by many women's private confessions that they would like to go but do not out of fear of possible consequences: gossip, censure, mockery, angry scenes at home, verbal or physical retaliation from a husband or parent-in-law, or problems for their family. This married woman's voice, coming from women as well as attributed to them, upholds the dominant gender ideology because, ironically, it is against her interests (as a wife, mother, and a lady of the community, a *kiria*) to assert her interests (as a woman, an autonomous person). And the woman's response to this intractable contradiction may involve not so much real acceptance but rather, a form of what Connolly calls "anticipatory surrender" (1983:91).

THE FIRST three voices, despite their complexities and ambivalences, reaffirm the validity of the segregation of unrelated men and women in public leisure space. Although the voices articulate this in part by assigning a moral quality to the *kafeteria* as a space, at the crux of their arguments is a particular conception of the female person and the meaning of her actions in the world. In this view, the female person actively "taking her pleasure" in the *kafeteria* constitutes a metaphor for an aggressive pursuit of sex. Thus, Stellios speaks of her as the archetypal and insatiable temptress; Katina defines the girl as a sort of "victim of pleasure"; and the third voice invokes the proper married woman as one who "repudiates" this sort of pleasure.

Yorghos

The fourth and fifth voices describe the *kafeteria* as a slightly different sort of place and the female as a slightly different sort of being. It is, in fact, in the final two voices that we first hear that she ought to be encountered not merely in terms of her sexuality but "as a person" (*san anthropos*). The fourth voice, that of Yorghos, remains ambivalent about the motives of either sex toward the other in the *kafeteria*, but because he finds the place agreeable, contemporary, and a sign of his own sophistication, he is unwilling to show himself an old-fashioned sort of patriarch.

Yorghos, a young single man in his early twenties, worked in the *kafeteria* but was well acquainted with the others in our group. Though at first he listened, silently, with Stellios, he spoke with easy familiarity to the girls. In the dynamics of the discussion, Yorghos was in a medial position, sometimes derisive of the girls' claims and opinions, sometimes agreeing with them against Stellios. His ambivalence, which demonstrated shifting assent to two mutually exclusive positions, is revealed in two statements.

The first was uttered at a point in the conversation when the girls were insisting that most married men of the town did not consider the needs of their wives for entertainment and release from the daily household routine. They felt that the men considered their obligations fulfilled when they took their wives out a few times a year, "on Christmas and Easter," as Soula remarked. This annoyed Yorghos, whose retort showed not only that he found their complaints exaggerated but also that he himself recognized a woman's need to get out (something that Stellios had explicitly denied). His sarcasm, moreover, was meant to convey that he would be quite liberal about permitting his future wife to fulfill these needs.

> Here you are, going on and on about all this, how do *you* get to come to the *kafeteria*? My wife, the young woman I'll marry one of these days, I can't—I'm not going to drag her along with me like a handbag. Let her take the kid, get her girlfriends, and come to the *kafeteria* for a cup of coffee. What, do I have to drag my wife along with me? Let her come.

Later on, however, after Stellios had pronounced that the woman in the *kafeteria* is the wrecker of marriages and happy families, Yorghos spoke up about what he was after in this sort of sociability:

> Let me tell you something. Every man, no matter how old, his mind is stuck on women. If I go into a store, to shop, even, or to the *kafeteria*, it doesn't stop me from seeing any woman that walks in,

married or single, if she isn't accompanied [by a man] I go right for her. It's in my mind straight away and I stalk her, like she's a chick, I don't regard her, in other words, as a woman. That's all natural, everyone more or less thinks this way. And don't forget that a person today[12] is mainly concerned with partying, with eating, and with figuring out how to make love with a woman and having a good time. I don't think he considers anything else. He doesn't see the woman, he sees her as an object, and thinks how to have a good time. Since he's had his good time, afterward, he acts as if he doesn't even know her.

In this aggressive monologue, Yorghos tells us how he thinks the world works. It is not a vision sympathetic to women, who seem to be excluded from his definition of a "person today." Indeed, in seeing women as objects of men's pleasure, he teeters toward the vision that Stellios articulates. The difference, perhaps, is that it discards the rhetoric of virtue, propriety, and complementarity and portrays the antagonistic struggles between men and women with a relatively straightforward rawness. It is also a significantly more individualistic vision, focused on desire and personal interest.

Soula and Amalia

The fifth voice is constituted by those of the two girls, Soula and Amalia. Though they have commented throughout on others' interpretations, they share a distinct vision of what a female is, and this they articulate in both what they say and what they do. First, they go to the *kafeteria*. Amalia, an unusually sophisticated student in her last year of secondary school, and Soula, the daughter of parents who in local terms are rather progressive, are striking as individuals, but in coming to the *kafeteria* they are not unique. To be sure, girls constitute a small minority among the customers, and their presence remains controversial. But townspeople identify the *kafeteries* as a meeting place for young people and they recognize, though they may disapprove, that girls increasingly spend time there.

Significantly, the use of the *kafeteria* by girls was viewed with relatively greater tolerance, grudging though it was, than that granted to married women. Their children's reality, parents admitted, was not the one they had known as children. They also recognized that girls have a comprehensible interest in seeing and being seen by young men. Being seen is, of course, an ambivalent process. Parents may quarrel

---

[12] Literally, "today's humanity," *i simerini anthropotita.*

with their daughters over what the latter "have been seen" doing there—such as smoking or flirting—whether this is rumor or fact. But the consequences for an unmarried girl are less serious—from the parents' perspective—than for a married woman.

It is also clear that despite its indisputably sinful connotations, the *kafeteria* carries prestige as a symbol of modern sophistication and civilized luxury. In a community that prides itself on being a bit of a bustling metropolis in comparison with the small sleepy villages surrounding it (yet one that is always painfully aware of its backwardness compared with the modern city of Thessaloniki), the *kafeteries* are part of the Sohoians' claim to being progressive. This explains, at least in part, why I, even as a woman, was taken to one on my first day by Mihalis, and why the mayor, an urban-bred and progressive man, arranged for the Women's Day speech to be held there. It is a lever that the girls use, as well, when they want to legitimize their presence there.

The conception of female personhood that Soula and Amalia defend is informed, first and foremost, by their understandings of a feminist discourse that emerges in the media and in the political agenda of the two major left-wing parties. It is informed, too, by the social position they occupy by virtue of their age and gender. Neither Soula nor Amalia is committed, in terms of interests or obligations, to a nuclear family in the same way that a married woman is. They are thus freer to articulate an ideal of the female person as autonomous and self-determining. Soula is indignant about the incessant and, to her, unreasonable demands for moral accountability that girls face in the village. She laments that girls constantly censor their own actions because of their fears of public disapproval:

> In the village, the one thing that everybody thinks about, whether it's to marry, to get engaged, to separate, or for the girl to do whatever, is *other people*. What will people say if I smoke, what will people say if I get engaged after I turn twenty, what will people say if I get engaged and break up, what will people say if I marry and get divorced, what will people say? They never say, What shall I do to make myself happy?

This complaint will sound familiar to anyone who has spent time in a Greek community of almost any size. But the assertion that a girl's own individual needs and desires ought to be recognized as legitimate is not typical.

Soula and Amalia insist that a woman should make decisions about how to act not on the basis of "what people say" but on the basis of

her own needs, desires, and interests. They see the concern with reputation as hypocritical and conformist, and they deplore the fact that
women organize their lives in terms of it. They do not believe that a
woman betrays her husband when she expresses an interest in a wom-
en's meeting or in a cup of coffee with her friends. Their sense of what
they want in a relationship with a man—which is not necessarily what
they think they can expect—is strikingly egalitarian and mutual compared with the hierarchical if complementary marriages they see
around them. They draw upon the rhetoric of individualism to argue
for a different conception of female personhood; they speak forcefully
of the woman as a "human being," as a "person."

After Yorghos' bleak description of the antagonism between men
and women and the supposedly "natural" objectification of women,
Soula responded. She argued that equality—a word they had been de-
bating all afternoon—was not a matter of sameness, of identical physical capacities. Equality meant regarding the woman not as object but
as subject.

> But Yorghos, *this* is what we want to do. To make it so that a man
> doesn't look at a woman as an object no matter what place she walks
> into. Why should he see her as an object? We want to get to the level
> where the man looks at the woman as a person.

At this point, Amalia—shyly, tentatively—added her own remarkable assertion. She argued that a female person's desires and her right
to act upon them in some way be allowed and be recognized as legitimate. After the men had smugly quipped to Soula that "the woman
also sees [that is, desires and objectifies] the man," Amalia countered:

> You know what happens? Everybody says, it's men who tease girls,
> and boys who tease girls, but if a girl likes someone, for her to ap-
> proach him first, he'll think she's "easy." If she's known as easy,
> that's it, she's had it. And yet that guy, he might not ever make the
> first move.

Soula and Amalia reject the equation of female moral goodness with
passivity, even as they feel it impinge upon them. In embracing an
alternative view of the female person, they redefine her power, her
interests, her desires, and the meanings of her sexuality and her actions
in the world. They enact their own independence by coming to the
kafeteria, and then (provoked by me, the anthropologist) they use it as
a forum to articulate and explore what "woman as person" means.
However weak and inchoate, their voices draw out and give tongue to
the contradictions that the other voices only indirectly express.

AMBIGUITIES OF RESISTANCE

Important social meanings of gender and sexual difference emerge in the discourse surrounding everyday sociability and are reproduced through the practices it entails. Pleasurable and trivial, these practices articulate, mostly nonverbally, particular dominant notions about the female person, her sexuality, power, and moral capacities, which help to organize how she is perceived as a social actor. The speakers articulate verbally the implicit meanings that inform these practices.

In describing the objects and sites of consumption, Sohoians portray males and females as acting out "natural" preferences for the sweet or the pungent and salty. Sohoians' use of gender as an adjective for objects in the material world (as in calling certain drinks "manly" and "womanly") further links these supposed preferences to constitutional differences. Consuming and enjoying sweets, a woman shows herself to be socialized as well as sociable. Acceding to the terms of this language of pleasure is not merely a performance of gender; it is a moral act, as well. Insofar as Sohoian explanations blur the natural with the moral, moreover, they veil the ways power and interests are at play in the very definitions of what males and females are and what they desire.

The emergence of a new leisure space, however, has provided a discursive space in which some townspeople are beginning to contest hegemonic ideas about women's nature and women's place. Sophisticated, European, and modern in its symbolic nuances, catering to a new kind of person as it engenders, in Williams' (1977:128–35) striking phrase, a new "structure of feeling," the *kafeteria* confounds neat gender boundaries. As it conceptually bumps against seemingly rigid categories of gendered space, shock waves rumble through the everyday world.

The entrance by young women into previously male-controlled public leisure spaces is undeniably a potent symbolic act of protest against locally configured patriarchal restrictions. And yet it does not make sense to see the *kafeteria* as heralding a new era of liberated pleasures for women. Such a conclusion could only rest on the assumption that gender inequalities reside uniquely in societies with traditional forms of gender segregation. It would also imply that by adopting Western—what scholars and Sohoians alike have often called "modern"—ways, the position of women is automatically improved.

The implications of such acts of resistance are more ambiguous. Though the *kafeteria* is a site where the traditional restrictions of the dominant local ideology of gender are being contested, it is hardly a revolutionary institution. On the contrary, and with no small irony, the recent appearance of *kafeteries* in Sohos exemplifies the hegemonic penetration of one Macedonian community by urban Greek and European institutions, symbols and forms of sociability that are displacing their indigenous counterparts. The *kafeteria* offers a new model of human "being," one stressing leisure, luxury, and males' and females' ostensibly equal opportunities to consume. In such a context, the subtler manifestations of gender inequality associated with the consumer society the *kafeteria* represents are easily obscured. The struggles of Sohoian girls and women to imagine and put into practice new definitions of female personhood will inevitably reflect, as they engage with, the contradictory dimensions of their everyday reality, with its competing discourses about gender and desire.

CHAPTER FOUR

Dancing Signs: Deciphering the Body in Wedding Celebrations

> Bodily *hexis* is political mythology realized, *em-bodied*, turned into a permanent disposition, a durable manner of standing, speaking, and thereby of *feeling* and *thinking*. The oppositions which mythico-ritual logic makes between the male and the female and which organize the whole system of values reappear, for example, in the gestures and movements of the body, in the form of the opposition between the straight and the bent, or between assurance and restraint.
>
> —Pierre Bourdieu, *Outline of a Theory of Practice*

IF EVERYDAY contexts of sociability entail a subtle semiotics of gender, ritual occasions often exhibit one that is more elaborate and stylized. Sohoian weddings provide an excellent locus for exploring how gender identities and relations are collectively celebrated, and not only because of their pomp and publicity. As a key rite of passage through which a man and a woman, each in different ways, acquire full adult status in the community, marriage is largely about gender and sexuality and the ways these are organized for the reproduction of the family, the community, and the state. Scholars working in Greece have long been fascinated by the symbolic and material dimensions of wedding ritual (see, for example, Campbell 1964:132–36 and passim; Skouteri-Didaskalou 1984:113–52). This chapter too focuses on the articulation of social identities and relationships, but less through words and objects than through the celebrating bodies themselves. Particular gendered social relations are perceptibly embodied in the conventionalized movements, gestures, and postures celebrants assume, in the spaces they occupy, and in the often wordless (but hardly silent) encounters they dance out with each other.

The main title of this chapter, "dancing signs," echoes the polysemy and instability of the bodies described. It also stands as a reflection of my own shifting analytical positions in relation to these events, as I employ several approaches to make sense of them. Most immediately, the title suggests a hermeneutics of spectacle, in which celebrating bodies are regarded primarily as "dancing signs" to be "deciphered." There is, admittedly, something disturbing about casting the problem in these objectifying terms, a reminder that the power relations implicated in any act of surveillance—even in seemingly "innocent" scholarly contexts—cannot be ignored (Bourdieu 1977:1–3; Foucault 1979). Yet inasmuch as the celebrants portrayed here are engaged in the creation of an unabashedly public performance, a spectacle in its most literal sense, my position—observing both as fieldworker and as analyst—seems reasonable enough.

This perspective of looking at the whole as if from outside is characteristically associated with structuralism, and indeed, I have found this method particularly useful in distinguishing the binary symbolism of gender encoded in the celebrants' visually emphatic bodily practices. The distinctively gendered bodily practices of the wedding celebrations, though obviously exaggerated, recall the taken-for-granted bodily "dispositions" that constitute the habitus; they reiterate culturally constituted meanings about male and female bodies in the everyday world. Insisting that social relations are always inscribed in the body does not mean that a body can be "read" in isolation from others. On the contrary, certain articulations about embodied selves may emerge only in the interplay of bodies, in the relations posed by the various participants. It is in the emphasis on the key role of contrast and opposition in human thought processes and on the location of meaning in the relations between terms, rather than in their essences, that the structuralist method provides a useful starting point.

Yet certain of its limitations should be noted. Questions of history are typically bracketed in structuralist analyses, yet the Sohoians' ideas about and relations to their own past are surely a central component of the event's meanings. Concerned as it is with the logical relations between symbols, moreover, a strictly structuralist account could not accommodate the nuances of performance and the social and historical awareness these presuppose. It could not account for the ways that celebrants not only play out the symbolic oppositions of gender embodied in their dancing practices but at times play *with* them.

"Dancing signs" also alludes to a textually oriented hermeneutics, concerned with Sohoian words about dancing bodies. Although seeming merely to comment upon dance-events, the various narratives in the text below in fact partially constitute them. For the ethnographer, shifting one's attention from "things seen" to "things heard" involves more than a methodological reorientation. Standing closer now in order to hear what is being said, the former "observer" inevitably finds it difficult to avoid being drawn into the conversation. The detached stance afforded by structuralism is disarmed. In my textual representations of Sohoian narratives, I try to evoke their dialogical origins, the ways they were elicited by and intertwined with my practices as ethnographer.

This hermeneutic exercise is textual in a second sense as well: its Geertzian narrative strategy of "thick description" is grounded in the metaphor of the event as a "cultural text" (Geertz 1973a). For all its problems (see Asad 1979; Crapanzano 1986), this analogy has the merit of emphasizing how the myriad nonverbal elements of an event, particularly one as conventionalized as a ritual usually is, are meaningfully patterned and susceptible to verbal unraveling.

But as Asad (1979), Keesing (1987), and others have insisted, a focus on meaning alone is not enough. For those who see the anthropologists' role as critical as well as hermeneutic, a focus on power is equally essential. Eliciting symbols and meanings must be followed by asking whose interests they serve and how they come to be embraced by the community at large. Wedding dances, then, must be approached in terms of both conceptual sense and physical sensibility, in order to explore the ways abstract social identities and immediate perceptual experience come together at the site of the body.

As a body of symbols, wedding dances evoke more than everyday bodily meanings. They evoke the multiple meanings of "the Sohoian wedding," which the townspeople see as second only to their Carnival in its beauty and uniqueness and which is to them a vivid signifier of the whole of their tradition, indeed, of "being Sohoian." The bodily forms and practices of the wedding can be understood as powerfully condensed representations—embodiments—of complex social identities: here, predominantly those of gender and place. These forms and practices carry the emotional force and authority of these identities, even as they are simultaneously the medium through which these identities are perpetuated.

Like Austin's (1975) "performative utterances," the performing bodies of the wedding celebrants visibly invoke a particular gendered order of things: they "celebrate" Sohoian ideas about the aggressive self-assertion of males and the vulnerability and social passivity of females. The heightened sensuousness that the celebration entails intensifies and gives value to these associations, enlivening them as a visceral, rather than just a cognitive, reality. Performed by dancing bodies, gender asymmetries, as well as other social asymmetries signified in terms of gender, become wedded to experiences of joy, celebration, and emotional and sensual engrossment.

THE WEDDING AS WORDS

A ritual event has textual dimensions: it is a set-apart sphere, bounded in time and space, which people talk about and interpret. The scholarly institution of folklore in Greece, too, also frames the Sohoians' consciousness of their wedding celebrations, which they now regard as a set of customs (*ethima*), a manifestation of tradition (*paradhosi*).

From the perspective of the anthropologist, ethnographic practice is a deeply textualizing activity (Clifford and Marcus 1986). My activities of photographing, tape recording, and eventually videotaping parts of Sohoian wedding celebrations constituted a fixing of the events out of their natural time, resulting in visual and aural "texts" on bits of plastic tape.[1] Playing back some of these tapes for those who participated in such celebrations stimulated further verbal texts, which now figure in the construction of this text. That making texts is an activity that both ethnographer and informant share can be seen in the account reproduced below—a description, originally tape-recorded, of a wedding in Sohos. The account also provides a general outline of the wedding as a series of activities, the context for the discussion of wedding dances and gender meanings that follows. Though fairly straightforward, Kiki's story is very rich, and not without its own textual tensions.

Kiki, a gregarious young woman in her mid-twenties, had married Stavros, an accountant working in the tax office, some five years earlier. I was visiting Kiki in her and Stavros' own shop in the market one March morning in 1983 when Kiki, no doubt trying to be helpful to me in my work as *laoghrafos*, asked me if I knew about Sohoian weddings. Pulling my tape recorder from my handbag and setting it between us on the glass countertop, I asked her to tell me about her wedding:

> *Jane*: We'll talk about your wedding, what happened.
> *Kiki*: At my wedding? We started on the Monday, here in Sohos, the wedding starts on Monday and it goes to Sunday, when the bride goes to the church. We, on Monday, hang out the trousseau, we'd had it ready from before, ironed, washed. We hung it up in my house. Later, on Thursday, we gave out invitations. We had them printed in Thessaloniki, what time the service would be, and it was put in an envelope. I gave them to a young cousin, and told him to pass them out to friends, relatives. And the groom handed out his own invitations, to his own relatives and friends. On Thursday afternoon, people brought over gifts, friends, and relatives. On Friday evening, the groom's relatives come over to see the bride's trousseau. The mother-in-law, sister-in-law, friends, from the groom's side. They come and look at these things. [See figure 6.]
> *Jane*: The bride, what does she do?

[1] Copies of videotapes and audiotapes that I made in Sohos are deposited in the Indiana University Archives of Traditional Music.

6. Two neighborhood women who have come to the bride's family home to admire her trousseau. Crocheted and embroidered pieces have been pressed, elaborately folded, pinned in geometrical patterns on swatches of dark fabric, and hung from the walls of the formal dining room.

Kiki: Nothing, she sits in the room.

Jane: Doesn't she give something?

Kiki: We offer a treat, a sweet. Either I or someone else, it's not absolutely required that the bride do the *kerasma*. They come and look at the trousseau, and they steal something from it. A table covering, a doormat, and they take it to the groom's to show what they got. From me, they got a doormat. Without my noticing—they told me the next day.

Jane: Is this a custom?

Kiki: Yes, a custom [*ena ethimo*], to steal something from the bride so that the groom will give them a gift for it.[2] They saw the

[2] During one Friday afternoon visit that I attended, a young woman from the groom's family surreptitiously snatched a pair of women's lace panties from the trousseau as the

trousseau, and then they left. Later, on Saturday morning, we got up, and prepared the food for the celebration [*ghlendi*].[3] The bride has a celebration, and the groom's is separate. In those years, we did the celebration in the house, but now, since lots of people go to the weddings, and houses can't contain them, we do it at rented halls [*kendra*].[4] At noon, the groom takes musical instruments [*daulia*][5] at his house, and in the afternoon, he brings the *ruba*.[6] That's when they put the wedding dress and slippers into a wide flat pan. They go, dressed up—all except the groom, who stays home—they go to "dance the bride."

Jane: They did that for you?

Kiki: Yes, they came, and I wore the dress we call the *Savvatiano*.[7] They came for me, I went down—you go down with your parents—to the dance. Later, the relatives of the groom take you and "dance" you. We dance for two or three hours, then they leave behind the bridal gown, and they leave. After this, we go back upstairs, and then go to the *kendro*. All the relatives gather there, and celebrate. But before we go to the *kendro*, we take down the trousseau [*prika* or *prikia*].[8] We have a big trunk, we throw in rice and coins, and the girls sing. If there *are* young girls. We put linens—sheets, pillowcases, and such things—in the trunk, because the blankets will be laid out on the truck. And then we celebrate until 5, 6 in the morning. The next day, the bride gets ready. About 11, the *daulia* come to take the

---

group was going out the door. Giggling and commotion followed. As soon as they were out of earshot, the bride's sister breathlessly protested to the assembled group that she had seen the theft but was too far across the room to be able to stop it. The bride's mother became very upset, worrying that "they will make a laughing-stock of us [*tha mas kanun rezili*]." Although this was a "custom," the theft of such an intimate item of clothing was a particular coup for the groom's family, and the bride's mother's sense of personal affront seemed genuinely intense.

[3] *Ghlendi* may be glossed "celebration," but in this context it refers to the feast held on Saturday night for the bride's relatives and friends.

[4] *Kendra* are large halls (literally, "centers") that normally operate as restaurants or grills but that may be rented out by families or voluntary associations on special occasions for celebrations.

[5] The *daulia* is a musical ensemble of one drum (*dauli*) and two double-reeded shawms (*zurnadhes*), to be discussed further below.

[6] *Ruba* is Turkish for "clothing." In this context it means the wedding apparel.

[7] The *Savvatiano*, the "Saturday dress," is worn at the Saturday night wedding celebration.

[8] Herzfeld (1980b) has discussed the tensions between official and local definitions of the notion *prika*. Sohoians recognize the distinction between *prikia* (household goods, especially textiles—woven, embroidered, or factory produced—brought by the bride into the new household) and *prika* (property in the more general sense, including the *prikia* but also land, animals, buildings, and money, which the bride brings into the marriage). Nonetheless, in everyday situations, they use the two terms practically interchangeably to mean the household items the bride brings with her to her new home.

trousseau. The bride sits on the balcony and watches. The relatives take her trousseau and arrange everything on the truck, so that they look nice, and the gifts, glass things, are loaded. And then they leave, dancing in the road, taking the trousseau to the house. On the truck go relatives of the bride, and when they get to the groom's house, they say, "Give us a gift and we'll give you the trousseau." And he gives them some money, so they unload the truck, and put everything in the groom's house. Then the groom is shaved, and everyone sings, and they cry: the mother, the brothers and sisters. They throw money in a towel which is set there. In the afternoon, they went with the *daulia* to get the *kumbaros*,[9] he lived far from us, then they came to us. The groom came up to us with a jug of wine, he treated all the relatives. The bride was inside a room, the *kumbaros* went in and put the shoes on her.

Jane: What happens with the shoes?

Kiki: On the bottom of the shoes we write the names of five to six single girls, and whichever one is "wiped out" first will be the first to marry. But at my wedding, we didn't do that. After that, the *kumbaros* goes down, and then my brother and sister took me down. As the bride goes down the stairway, she makes the sign of the cross and—we'd made these large rings of bread [*kuluria, pleksidhia*][10]—the bride throws pieces of them from the stairs. The single girls take these and put them under their pillows. Then, they took me to the church with the *daulia*. The whole ritual with the crowning took place; we went outside, we danced.

Jane: How did you dance? Is there some order?

Kiki: Sure, there's an order, the bride with the groom and the *kumbaros*, and afterward friends, whoever wants to, join in, but we only dance *kalamatianos*.[11] Just that dance.

Jane: Why only that?

Kiki: Because only that is appropriate for the bride. What is she going to dance, *tsifte teli*?[12] *Zebekia*?[13] At that moment, only kala-

[9] The *kumbaros* (fem., *kumbara*) is the wedding sponsor, who in Sohos is generally a man but occasionally a woman. As in some other Greek communities (see du Boulay 1974:162–63), he or she is likely also to be the *nunos* (fem., *nuna*), that is, to have baptized the groom or to be the son or daughter of the person who baptized the groom.

[10] *Pleksidhia* and *kuluria* are made especially for the wedding.

[11] The *kalamatianos* is a circle dance of moderate tempo in 7/8 time with a "slow-quick–quick" pattern of steps.

[12] Kiki is being ironical here. The Greek form of *tsifte teli*, the "belly dance," usually danced in Sohos as a couple's dance, is associated with high-spirited, festive occasions, not the highly formal, serious moment of dancing after the wedding ceremony.

[13] *Zebekia* is a local variation of the word *zeibekiko*, a highly individualistic solo dance

matianos is appropriate, and another dance, the *sighanos*,[14] an old dance. The father-in-law, mother-in-law, bride, groom, *kumbaros* dance, they give "gifts of money" to the *daulia*, and afterward, they take their cars and leave. That's it, it's over. Afterward, we went to Thessaloniki to get our photographs taken, and we stayed in a hotel that night. The next day, we left for a week in Athens. But in those days, we did it very differently—there was much more work, more hassle. My wedding, that's what it was like. Now, my mother-in-law will tell you other things.

Eloquent and complete in its own terms, this text announces in many ways that it is an interview between scholar and native informant. At the same time, a careful look reveals that Kiki and I do not agree about what such an interview implies. Although I begin by asking her to tell me about *her* wedding, she takes the conversation in another direction. From her first utterance, when she shifts from "I" statements to "she" statements (which also entail a shift from past to present tense), Kiki adopts a particular "informant" posture consistent with her own perception of the proper folklorist/folk relationship. Authoritatively and confidently, she describes a collective phenomenon ("our wedding") in the grammatical tense characteristic of both eternal verities and ideal types. As we talk, I also intermittently slip into this version of the folklorist role.

As the conversation continues, however, Kiki's narrative fluctuates between first-person and third-person stances, between "her" wedding and "the" wedding. This she acknowledges in her final remark, "My wedding—that's what it was like. Now, my mother-in-law will tell you other things," implying that her mother-in-law, being older and having witnessed the weddings of past years, would be able to give me a more "complete" account. Such textual tensions reveal contradictory aspects of the wedding as a conceptual and experiential category for Kiki: at once individual and collective, contingent and continuous, historically changing and eternal, and finally, narratively constructed (for the benefit of a real and present *laografos*) using the conventions of a folkloric discourse that, however foreign, has penetrated local discourse to the extent that Sohoians use it to describe their own traditions.

As Kiki's narrative suggests, the townspeople often regard local

in very slow 9/4 time, especially popular with young men. It is discussed in more detail in Chapters 5 and 6.

[14] The *sighanos* ("slow"), also called the *siryani* ("stroll"), is a slow, stately circle dance, the town's most formal dance.

weddings as approximations, better or worse, of some ideal type, as—in the words of my young friend, Yannis, disgruntled that I would miss a Sunday afternoon session playing music with him in order to observe yet another wedding—"all the same." Consequently, despite the dangers inherent in any such generic description (see Fabian 1983), I will in my own "thick description" remain faithful to this local proclivity and approach the wedding as a set of collective and constantly reiterated practices.

JOY AND DOMINATION IN THE PERFORMANCE OF MASCULINITY

Most of the weddings I observed during fieldwork were very similar to Kiki's. The formal encounters between the groom's and bride's houses begin on Friday. Now, as then, the groom's female kin make a ritual visit on Friday evening to view the bride's trousseau and the wedding gifts. After this, the groom's party visits the bride's house three more times: first, on Saturday afternoon, to deliver the bridal gown; second, on Sunday morning, to fetch the trousseau, which is elaborately arranged on an open pick-up truck; and finally, on Sunday afternoon, to take the bride to the church for the ritual "crowning." These last three visits are highly public movements and are always accompanied by the loud, raucous music of the *daulia*.[15]

For those in the community who are not immediately involved as either kin or friends to the bride or groom, it is the sound of the *daulia* that publicly announces an imminent marriage. A *dauli* is a large drum, carried at waist level by a strap slung over the shoulder. In his right hand the *daultzis* (*dauli* player) carries a thick mallet, and with this he marks the heavy, stressed beats of the melody. In his left hand he carries a long, light wand, with which he taps out the unstressed beats. Although he is responsible for maintaining the beat and controlling the tempo of the whole ensemble, a skilled *daultzis* can use this interplay between heavy and light striking to create subtle and exciting syncopated rhythms.

The *dauli* is accompanied by two *zurnadhes*. The *zurna* is a Balkan double-reeded shawm with a reedy, piercing sound. The *primo*, or first *zurna* (also called "master" or *mastoras*), plays the melody part, which includes elaborate improvisations and embellishments. The second *zurna*, the *voithos* or "assistant," plays either in unison with the first or

[15] Vlach weddings, when both bride and groom are from Vlach families, continue to use the Vlach ensemble of clarinet, trumpet, and drum, which Sohoians call *to tzaz*. I saw one wedding with this ensemble. When at least one member of the couple is *dopyos* (-*i*), "from this place," *daulia* are almost certain to be employed.

a major third lower, and provides a steady or rhythmic drone (*ison*) for the *primo*'s long improvisations.

Although the musical ensemble always includes one *dauli* and two *zurnadhes*, it is always referred to as "the *daulia*" (the plural form of *dauli*).[16] This is significant not only in terms of the way Sohoians conceptualize music and sound; it also hints at the way they configure social relations when they dance. *Daulia* do not "play" songs, they "hit" (*htipan*) or "beat" (*varan*) them. In these ways Sohoians emphasize the percussive aspect of the ensemble. In a sonic idiom, the *daulia* declare the joy of the groom's party to past and present inhabitants of the town. "The *daulia* wake up the dead!" people often say enthusiastically. The *daulia* define, through sound, the space of celebration, to the public and to the celebrants alike.[17]

On Saturday, before the first public manifestation of the wedding celebrations in the afternoon, female members of the groom's household and female relatives and immediate neighbors prepare the food that will be used that night in the groom's celebration. They cut up vegetables for salads and potatoes for frying and make small fried meatballs and meat pies, while the men of the household and nearby neighbors deliver quantities of meat, preferably lamb or beef, to be roasted at the *kendro*. The groom's family will have arranged for the services of the *daulia*, which arrive after the midday meal and rest period. Relatives, neighbors, and friends of the groom's family gather in his yard, and as the *daulia* play joyful songs, the groom's party dances circle dances (*kalamatianos*, *sirtos petahtos*,[18] *sighanos*). This dancing is dominated by married women and girls, most of whom are also assisting in the massive labors of cooking, cleaning, and arranging the house in anticipation of visitors. After about a half hour of dancing, a party of celebrants led by the *daulia* moves into the street to proceed to the bride's house. Both the procession and the dance step associated with it are called the *patinadha*, which means the "stepping."

The group of celebrants is composed largely of unmarried male youths (the groom's relatives and friends), but it also usually includes some adolescent girls and several older men. The groom himself and

---

[16] The musicians, on the other hand, tend to refer to themselves as a *parea* ("company"), or a *zighia* ("team").

[17] Older townspeople told me that poor families who were unable to afford *daulia* (particularly in the years before easy transport, when men had to go on horseback over the mountains—a long day's journey—to fetch the *daulia*, who are not native Sohoians, as we shall see) might instead use a *laterna* (a sort of piano-organ) for weddings. Much greater prestige was attached to the *daulia*, however.

[18] *Sirtos petahtos* is a dance with the same steps as *kalamatiano*, but in even, double rhythm, usually a lively 2/4. The steps are light and bouncy, hence "*petahto*," or "springing."

his father are absent, and so are married women. The character of the groom's party is primarily male and youthful, like the groom himself, and in many ways, this group collectively "stands in" for him in its ritualized encounters with the bride's household and with the community. The masculinity of the group is marked many times over, from the way young men wear their coats and hold their cigarettes to the ways they use their bodies. In these encounters, masculinity is characteristically demonstrated—indeed, performed—through domineering gestures and coercive acts toward others.

The groom's party's first collective gesture of their power is their loud and boisterous appropriation of the public space of the road. The *patinadha* is most of all a spectacle. The throbbing *dauli* and penetrating *zurnadhes* can be heard long before the celebrants can be seen, and the sounds create excitement among the crowds that gather to watch the *patinadha*. The route of the *patinadha* always goes through the actual and conceptual "center" of town, the marketplace, even if the bride's house and the groom's house are in adjacent neighborhoods on the same edge of town. The appropriation of space on the road and in the marketplace is especially significant in the Saturday afternoon *patinadha*, because Saturday is the busiest afternoon of trading in the whole week.

The celebrants, an amorphous and constantly fluctuating mass of bodies, move through the streets slowly, stepping in tiny steps to the quick 9/8 rhythm, their arms raised in front of them, palms forward, in the conventional posture Sohoians use to denote celebration. Many of the men wear their jackets draped over the left shoulder, with only the left arm in its sleeve, in a style that is described as *pallikarisio*, having the flair of "virile youthfulness."[19] I have also heard this style described as *saltanat*, a Turkish term meaning "sovereignty, dominion; authority, rule; pomp, magnificence" (Alderson and İz 1959:287). *Saltanat* emphasizes the performative conjunction of power and splendor in the men's dress and bearing; at the same time, it reinforces the connotative link of this spectacle with the town's Ottoman past.

Most of the celebrants, both male and female, carry a small bottle of ouzo. Though the celebrant may sip from it, it is used primarily for treating those who come out to watch the procession. The ritual is simple. The celebrant wordlessly hands the bottle to a man or woman, who is usually an acquaintance. The recipient raises the bottle and says a conventional well-wishing, "To your health [*stin iya sas*]," or "May

---

[19] *Pallikari* is a term for youthful "warrior," and for an unmarried young man when positive qualities of daring, courage, and manliness are being emphasized (see Campbell 1964:279). Old men, wearing the traditional costume at the Carnival festivities, often drape their jacket over their shoulder in this way.

you enjoy him [the groom; *na ton hereste*]." To an unmarried celebrant, the recipient will say, "To yours [your own marriage; *sta dhika su*]." He or she then takes a drink, and hands the bottle back to the celebrant. An onlooker may be offered many bottles in succession.

The *kerasma*, already explored in Chapter 3, is a conventionalized exchange within many contexts of Greek sociability that establishes the relationship between host and guest. As Mauss (1967 [1925]) long ago pointed out, it is a relation of unequal power. The individual who receives is always contextually inferior, whether that person is a guest in someone's house or is the man who enters a coffeehouse and is treated by an acquaintance already "sitting" there (see Herzfeld 1985a:154; Kenna n.d.). Despite this clear implication, the *kerasma* is conventionally described by Sohoians as a gesture of largesse, of unmotivated generosity. It is, moreover, considered insulting to refuse the *kerasma*. Refusal is seen as a demonstration of arrogance, a refusal to become beholden to the giver and thus a refusal to engage in what should be reciprocal relations of exchange over time.

In the *patinadha*, though the motivation for the *kerasma* is said to arise from the "joy" (*hara*) of the groom's family at the upcoming wedding,[20] the element of raucous coercion in the offer of ouzo is striking. When a vehicle drives down the road toward the celebrants, for instance, they block its way. Several youths from the procession approach the driver, and usually any passengers, as well, and thrust a bottle of ouzo through the window. Until the driver toasts (sometimes simply by wordlessly raising the bottle in front of him) and then drinks, the vehicle is not allowed to pass.[21] At later stages of the procession, particularly on Sunday, as the celebrants themselves become progressively more drunk, the *kerasma* becomes increasingly physical and brusque. The driver may have the bottle pushed into his mouth and upturned, so that he splutters and chokes as ouzo runs down onto his shirt. Even here, the onlooker is obliged to indulge the desire of the celebrant, and these assaults are endured with good humor most of the time.

A third mode in which the groom's party imperiously displays its collective masculinity inheres in its interaction with the *daulia*. While the group processes, offering the *kerasma*, the *daulia* strike up an almost nonstop stream of tunes, mixing popular songs gleaned from the radio with a few local songs. It is the responsibility of the *primo* to keep the songs continuously flowing. Celebrants often sing along with the tune initiated by the *zurna*. A celebrant can also "request" (more accurately,

[20] In many Greek communities, though not in Sohos, *hara* is used as a synonym for "wedding."
[21] Drivers of vehicles in this community are almost always male.

"demand") a song he particularly likes. Requests are made most frequently in two contexts: during the "circle" dances that occur at crossroads and in the road below the central square[22] and during the later
stages of the *patinadha*. The encounter between the celebrant and the
daulia over a song, and the dance that goes with it, embodies relations
of domination in a graphic way.

In other dance contexts, this process is called *parangelia*, "ordering"
a song. "Ordering" is a peculiarly apt translation. *Parangelia* in a nightclub, for instance, involves a negotiation between a male dancer and
the musicians, which entails both an "order" for a particular song that
he (or his table) alone will have the privilege to dance to, and a place in
the "order" (*sira*) of these requests. Celebrants in the *patinadha* only
occasionally refer to their song "requests" as *parangelia* (though musicians do call them this), perhaps because the sense of competition
within the group cannot be explicitly acknowledged (a subject to
which I will return below). The encounter is structurally the same,
however. Once the tune appears to be finishing, the male celebrant
approaches the *primo*, shouting into his ear and telling him to strike up
a particular song.

When compared with the often awkward and reticent conditionality
of English, the Greek grammatical imperative is starkly direct, but this
form is appropriate in all except the most formal of situations. Ordering a song with such directness is not in itself considered rude or pre-
sumptuous. What marks the encounter between celebrant and the *daulia* as one of domination are several other features.

First, the process of ordering is shaped by the attitudes that Sohoians
hold toward the *daulia*. In referring to the musicians as *daulia*, "the
drums," or *orghana*, "the instruments"—a "disembodied" usage—Sohoians emphasize their interest in the sounds they make. They are
viewing the musicians "instrumentally." Indeed, I rarely heard townspeople refer to these men as "musicians" (*musiki*) or even use the less
respectful title of "instrument players" (*organopektes*). It is true that
older people, particularly those most familiar with the traditional repertoire of Turkish songs, appreciate the differences in skill among these
musicians, and may be on friendly terms with a few of them. Yet few
Sohoians know the names of more than one or two of the perhaps
fifteen musicians (about five troupes of fairly stable membership) who
play, year after year, for nearly all of the community's weddings, its
Carnival, and its summer feast days.

---

[22] Though often labeled "circle" dances (*kikliki hori*), these in fact comprise a line of
dancers who circle (in most cases) in a counterclockwise direction, typically around musicians standing in the center. All Sohoian "circle dances" are *open* circles, with the first
and last positions clearly distinguished.

The Sohoians' tendency to ignore the humanity of the musicians is also linked to the fact that the musicians are Gypsies. Some people call them Yufti (a coarser and more intimate form of the word Yifti). The derisive overtones of this term were underlined by a young man who, after using the word Yufti in his own commentary, advised me (as a relative outsider, and potentially unaware of such nuances) that I should never say this to their faces, that it would make them angry. Most of the musicians who play in Sohos come from two farming villages, Anthi and Flambouro, about an hour's drive by car.[23] These settled Macedonian Gypsies have since Ottoman times provided music for Sohoian celebrations: they constitute a hereditary group of semi-professional musicians.[24]

Because of the traditional contempt of Greeks for Gypsies, these musicians do not always embrace this label. They insisted to me that they were "indigenous" (dopii). Those who acknowledged the designation Yifti gave their own etymology of the word. They saw it as a corruption of Eyiptii, or "Egyptians—See? Our skin is black, like the Egyptians," they remarked—who had been brought to Macedonia by Alexander the Great. Whatever their real origins, they differentiate themselves fiercely from the itinerant, landless, and often Moslem Tsingani, whom they despise. Sohoians also make this distinction. They point out that "their" Gypsies are Christians, not "Turks" (that is, Muslims), and have houses, and that their sons serve in the army. They see "their" Gypsies as "good" Gypsies. Nonetheless, though interdependent and even intimate (in a typically Ottoman sense), the relation between the townspeople and Gypsies is clearly hierarchical.

When a youth orders a song during the circle dances, he takes the position at the head of the line of dancers. In Sohoian dance-events generally (and also elsewhere in Greece), this position is considered the most important. The person occupying it is called "the first," "[the one in] front," and occasionally, "the standard-bearer" (bayraktar).[25] The person (usually male) who orders the song has the privilege of dancing first (or of choosing a substitute, for example, a female relative or his

[23] Two troupes that I knew came from Iraklia (previously called Djumaia), an industrial town near the Bulgarian border. These men did not farm but instead made their living almost entirely by playing music for celebrations throughout central Macedonia.

[24] In many areas of Greece, especially the mainland, and throughout the Balkans, Gypsies have dominated the ranks of musicians. Family troupes (almost exclusively male) are common, and particular families have established powerful reputations over generations as unusually gifted musicians within a region (for instance, see Auerbach's [1984] discussion of the Halkias family of Epirus). At the time of my fieldwork, no particular troupe had achieved special preeminence among Sohoians, though some pointed out to me who they thought was the "best" zurnadzis.

[25] Bayrak, a Turkish word meaning "flag" or "standard," alludes to the white kerchief (mandili) used by the lead dancer during the stately sighanos.

fiancée). It is to him that the musicians direct their playing and from him that they can expect gifts of money. The first dancer leads not only literally, by drawing (*serni*) the other dancers with his or her body; it is also the first dancer's prerogative to set the tempo and steps, and to execute improvisations (variously called *fighures*, *skertza*, or *kolpa*). The first dancer is thus set apart from the other dancers; for the watching public, this dancer is the object of vision and of commentary. "Everybody watches the first one," people say, and as I explore here, the experience of being watched can give rise to complex and ambivalent emotions (see Danforth 1979a). For most first dancers, being set apart is an ephemeral condition, lasting only until he or she pulls up a new first dancer. But some dancers are set apart in a more enduring sense, by their exceptional skill, confidence, and imagination: a good dancer or "master" (*meraklis, -u*, one who excels; see Caraveli 1985) is one who "somehow sets himself/herself apart" (*kapos ksehorizi*) (see figure 7).

The male youth who has ordered the song takes the position as first dancer, and dances for as long as he likes.[26] The *daulia* ensemble stands in the center of the circle; usually, the *daultzis* walks along with the lead dancer, facing him and beating the rhythm in a sort of incitement to more enthusiastic improvisations. During this dance, or just after, the first dancer throws a bill or two onto the ground—100 and 500 drachma bills were most common—which one of the troupe eventually stoops down to pick up.[27] This practice is not considered payment. It is called "gifting money" (*dhorizume lefta*). The individual gifts of money are called "[things of] chance or luck" (*ta tihera*) (see also Loutzaki 1985:21).

"Gifting" is crucial to understanding what dancing means in this context, and how it is structured by and reproduces the hierarchical relations between Sohoians and the Gypsy musicians.[28] When the groom's family engages ("takes," *pernun*) a troupe of *daulia* for a wed-

[26] When finished, he pulls up a friend, often the second dancer, to his position, and joins the end of the line.

[27] Currency rates fluctuated during the period of my fieldwork, but 100 drachmas was in 1984 worth about $0.80.

[28] "Gifting" occurs elsewhere in the wedding celebrations, for example, when the bride gives small gifts to her close relatives on Sunday just before she leaves the house for the church, a custom referred to by Kiki. She gives a hand-towel to her mother and socks to her father and close uncles, laying the items on the right shoulder of the recipient and kissing his or her hand; each gifts her by slipping a coin or a bill in her hand (cf. Rheubottom 1980). Similarly, when a young man leaves for the army, he bids farewell to his father and his father's colleagues and male relatives in the market, and they gift him. It would appear that these involve the same relation of hierarchy between giver and recipient. They involve hidden, almost secret gestures (for example, placing the coin in the bride's hand), however; they do not involve the extravagant display that one sees in the *patinadha*.

7. "Only the first dancer counts," Sohoians say. One friend leads another in a *kalamatianos* during an evening celebration for the feast day of the Twelve Apostles, Sohos's major religious festival (*paniyiri*).

ding, they do not normally promise them any money at all, except for traveling expenses.[29] The musicians accept this because they know they can usually make between 40,000 and 60,000 drachmas in a wedding from *tihera*. The musicians I spoke to consider Sohoians to be particularly extravagant in their celebratory habits and thus they rarely insist on an explicit financial agreement (*simfonia*) with them, though

[29] I found that sometimes a family would promise to pay a minor sum—no more than 10,000 drachmas, or about eighty dollars, for three men working two full days, usually in cold, inclement weather. This tends to be offered in situations where the *daulia* have reason to believe they will not be able to earn an adequate amount from "gifts." Eleftheria (see Chapter 7), for example, a young Sohoian woman who had immigrated to Thessaloniki as a child and wanted to have a "Sohoian" wedding with *daulia* at the Saturday evening celebration and before setting off for the church ceremony in Thessaloniki, guaranteed this sum (see also Loutzaki 1985:21).

they often do when performing in other places. For the musicians, however, the price of this insecure if potentially profitable arrangement is, as they admit, acceptance of the indignities of a plainly subordinate position.

Distinguishing these "chance gifts" from "payments," the Sohoians do not "pay" the musicians for their labor in making music. The relationship between making music and its remuneration is much more contingent. Many Sohoians insist that they are not obliged to give a gift and that they will not give one unless they like the way the *daulia* play. And even the money "thrown out" is not seen primarily as a gift in appreciation of a satisfying performance by the *daulia*. Rather, it is thought to be an expression of the dancer's *kefi*, a term difficult to translate but perhaps best rendered as "high" or "high spirits."[30] What the *daulia* receive depends entirely on how successfully they are able to inspire the dancer's *kefi*. As will be discussed more extensively below, the notion of *kefi* has both private and public dimensions. *Kefi* is performed as well as felt, and gifting is one means of performing it in the highly public context of the *patinadha*. It is a display of the expansiveness of not only the dancer's mood but his wallet. Moreover, it is not just the extent of his wealth being displayed but the extent of his willingness to part with it (see figure 8).

Both in the circle dances and in the requests that occur as the *patinadha* moves along the road, male celebrants "throw out" money in a very dramatic way. One method is to hurl a slightly crumpled bill onto the ground, where it is left for a while to be observed by the crowd.[31] Another method is to spit on the bill (often a higher-denomination bill, perhaps 500 or 1,000 drachmas) and stick it on the forehead of the *primo zurna* or place it behind his ear. Dancers also lay bills across the *zurna* bell or twist bills into cones and stick them into the holes on the bottom of the *zurna*, a gesture that does not affect the musical notes being produced. Dancers may, finally, tuck bills into the ropes which bind the drumhead to its frame. Musicians cooperate in this display by leaving these bills where they are stuck for a minute or so, and then they remove them and put them in a coat pocket so that other bills will be proffered. One *zurna* player often took the bills he received during a dance and folded them around his fingers, so that they stood upright as he played. But however clever the musicians' flourishes, it is the

[30] *Kefi* derives from the Turkish *keyif* or *keyfi*, whose range of dictionary meanings includes "health; bodily and mental condition; merriment, fun, good spirits; pleasure, amusement; inclination, whim, fancy; slight intoxication" (Alderson and İz 1959: 188).
[31] The different denominations of Greek paper money are distinguished by size and color, so it is possible to identify them from a distance. I saw the 5000-drachma bill, which is a dark blue, used in gifting only a few times, and never in the context of a wedding.

8. Gifting the *daulia* in the *patinadha*. Bills are laid across the bell of the *zurna* for display.

dancers' show. As in the *kerasma*, the abundance of these bills is associated more with the giver than with the recipient, and confers prestige on the former.[32] Sohoians do not see the bills as evidence of the *daulia*'s special skill, except in an indirect sense. They seldom know or remember which *daulia* were playing but they do remember whose money "fell" and frequently, how much.

BODY AND SPIRITS

As the *patinadha* moves beyond the marketplace and onto the road leading to the bride's house, it remains a public spectacle, yet its intra-group dynamics begin to intensify. The physical interaction among the young men is rougher and rowdier, yet at the same time individuals are becoming increasingly self-absorbed. Sohoians recognize that this is a consequence of the quantities of ouzo the youths are drinking, and so they say "they are becoming drunk" (*methane*) or "they are drunken men" (*ine methismeni*). The altered state that they are striving to achieve

---

[32] Sohoians acknowledge that grandiose gestures of gifting may at times be cynical and unrelated to *kefi* (therefore "inauthentic," *pseftiko*). This is indicated in the assertion I heard several times that some youths throw down large-denomination bills, then secretly ask the musicians to give the money back (something I myself never observed).

and to perform is not simple inebriation, however, but rather that of *kefi*.

Kefi is a centrally important cultural construct in Sohos, as in many other Greek communities.[33] Throughout Greece it is a term particularly, though not exclusively, associated with celebratory occasions, where feasting, drinking, dancing and music making occur. In Sohoian celebrations alcoholic "spirits" are complexly linked to the psychological "spirits" of *kefi*. Despite the importance of convivial drinking in the creation of *kefi* among men, *kefi* is not really an alcohol-centered notion. Indeed, though a specific kind of *kefi*, *tsakir-kefi*, is defined as a "slight inebriation" and is seen by some as the first stage of *kefi*, alcohol is not absolutely required for *kefi* to be created. *Kefi* is a much broader notion. More than just a label for a kind of high spirits, *kefi* has philosophical dimensions, particularly concerning the relation between self and collectivity.

Some who have written about *kefi* have recognized this. Most have stressed *kefi* as an ideal state in which individual and collective interests are happily congruent (but see Auerbach 1984:144–74). Thus, Caraveli emphasizes *kefi* as a "heightened form of experience," whose correct expression (according to the Karpathiot Olymbites) nonetheless involves disciplined adherence to "precise and well-articulated rules and patterns"; these enable, rather than inhibit, a deeply satisfying emotional engrossment (1985:263–64). Similarly, in his examination of notions of male personhood and emotion in the fiction of twentieth-century Eastern Aegean writers, Papataxiarchis suggests that although *kefi* expresses the emotional and moral center of the person, represented by the heart—in his words, "*kefi* represents the natural predisposition of the heart"—it is realized most profoundly within the collectivity: "Ideally, *kefi* is reached in *glendi*, a collective field of expression and festivity where male communion reaches its highest form" (Papataxiarchis n.d., 8).

Although the sense of *kefi* as an ideal state of communal sociability is extremely important in Sohoian contexts, too, *kefi* is a more ambiguous notion than this implies, and one that has gendered nuances. For Sohoian men, *kefi* is a mode of both action and feeling in which male individuals explore tensions and boundaries of their social world *as men*. These tensions and boundaries concern particularly the conflict between individual will and obligations to the collective. This conflict is one that emerges frequently in celebratory situations; the specific

---

[33] As Caraveli's work makes clear, *kefi* is a notion whose forms of expression and emotional content may vary subtly from one locality to another, and which needs to be understood in relation to what she calls "indigenous folk aesthetics" (1985:265; see also Auerbach 1984; Papataxiarchis n.d.).

character of the *patinadha* as a collectivity of kin and friends affects the form it takes here. In the *patinadha*, both *kefi* and the tensions it entails are articulated through specific configurations of body and spirits.

During this phase of the *patinadha*, the youths offer ouzo not just to spectators and oncoming cars but increasingly to each other. At least one youth always carries a large ten-litre glass bottle, encased in plastic, from which a funnel hangs by a grimy string. He balances it on his shoulder as he dances. Filled with ouzo, this bottle (*demitzana*)[34] is meant to refill the small bottles as they are diminished through the *kerasma*, but as the *patinadha* progresses the male celebrants increasingly drink directly from it. In an often-repeated scene, several youths grab one of their numbers, hold him tightly, and pour ouzo from the *demitzana* down his throat.

Youths tend to form clusters and go down the road with arms intertwined, leaning heavily on each other, pushing and pulling each other along. These are conventional gestures of intimacy and camaraderie. Townspeople watching my videos remarked that the young men's gestures stemmed from (nonerotic) "love" (*aghapi*) or "friendship" (*filia*). When a youth wishes to order a song, he drags his whole cluster to the ground. They form a huddle, squatting, and emphatically shout and beckon the *daulia* to come over to them, and then one or several shout to the *primo* to play a particular song.

The songs requested and heard over and over again, and to which the celebrants sing along in the *patinadha*, tend to be of two sorts: love songs and songs of exile. These themes, quite appropriate to the groom, are also relevant to the young men themselves. Songs of the first category are "popular" songs, including popularizations of traditional Macedonian folk songs, by singers such as Yorghos Dalaras, Haris Alexiou, and Glykeria. First lines of some repeatedly requested songs are "What did I want falling in love with you?" (also known as "Two knives in my heart"), "Tonight my heart is ripped to pieces," and "You threw away my ring and went far away." Among songs of exile are "Heavy is the foreign land" (*Varia ine ta ksena*) and "Anestaki," a Macedonian lament in which a mother cries out for her son away at sea.

The love songs, which predominate in the requests, express a particular conception of love. They brim with pain, hopelessness, and anger. Words that Sohoians use to talk about these songs, and the emotional states that they produce in the listener, include "madness" (*trella*), "dizziness" (*zaladha*), "anxiety and suffering" (*stenahoria*), "intense yearn-

---

[34] Some Greek readers have suggested that *demitzana* should be rendered *dramitzana* or *dermitzana*. It is probably a Greek form of the English "demijohn."

ing" (kaïmos), and "burning passion" (kapsura). Young men who work
themselves into a state of intense emotion and constantly demand
songs from the musicians so that they can express this in dance are
often called kapsuridhes. This term is often used with a tone of amused
irony, suggesting the speaker's recognition that the young men's emotion is "performed."

These songs provoke a particular emotion; they also structure it.
Each youth has a favorite song, one that is meaningful to him.
Through listening to this song and responding with his movements he
gives his emotion a coherent form and also authenticates it in the eyes
of his peers. A youth who is trying to get his song played badgers the
primo zurna, throwing money at him even before the song begins. As
the zurnadzis crouches down next to him, a youth often holds the bell
of the zurna close to his ear. Leaning backward, his eyes closed, he
waves the other hand in the air, forcefully beating out the song. The
others around him form a circular audience, supporting his body, silently holding their arms in the air like a miming chorus, or shouting
exclamations and pouring more ouzo into his mouth (see figure 9).
Alternatively, the youth may stretch out on the road in a kind of
grounded, horizontal dance. He thus assumes a supine, almost "feminine" posture, as if he cannot but succumb to the erotic power of the
zurna's song and the emotions it provokes (see figure 10). Demonstrat-
ing this surrender, he may emphatically smash a bottle of ouzo on the
ground, splashing his clothes.[35]

For a youth in the patinadha, this is a moment of climax. Both private and theatrical, it is a moment of dramatic embodiment, and of
engrossment in music, motion, and his private world of emotions. In
drawing the zurna to his ear, he claims it as his song. He is the center
of the performance. This is when he "makes" or "acts out" his kefi
(kani to kefi tu), all the while appearing—and making sure he appears—
oblivious to all else around him.

Yet this is also the moment of breakdown, when quarrels tend to
erupt among the celebrants. For the young men are all, more or less,
in the same state. They do not take turns "entering" this kefi and tend
instead to compete simultaneously for the attention of the daulia. Each
struggles to get his own song played. Because this kefi is thought to be
so overwhelming, each youth is desperate to express it. Paradoxically,
therefore, amid the signs of abandonment to song and sentiment, a
youth "in" his kefi assumes a willful and egoistic pose. His immediate

[35] Sohoians say such gestures are done for "embellishment" (fighura, skertza), the same
terms used for dance improvisations.

9. A youth listens to the song he has ordered. He marks his exclusive rights to it by drawing the *zurna*'s bell close to his ear, while the groom's brother pours ouzo into his mouth.

10. A pose of engrossment. Pelvis raised, arm extended, cigarette gingerly grasped, this youth gives his emotion bodily form. How long should he be permitted to delay the procession? His friends disagree. One attempts to pull him up by the wrist, but a second, objecting, protectively lays his arm across the supine body.

sentimental interests conflict with those of his peers. The *kefi* that united them now threatens to divide them.

Sohoians recognize the ambivalent qualities of *kefi*. They are clearly encoded in the remark that someone is "making [acting out] his *kefi*." It can convey the speaker's approval, admiration, amusement, or patient indulgence for a man who, say, gets carried away in his dance improvisations, or who, in his enthusiasm, breaks a minor rule of etiquette, or who behaves extravagantly in a manner that is not ultimately harmful or offensive. The coercive *kerasma* during the *patinadha* was sometimes described to me as an excess of *kefi*. On one occasion when I refused a proffered bottle, I found myself chided by a woman spectator that I must not "ruin the *kefi*" of the giver.

The phrase can have very negative connotations, however. "He's making his *kefi*" can mean "he does whatever he wants, he doesn't care what the world thinks, he doesn't care about anybody but himself." People use this phrase with anger, disapproval, disgust. This dual aspect of *kefi*, especially for men, echoes—and indeed, may express—the double-edged, morally ambivalent qualities of *eghoismos*, which Campbell defines as the "sentiment of self-regard" (1964:307) and which he sees as closely related to *filotimo*. Campbell explores this ambivalence, pointing out that *eghoismos* "contains the notion of a positively competitive attitude" (ibid.:311). This competitive posture, seemingly that of the individual male against the community, is in fact a normative expression of Sarakatsani values concerning manhood. Thus both the man who, struggling to show himself as superior to others, assumes the arrogant pose, and the man who, feeling that his *eghoismos* has been molested, reacts aggressively, causing a quarrel, are conforming to communal expectations, even though those witnessing it may see the quarrel as a "bad" thing.

Just as *eghoismos* remains a double-edged virtue, so can the pursuit of *kefi* destroy a valued sociability even while expressing social values. A man can "make his *kefi*" in ways that are either supportive of or subversive to collective celebration. In the first sense, *kefi* represents an escape from ordinary self-control and social constraint. Thus did one dignified elderly man assure me that drinking ouzo during the all-night and mostly all-male Carnival celebrations "gives you courage, so that you can leave behind your *dropi*." *Dropi*, usually translated as "shame," here describes impulses of reserve and self-containment. In the second sense, *kefi* represents the same escape carried too far, in which a man's engrossment in sociability is preempted by his own selfish and antisocial willfulness. In practice, the line between these two is thin and fragile, and what is "too far" is open to negotiation.

In a way, these youths are standing (or lying, in this case) precariously on this line. When more than one youth (and more than one cluster) is shouting for a song to be played, somebody is bound to be disappointed. Most of the time these things are taken in stride, but occasionally there is a small scuffle: angry shouting, aggressive jostling, a blanket thrown on the ground in a fit of pique. Believing that his demand has not been recognized, a youth makes this dramatic performance of anger, as I was told, "in reaction" (*apo andidhrasi*). This is called a "misunderstanding over, or because of, the dance" (*pareksighisi ya to horo*). An old man watching a video I had made of one wedding in which such a fight broke out explained (in highly conventionalized language), "One guy wants his song, and the other one wants his, and the first guy thinks, 'Why should they do his song and not mine?' and a fight breaks out."[36]

In fact, contrary to many other dance contexts, these eruptions are momentary, and to a casual observer may pass almost unnoticed (though Sohoians never miss them). What is remarkable is how quickly they are handled. It is here that the older men of the *patinadha* intervene. Their intervention is gentle: a firm hand on the shoulder, a mild rebuke (but just as often it is wordless), a frown. The transgressing youths, like the Sarakatsani shepherds whose "knives are drawn with greater bravado when it is certain that others are present to prevent their use" (Campbell 1964:310; see also Herzfeld 1985a:51), do not really try to resist this intervention. It is as if, having decisively performed both the depth of their feelings and their manly self-regard, their *eghoismos*, they are willing to go back to the compromises of collective celebration. By their very presence and with a quiet, dignified authority, the older men invoke the collective character of the *patinadha*. They remind everyone that these boys are, after all, cousins and friends.[37]

GIRLS IN THE PATINADHA

The configurations of *kefi*, body and spirits just described are clearly a male prerogative. These performances are, moreover, fundamentally

---

[36] This conventionalized explanation is itself a variation of the commonly heard expression: "Why you and not me [*yati esi ke ohi egho*]?"

[37] There are two ways in which the divisive aspect of these "misunderstandings" can be denied in the ideology of the *patinadha* experience. One is by scapegoating the *daulia*. Sohoians like to grumble that the Gypsies are greedy, overpaid, and will disregard the "order" of requests if they receive an extra large gift. The musicians deny this, but they recognize that they will be blamed for such conflicts. They say that "everything falls on top of us," but that only by not protesting at their abuse can they reap profits from the celebrants' extravagant *kefi*. "They respect us because we do not speak [that is, speak out or protest]," remarked one musician. The second way to dismiss the seriousness of the quarrel is to blame the ouzo: "It's the ouzo talking [*to ouzo milai*]."

about masculinity, male experience, and male relationships. But what of the fact that these youths have other social identities that are relevant in this context, that they are not only males (and young males, at that) but also members of the groom's party? Perhaps these performances ought to be seen, rather, or in addition, as the jubilant antics of the situationally dominant "wife-takers," a kin-based collective entity, ungendered as such and including both males and females.

Certainly, in a traditionally patrilocal and still patriarchal community like Sohos, these two readings of the male youths' performances are not mutually exclusive. The relations of authority between husband and wife, man and woman, replicate those obtaining between the groom's entire kin group and the bride, as they are manifested in the couple's new household, and also those obtaining between the groom's and the bride's respective kin.[38] Still, the distinction between a performance about relations among men and one about relations among kinship groups is real. The predominance of young men in the groom's party and the flamboyance of their performances can easily distract us from investigating this distinction.

Turning our attention to the adolescent girls in the *patinadha*, however, clarifies the specifically gendered dimensions of the groom's party's social and bodily practices. For the symbolic position of the girls is more awkward. As members of the groom's party, the girls "stand for" the groom. Yet they are girls, an age-specific gender category with particular connotations. These propositions are not wholly compatible, and the contradiction manifests itself in the bodily practices of the girls within the *patinadha*.

Although it is considered entirely appropriate for an adolescent girl who is a close relative of the groom to participate in the *patinadha*, there are certain ways in which her participation defies everyday codes of gender. The location of the *patinadha* on the road is significant, since the road, in traditional thought, is both public and male-controlled space. It is also, metaphorically, a place of danger. "Woman of the road" is in Greek as in English an old euphemism for a prostitute, and though unmarried Sohoian girls today have considerably more freedom than did their mothers to move about in public, they are still re-

---

[38] Although normatively equal as co-in-laws (*simpetheri*) with the groom's parents, the bride's parents often find themselves constrained both practically and (given dominant assumptions about male authority and the integrity of the household) morally against intervening in the newly created household on behalf of their daughter's interests. Several older women, each of whom had, as a young bride, returned to her mother with the complaint that she was being mistreated by her new husband, were thus all given similar advice: to return to her husband and make the best of things. The groom's parents, by contrast, are typically much more involved in the new couple's domestic affairs, particularly if the two families share a house or apartment building.

11. Girls in the *patinadha* carry small bottles of ouzo as they dance through the marketplace on their way to the bride's house to deliver the bridal gown, or *ruba*, early Saturday evening.

quired to account for their time and their actions to an extent that would be inconceivable for their brothers. Both the good names and the bodies of girls are considered vulnerable to the predations of men. The road, of course, may no longer be the actual site of a girl's exploitation; I have already suggested that the *kafeteria* has recently superseded it as the quintessential "den of iniquity." But the road continues to have metaphorical power, nonetheless.

A girl's participation in the *patinadha* violates this prohibition. She dances in the street with joy and enthusiasm. She may be exhilarated by dancing in public and by being seen.[39] She also carries the bottle of ouzo, that symbol of male sociability, and "treats" onlookers. Her membership in the groom's party legitimates her participation in these ordinarily masculine prerogatives to an extent that eyebrows are seldom raised in disapproval (see figure 11).

Yet there are certain contrasts between the bodily practices of the girls and those of their young male co-celebrants. These manifest what are largely implicit limits to female comportment, incorporated through the habitus and linked to local ideas about gender, sexuality,

[39] That girls and young women participating in the *patinadha* are intensely aware of, and take pleasure in, its exhibitionist character became clear to me during a video showing. A young woman, arriving late, excitedly began to interrogate the others about which parts of the performance I had videotaped. "Did it show us dancing in the marketplace?" she asked.

and morality. Here, the opposition between male and female is salient *within* the collectivity of the groom's party.

Specifically, though girls treat spectators they encounter on the road to ouzo, they do not participate in the coercive treating of those who are part of the public audience or the other members of the collectivity of celebrants. In fact, the girls' postures when treating retain some of the sedateness of the household *kerasma*. The forceful and usually reciprocal treating of ouzo to co-celebrants is an activity confined to men, and usually to young men.

Partially in consequence, girls do not become drunk, at least insofar as "drunkenness" is a socially defined state with publicly discernible symptoms. My experience is that girls dancing in the *patinadha* do not become quietly or privately drunk, either. When I asked why girls did not get drunk, I was often given the "explanation" that "girls don't drink." This apparently simple statement is ambiguous. Is it description or is it normative injunction? Is the verb "to drink" understood to mean, contextually, "to drink to excess"? The ambiguity indicates a point of tension within the ideology of gender in Sohos. But one thing is clear: if "girls don't drink," young men most certainly do. Drunkenness and its absence are opposing modes for elaborating and experiencing maleness and femaleness.

A second contrast between male and female practices in the *patinadha* is that girls do not initiate *parangelia* (ordering) with the Gypsy musicians, though they may lead a circle dance if a male relative places them there and/or gifts the *daulia* on their behalf. By avoiding *parangelia*, girls differentiate themselves from their male counterparts in a number of ways. They demonstrate their economic and social dependency on males, at least within the celebratory context. They distance themselves from the aggressive displays of domination toward the Gypsies that are characteristic of the youths. And they distance themselves from the conflicts among the male youths within the groom's party, conflicts that concern the opposed interests of individual celebrants in their pursuit of, and performance of, the emotional intensity of *kefi*.

Finally, in opposition to the extreme and progressively less controlled body postures of the male youths, the girls' bodies are extremely composed and controlled. Girls never lean precariously on each others' arms as their drunk brothers and male cousins do, nor do they fall down, sprawl, or lie on the ground. At most they are pulled down by the males in the group, and squat with them good-humoredly, indulging them in their drunkenness, entwined within their arms, waiting to arise and resume their more restrained postures, laughing and clapping and waving their arms in the air.

My attempts to get townspeople to elaborate on the "obvious," to explain exactly *why* girls did not fall down in the road like the youths did, were often greeted with: "What are you saying? They certainly do *not* do it!" Others obliged the apparently dull ethnographer with the verbally more explicit explanation that "a girl does not want to degrade herself."[40] Some of the girls I queried recoiled in giggling embarrassment at the very thought of using their bodies this way: "*A pa pa!*" they exclaimed. Their exclamation merits a closer look. Translatable, perhaps, as "No way!" or "Don't even think about it," these seemingly "nonsense" syllables constitute not just a practical consciousness of official local morality but a rather explicit theoretical consciousness.[41] Yet by uttering these nonlexical sounds girls also maintain the taboo against speaking about sexuality directly in a public context. These reactions underline the implicit yet powerful connections that Sohoians see between a girl's ability to control her body in dance and imputations about her sexuality, which for the girl has real repercussions.

The ambiguity of the girls' symbolic position, then, is expressed in contradictions within their ritually prescribed bodily practices. As part of the groom's party they are permitted to assume certain "masculine" practices, yet they are constrained by the fact that they are "girls." As such, they provide a corporeal contrast to the flamboyantly masculine excesses of their brothers and male cousins.

THE BRIDAL BODY

The other female figure important in wedding dances is the bride. She is in many ways the central and most symbolically elaborated figure in the entire wedding ritual. Her ritual and symbolic position is much less ambivalent than those of the girls in the groom's party and, indeed, embodies a dramatic opposition to the representations of maleness described so far.

According to local custom, the bride stays inside her parents' house

[40] This explanation was also sometimes given in answer to the question, "Why don't girls get drunk?" and this demonstrates the conceptual links between drunkenness, loss of bodily control, and social degradation for girls. Although girls' and women's everyday bearing is much less restrained than that which Campbell (1964) describes for the Sarakatsani, the conceptual links are similar: thus, Campbell reports that Sarakatsani women avoid running for fear of falling.

[41] The expression can be used ironically, as when a female speaker (through subtle changes of gesture) imagines this utterance on the lips of elders or members of the community, as an anticipated response to a particular act the speaker imagines carrying out. Such ironic usages express—but at the same moment, question—hegemonic gender ideas.

for the entire week preceding the church ceremony.[42] People explain this custom by saying that the bride must remain at home to receive the guests who visit and bring her gifts. This prescribed enclosure in the house may be in marked contrast to the everyday experience of young women who work as hair stylists, nursery school teachers, and seamstresses at local workshops. But for symbolic and sentimental reasons, Sohoians believe she should spend her last week in the family house.

Within traditional Sohoian thought the resonances of the girl's association with the house are rich and powerful, if not without contradictions (see also Hirschon 1978). Older women who grew up while Turks still lived in the town (until 1923) describe the streets of their childhood as a place of danger. They tell stories of two Christian girls who encountered Turks on the street, were seduced by love magic, and eloped with them. Middle-aged women recall the dangers to the self and the reputation that ten years of war and the intermittent presence of German, Italian, Bulgarian, and Greek soldiers presented to girls who left the household's protective enclosures. They repeatedly lament that they were confined to the house and immediate neighborhood except for the formal stroll on Sunday afternoon and communal festivities such as Easter and Carnival.

This selective insistence on the girl's confinement to the house is all the more striking in the context of the historical participation of Sohoian girls, as young as eight years old, in agricultural production and in waged work outside the house. In light of this, the statements often repeated within Sohos that girls in the past were literally cloistered inside the house cannot be accepted as wholly accurate. But if they reflect a selective memory, they also enunciate a certain truth: that in those days, only economic necessity legitimized a girl's entry into the world of work outside the house, and that her reputation depended on how well she carried domestic virtues—modesty, obedience, cleanliness, order—into this new domain.

Passivity as a female ideal is encoded in formal courting practices and its culmination: the negotiations leading to engagement. Though some older women admit to marrying "for love," typically, the girl was supposed to wait to be asked for, and the *proksenitis* (go-between), a friend or relative of the groom, always approached the bride's family first by making a formal visit to her house. Traditionally, the prospective bride offered a *kerasma* to the groom's representative and then left

[42] The exception to this is the occasion of the Saturday night *ghlendi*. This, however, is a celebration of her kin and close friends; though it is festive and occurs in a *kendro*, a public space, it is in a sense a household transposed. The bride is accompanied to and from the *ghlendi* by her kin, and enveloped by them during the actual celebrating.

the room, leaving the negotiations to her parents. Arranged marriages are very much on the wane in Sohos, yet even today any overt initiation of courtship, and certainly of marriage negotiations, by the girl is considered unseemly by many.

This idealization of female passivity remains evident, even though courtship practices have changed radically. Wedding celebrations of the past included a ceremony, observed as late as the 1960s, in which the proof of the bride's deflowering (the bloody sheet) was shown to the groom's female kin. It was publicly announced and celebrated with special tunes by the *daulia* in a final *patinadha*, in which the groom's family carried red-colored ouzo or raki back to the bride's parents' house (see also Danforth 1978:145–47). This final *patinadha* was said to be in honor of the bride's mother, for keeping her daughter *endaksi* (contextually, "chaste," but literally, "in order"; see Douglas 1966). Today the ritual of engagement initiates the new social relationships. The young man's parents begin to call the fiancée "our *nifi*," which means "bride," "daughter-in-law," or simply "in-marrying woman"; she addresses them as "mother" and "father" but refers to them as her "mother-in-law" (*pethera*) and "father-in-law" (*petheros*). The young woman's parents also call the young man "our *ghambros*," meaning "bridegroom," "son-in-law," or "in-marrying male." From this point, too, the couple's sexual relations become more or less acceptable to the community.[43] Though premarital sexual encounters were not highly unusual, many girls I knew were convinced that any man, discovering that his fiancée had "gone with others," even if this had occurred before she had met him, would become extremely angry. Female chastity thus remains a value, particularly for a man; it signifies his exclusive rights over "his" woman's sexuality—past, present, and future. The initiation of sexual activity between the couple is temporally moved forward, however, to the period of engagement (see also Herzfeld 1987a). The pregnancy that often soon follows may hasten the actual wedding date, but it rarely causes great dismay. As the surest proof of her child-bearing ability, the bride's pregnancy may even be welcomed by her anxious kin. In any case, well over half of the brides marrying during the period of my fieldwork were (or were claimed to be) pregnant.

While the groom's party appropriates the streets, the bride "waits in

[43] Sohoians express some ambivalence about this situation. After engagement, the male fiancé regularly visits the fiancée at her home, often spending the night. Secrecy shrouds the sleeping arrangements, however. One mother who admitted that her daughter was sleeping with her fiancé laughingly exonerated herself by pointing out that the fiancé had been so insistent that she (the mother) had been forced to give in. Again, this reiterates that what counts in maintaining the girl's reputation is the female pose of passivity toward sexual relations rather than the actual fact of chastity.

her house." In a ritual and public sense, it is the wedding that represents a young woman's social "coming out," or more precisely, being "taken out." This phrase, "he will take her out" (*tha tin vyali*) can have sinister overtones: it can imply that he will "take advantage." But in marriage, this act of taking a woman out into the world is ritualized and legitimized. Her name is "wiped out," and she assumes her husband's last name.[44] The goods that she brings into the marriage, symbolized by the trousseau, are also "taken out" of her house and transferred through the second *patinadha* from her house to the groom's household, where she and her husband are likely to occupy a separate floor. (Regardless of where they are to live, the trousseau is brought here first and only later is taken to their new apartment, if it is distant from the groom's parents' house).

But the bride's passivity is most dramatically embodied in her position as a dancer. She is placed in a passive position both grammatically and physically. This is linguistically encoded in the conventional phrase, which appears several times in Kiki's text, that a specific group (especially, here, the groom's party) "dances the bride" ("*horevun tin nifi*").[45]

When the groom's party arrives at the bride's yard with the bridal gown early on Saturday evening, in the middle of the first *patinadha*, the bride and her relatives are waiting.[46] They dance out to meet the groom's party. The bride's father and mother and possibly other male relatives offer them ouzo in small glasses—the "domesticated" mode of offering ouzo—and tidbits or *mezelikia* (customarily bread, cheese, and sausage). The wedding is the only context when males offer the household *kerasma* (see figure 12). As the groom's party, themselves now in the position of guests, are receiving the *kerasma*, the *daulia* begin to play music for the circle dances.

At this point, the most important male in the groom's party (an uncle, an older brother) stuffs a bill into the pocket of the *primo*, calls

[44] As of 1983, with the introduction of the new Family Code, all Greek women are required to retain their natal surnames for legal purposes. They are free to use this surname, their husband's surname, or a hyphenated combination, however, for all other social purposes. As before, nearly all Sohoian women still assume their husband's surname at marriage.

[45] See Hirschon (1978:85) for the Asia Minor custom of "speaking the bride."

[46] This "waiting" is a transposition of the state of the girl waiting to be sought in engagement, which in both cases constitutes a state of anxious expectation. In one conversation about marriage I had with a fifty-year-old man, Serafim, and Maria, his forty-five-year-old *simpethera* (affine; his son and her daughter were engaged to be married), Serafim made the following aside about the moment when the bride is waiting to be taken to the church: "I'm thinking how difficult it is for the bride—for the groom, too—but for the bride, very difficult, to wait and wait." Maria concurred: "Waiting for him to come. And if he doesn't come?"

12. Male relatives of the bride offer the *kerasma* of ouzo and tidbits to members of the groom's party on Saturday evening.

out the name of a song, asks the bride if she knows how to dance it, and then, standing at the head of the line, takes her hand and "dances her."[47] He dances proudly, with improvisations, and when he chooses, he "puts her in front" (*tin vali brosta*). After a short while, a second man gifts the *daulia*, and takes the bride's hand, ordering a new song if he wishes. This continues until all the principal representatives of the groom "dance her," at which point members of the bride's family (male and female relatives) "dance her" (see figure 13).[48]

After they have danced for about an hour, the *daulia* and the groom's party leave. Later that evening, the bride's and groom's households hold separate celebrations. At the bride's celebration, the bride often takes a visibly active role in facilitating an atmosphere of unity and enjoyment. This is expressed most vividly in her solicitous efforts to cajole guests into joining the dancing. Her specially active posture among her own kin is a striking contrast to that considered appropriate among her new in-laws.

Very late the next morning, after a long and slow *patinadha*, the

[47] Until the 1970s or so, this man also gave a gift of money to the bride for the privilege of "dancing her," which she then handed to a small girl.

[48] Some informants insisted strongly that all the important members of the groom's party had the privilege of "dancing the bride" first; others did not emphasize this ordering very much, beyond the groom's party's prerogative to have the first few dances with the bride. In practice, there was significant variation in the way the order of lead dancers actually proceeded. In contrast to these dances in the bride's courtyard, the order is more strictly observed in the final dance, after the church ceremony, in the churchyard.

13. The groom's party "dances the bride." The bride, wearing her "Saturday dress," has been placed in the lead position by the groom's first cousin. Her own kin join in the second half of the line, while friends and neighbors look on behind her.

groom's party returns for a second time to the bride's house to collect the trousseau. According to Kiki's account, the bride sits on the balcony and watches. In the weddings I observed, the groom's party was again treated, and again demanded to "dance the bride." The encounter between the two families at Sunday midday is characteristically rather tense. After a full twenty-four hours of dancing and drinking ouzo, the youths in the groom's party are usually drunk and rather belligerent. They customarily demand a crate of wine or beer from the bride's father when they enter the yard. They may stumble from drunkenness as they "dance the bride," and they may also dominate the dance space so that the bride's family cannot dance. While the women of the bride's house hurriedly decorate (*stolizun*) the truck by hanging blankets and pillows in precise patterns, other youths of the groom's party boisterously and almost carelessly move trunks, boxes, and other objects from the bride's house, heaving them onto the truck, loudly muttering all the while that the trousseau is shoddy and inadequate. Like their female relatives during the viewing of the trousseau, the youths often try to steal something, an act that reiterates the adversarial relations between the two households while also alluding to the groom's conquest of the bride.[49]

The *daulia*, on whose lapels white handkerchiefs—signifying the union between the bride's and groom's households—have been pinned by the bride's parents, stand to the side and play sad (*lipitera*) songs. These very slow, even-tempo, and highly embellished songs are meant to be sung rather than danced.[50] Only occasionally does anyone sing at this moment in the proceedings, but Sohoians, particularly those over thirty or so, recognize and are visibly moved by the tunes and the words that go with them. One of the songs played at this moment implores:

> Mama, your flowers, water them often,
> You won't see me anymore, sweet mother.
> I am leaving, mama, I'm going to the foreign land.
> Give me your blessing.
> Health to my mother, and to my sister,
> Health to the girls and boys.
> I leave to my mother three vials of poison
> Sweet mother,
> One to drink at morning,
> Sweet mother,
> Another at midday,
> Wicked mother,
> And the third, the most bitter,
> To drink late, late at night,
> Sweet mother.

A second song portrays the bride's ambivalent sentiments of sorrow and anger even more directly:

> One Friday and one Saturday evening
> My mother drove me from my grand house.

[49] At this point in one wedding, the youths found a huge, thirty-pound sack of almonds in a shed; though caught in the act of dragging it out, they got the bag because the bride's parents felt "ashamed" to publicly refuse it to them, since it was "for their child." At a second wedding, however, a large radio the youths had lifted from the bride's parents' house as they were loading the trousseau onto the truck was retrieved by an angry female member of the bride's household, who scolded them for their obstreperous silliness.

[50] They fall into the category of "songs of the table" (*tou trapeziu*).

My father, too, ordered me to leave.
I leave, weeping.
I leave, complaining bitterly.

These wedding songs, following a pattern similar throughout Greece, are with their images of exile and death essentially laments: indeed, they are sometimes sung to mourn the dead. Here, they mark the ritual transition from the bride's old life to her new married state (see also Alexiou 1974; Caraveli-Chaves 1980; Danforth 1982; Herzfeld 1981).

After the loading and decorating of the truck is completed, the bride's family attempts to send the groom's party back home. The youths in the groom's party, however, refuse to be rushed. Indeed, in their insistence—enacted through bodies, not words—on enjoying themselves as long as they themselves wish, they assert their prerogative and power yet again. This is achieved by (again, nonverbalized) appeals to the sanctity of *kefi*. In one wedding I observed and videotaped, the dowry truck and nearly all of the groom's party had left the bride's yard and were beginning to move in procession to the groom's house in preparation for the wedding. Things were running quite late: the wedding was set for three o'clock and it was already half past one. Despite this, the liveliest *parea* in the groom's party huddled on the ground just under the raised front porch of the bride's house, singing, refusing to move until the *daulia* came back to play their tune. The bride's aunt shouted down at them from the porch, saying, "Get a move on, now! When are we going to get to the church?" After a few moments, when she came down to plead with them, one fellow grabbed her hand. As if not wishing to spoil their *kefi*, she smiled good-naturedly and waved her hands in time to the tune. They smiled back and did not move. They still squatted and continued to sing in a drunken huddle until, a few minutes later, the *daulia* were fetched from down the road where they had been playing for the rest of the celebrants. Time—the control of it, the ability to delay others and even the progress of the event as a whole—is a further symbol of the power of the groom's group over everyone else (Bourdieu 1977: 6).

After such delays, the groom's party finally sets off down the road, led by the truck, continuing the *patinadha* back to the groom's house (see figure 14). Those celebrants who are closest kin to the groom join the other relatives already gathered there. They share a final midday meal. This is followed by the shaving of the groom by a local barber, an emotionally charged ritual accompanied by *daulia* and songs. Relatives weep as the songs describe how the groom is forced to leave his mother for his wife:[51]

---

[51] Typically, in a patrilocal community, one would expect such songs to be sung only for the bride. Sohoians saw no impropriety in singing for the groom, however. They

14. Those in the groom's party make a final collective gesture of joy and loss on their return to the groom's house with the dowry truck at midday Sunday.

Manly vigor does not last
The time of youth passes quickly
My neighbors and all the town's rich men were jealous of me
Even my mother was jealous of me
And wanted to drive me away.

Drive me away, Mother,
Far away to the foreign lands.
To take foreigners as sisters
To take foreigners as stepmothers.

Foreign women wash my clothes
Once, twice, three times, five times,
After that they throw them in the streets.
"Here, my boy, take your clothes
Send them to your mother to wash."

---

pointed out that though he might remain in the same house (perhaps in a separate apartment), his ties with his mother were necessarily attenuated at marriage as he turned his energies to another woman, his wife.

If I had mother or sister
I would not have come to the foreign land.

After the groom is shaved, the third and final procession to the bride's house begins. Despite the slow and majestic meter of the music, this final procession has a hurried quality.[52] The groom, his *kumbaros*, and all his dressed-up relatives (minus those brothers and cousins too sick with drink to attend) stride quickly, even the high-heeled women, who gingerly negotiate the potholes littering the muddy streets.[53] Arriving at the bride's house, the *kumbaros* offers a glass of wine, from a full pitcher in which a cut lemon has also been placed, which he (or the small boy, the *dever*, who assists him) carries to the bride's parents and other close relatives. He is then ushered into the room where the bride is waiting. He gives her white shoes (which she laughingly pretends do not fit, forcing him to add more and more bills until they magically do) and her bouquet. She moves to the threshold, tearing and scattering bits of the bread ring she holds. As she is led out of the courtyard, her father pours a glass of wine on the ground in front of her and sprinkles rice behind her. Flanked by one kinsman and one kinswoman of her own age, ideally a brother and sister, the bride takes her place at the head of the procession, just behind the musicians. With the groom now in the rear, the rest of the celebrants briskly and wordlessly follow. In this procession, so utterly different from the previous two, the stately strains of the two *zurnadhes* are punctuated only by the soft clattering of shoes on pavement.

Reaching the churchyard, the procession enters the church. The couple goes through the ecclesiastical wedding ceremony which normally lasts about 45 minutes. When this is finished, the couple, their parents, and the *kumbaros* stand near the church entrance, receiving gifts of money from the guests as they file out.

The final event of the wedding is the "dancing [of] the bride" in the large courtyard of the church, the town's central square. Neighbors, people out for a stroll, anyone who wants to (women, especially, want to) hang at the edges of the church in the cold, waiting for the dancing to start, "to see the bride" (*na dhume tin nifi*). After the photographer has taken group photos at the doorway of the church, the *daulia* go to the center of the church courtyard and begin to play. By custom, the *kumbaros* should clasp the hand of the bride, who clasps the hand of the groom, and walk them counter-clockwise in a circle three times. The

---

[52] Not unusually, given the very long duration of the Sunday *patinadha* (typically three to four hours to cover rather short distances, rarely more than a mile round-trip between the groom's and the bride's houses) the church wedding may be up to several hours late.

[53] Because the demands of agricultural work are heaviest in the spring, summer, and early autumn, weddings are customarily celebrated in winter.

kumbaros often foregoes the walk, however, and begins leading them (still three times around) in a moderate *kalamatianos*, a relatively sedate dance in 7/8 time. After the *kumbaros*, the groom's father and mother, then the bride's father and mother, then more distant relatives and friends who gradually join the line take turns dancing the bride. The person leading the dance, particularly if male, may pull bills out from a pocket and throw them onto the ground. When a female relative takes the lead, it is often her husband or father who gifts the *daulia* on her behalf. Though it is unusual, no stigma attaches to a married woman who gifts for a son or daughter, especially if she is a widow. Totally surrounded by a dense crowd, the dancers continue for at least half an hour. The end of this dance signals the end of the wedding.

The custom of "dancing the bride," articulates through dancing gestures the bride's status as the object of actions which "take hold of her" (*tin piano*) or "take her" (*tin perno*, a phrase that also means "I take her as a wife"); "draw her out" (*tin vyazo*); and "put her in her place" (*tin vazo stin thesi tis*) (see Hirschon 1978:71). This occurs first in the courtyard of her parent's house and culminates in the public performance in the churchyard, which is also the central square. As she is "brought out" in the dance, she is also brought out into society.[54] Though she occupies a position of honor, it is a passive position.[55] She is watched, admired, and judged.

OF GENDER AND GYPSIES

I have stressed the hierarchical interdependence between Gypsy musicians and male youths in the performance of gender. These youths need the Gypsies' tunes in order to structure their dances and, thereby, to structure their emotions. And they need to appear to dominate the Gypsies in order to enhance their own masculinity. In turn, the Gypsies need the money that falls as "gifts of chance," and so they are prepared to accept, to a certain point, the humiliation this entails.

The musicians' bodies provide a contrast with both the male and the female young people in the wedding processions. Unlike the young men, who "perform" the physical abandonment that comes with *kefi*

[54] An older man assured me that a great scandal occurred in the 1920s when a young man presumptuously placed a young woman in the front of the dance line before they were officially betrothed.

[55] This was further reinforced in past days in a ritual no longer observed. During festivities honoring the *kumbaros* at the groom's house following the church ceremony, the bride was required to stand in all her finery in the corner of the room, neither eating, drinking, resting, nor relieving herself, often for several hours, waiting for the *kumbaros* to finish his own feasting and then offer her some. Several elderly women, remembering this custom with distaste, explicitly pointed to it as a sign of the "barbarity" of the past.

and drunkenness, and unlike even the girls, who, though decorous, nonetheless show enthusiasm in their faces and gestures, the musicians are always upright, physically composed, their faces often expressionless as they play (see Rice 1980).[56] While the celebrants shuffle or skip to the quick-quick-quick-slow steps of the procession's predominantly 9/8 rhythms, the musicians stride in slow, even steps. When a youth lies stretched out in dramatic gestures on the road, swooning before the *zurna*, the musician crouches down, dignified and composed. When the youths shout roughly and gesture emphatically, often in demands for songs, the musicians shake their heads obligingly (yet without servility), wordless except for an occasional gentle murmur of irritation. Whereas the youths' extravagant gestures constitute a stylized performance of sexuality in which the prescribed sentiments and the gestures together evoke the sexual encounter, the Gypsies' comportment is a total inversion of such explicit, stylized, slightly parodied sexuality. In a symbolic sense, then, the Gypsies appear not as feminine but as sexless, neutered men. In this play of gender, gender is a code of power as well as of difference.

The symbolic position of the Gypsy musician in the performance is thus complex. He is at once, paradoxically, a man, a socially inferior and thus unsexed man, and an instrument. He must be cajoled as well as dominated. He is, through his music, the one who constitutes the performance itself, and at the same time his performance, according to Sohoian norms, is and should be in a gestural sense invisible, neutral, without qualities, symbolically reflective. The performances of the Sohoian dancer and the Gypsy musician are a subtle, uneasy choreography of mutual interdependence.

The sense in which the townspeople view the Gypsy musician as a corporeal foil to the dancer was articulated in a discussion I recorded with a group of middle-aged men at the *kafenio* owned by Triandafillos Sofulis. We were discussing the interaction between the *daulia* and the first dancer in the circle dances that are a feature at weddings and other celebratory occasions. The men discuss quite explicitly how the musician (here, the *daultzis*) should provide a bodily contrast to the dancer, stressing that the bodies can be understood "relationally."

> *Yorghos:* Yanna, when you don't know the song, your feet just won't go, you can really kill yourself! First, you have to understand

---

[56] Timothy Rice's account of *surla* (*zurna*) players in Yugoslav Macedonia provides an interesting contrast. It suggests that in that context the musicians' bodies, as well as their music, become more expressive and dramatic as the music builds: "They stood, arched their backs and stabbed their *surlas* straight up into the air, playing with one hand in carefully controlled abandon" (1980:124).

the meaning of the song, then the feet come later. Otherwise, it doesn't work.

Panos: Listen, Yanna, there—where the *dauli* thumps, *dang! dang!*—that's where the meaning of the song is. The *dauli* is the one directing everything.

Yorghos: You have to know how the steps fit with the *dang! dang!*—with the meaning. It's the *dauli* who is the "director" of the pulling of the dance. The stepping has to follow that beat. Otherwise, you end up running like some kind of animal. *Baba bum!*

Panos: That guy who is hitting the *dauli*, he can tell when you don't know the dance. So he comes here right here in front of you, he beats the *dauli* and he dances. To show you how.

Stavros: He beats it [exaggeratedly gestures the beating]. For "security."

Mihalis: He shows the dancer how to do it, so the dancer can pull himself together.

Yorghos: If you see the *daultzis* dance, you know that the other guy doesn't know the dance. For a man who knows how to dance, *this* is how the *daultzis* stands: straight up! He just beats [the *dauli*]. But as soon as somebody loses the step and can't do it anymore, the *daultzis* starts dancing. He helps him a little, he directs him.

Stavros: Since the man has "insisted" [upon ordering a dance he doesn't know], the *daultzis* hits: [intones slowly and emphatically] *Dang! dang! dang!* He says to you, "Go ahead, do it, since you think you know so much!" [parodies the emphatic gestures of the *daultzis* and everybody laughs]. "Here, see? I'm hitting it *for* you since *you* don't know how to do it!"

Mihalis (speaking as if he were the *daultzis*): I'm helping you but your legs just won't 'break' [that is, move rhythmically with subtle improvisations].

Yorghos (as *daultzis*): Dance it however you want to, just so you throw your money!

Panos (as *daultzis*): Bang! Bang! Bang! and just get on with it [*dupa dupa dupa ke aide*]!

This discussion is about a hypothetical performance that breaks down because of the dancer's lack of skill. Discussions about a failed performance reveal more than any successful performance (Stone 1982:9). Ordinarily, the *daultzis* and the skilled dancer negotiate the meter. Such a dancer knows the music and the steps, and he or she is able to manipulate the tempo (shortening or lengthening steps) with-

out losing the beat. Ideally, the first dancer, and not the musician, has
the prerogative of controlling the musical pace.

In this conversation, however, the men portray the musician's gestures as responses to the dancer's lack of knowledge about the dance.
These men's gestures, as they assume the persona of the *daultzis*, are
grotesque parodies of movement. They mimic the ways the musician
exaggerates the beat and the steps with his own body as he mocks the
incompetent dancer. The words that the men as *daultzis* "say" to the
dancer are probably, given the power relation between musician and
dancer, rarely literally said in the midst of real-life performance. The
men, explicating on my behalf, are putting into words what they read
the *daultzis* to be "saying" through the way he moves his body. The
daultzis' gestural "silence" in a successful performance is a purposive
and significant feature. His very lack of movement mutely testifies to
the dancer's skill or, as in the *patinadha*, to the enormity of his emotion,
his *kefi*. The *daultzis'* posture highlights, by inversion, the postures of
his client.

The men I interviewed clearly recognize the subtleties of power between the dancer and the musicians. They explain that the *daultzis* "directs" (*odhigai*), but not with his body: rather, he directs through his
instrument, through its sounds. Here we return to the paradox that
though the musician must be seen as a man (though inferior, muted,
symbolically neutered), he is also seen as an instrument or an extension
of the instrument. In this identification, the human essence is subordinated to the musical one. Similarly, in the pauses of the *patinadha*
when the youths are moving and swaying to the *zurna*'s melody, their
encounter with the instrument itself is sensuous. They interact intensely with the *zurna*. Cradling the *zurna* bell in their hand and drawing it to their ear, laying bills across it, they encounter it as an erotic
object. Its beauty and power lie not in the wood or its shape but in the
zurna as a sounding instrument. The tunes it plays are both a provo-
cation to and a tonal incarnation of the youths' passion. They tease and
caress the *zurna* without ever (nonverbally) suggesting that the over-
ture extends to the man playing the instrument.

There is, perhaps, one further way that the Gypsies figure semiot-
ically in the performance, and that is by framing the performance, and
the event as a whole, as a Sohoian performance. The Gypsy musician
is, again, symbolically liminal, a paradox (Turner 1967). From the perspective of the townspeople, he is an "outsider" who is nonetheless
"their" outsider, without whom "their" wedding cannot be performed
and is even unimaginable. His virtuosity is a prerequisite for their
collective, virtuosic performances; the skills of musician and dancer
coordinate together in the same moment of performance, the product

of a mutual but hierarchical partnership. The Gypsy musician corporeally defines Sohoian males and even, to an extent, Sohoian females, by inversion, by *not* being Sohoian. He is in the center of the performance, literally and materially, but he performs "difference," a difference that is also always subordinate.

REFLEXIVITY AND RITUAL

To most people, most of the time, gender is a natural, not a social, fact. Although the limits to what a male is permitted to do with his body and a female with hers are in fact inculcated from birth, in the commonsense framework of everyday life they come to appear both natural and self-validating. The fact of being male or female is perhaps the most fundamental truth a child takes into its body, where it becomes a virtually incontestable core of being, but it is never merely this brute, biological fact that is thus embodied. What are being embodied are the socially encrusted ways of being male or female in the world, ways encountered and learned through the child's practical engagement in the quotidian social activities within a particular society.

Ideas about male and female persons that are hegemonic in the Sohoian social world are, indeed, incorporated in the bodily and social practices of Sohoian wedding celebrations. The brusque swagger that boys publicly assume from early adolescence, especially in the presence of their peers—a youthful bravado that is gradually replaced by the assured, authoritative poses of the mature man—is amplified in their boisterous activities in the *patinadha*. Even the evocatively "feminine" poses of submission to erotic passions (which in any case corporeally reiterate the notion that a sexually aroused man cannot control himself and thus is not responsible for his sexual behavior) are predicated on the emphatically "masculine" stance of *eghoismos*, the insistence on commanding the spotlight and having one's own way. Likewise, the relatively more restrained demeanor expected of adolescent girls in public situations is rendered in their muted performances in the *patinadha* and in the ritually exaggerated modesty and passivity of the bride.

Acknowledging the enduring force of the lessons deeply learned by the body (see also Scarry 1985:108–121 and passim), Bourdieu insists that the principles thus embodied "are placed beyond the grasp of consciousness and hence, cannot be touched by voluntary, deliberate transformation, cannot even be made explicit" (1977:94). Perhaps, as some have suggested, Bourdieu underestimates the capacity of actors to reflect upon the conditions of their existence (Karp 1986:133; see also Giddens 1984). But even if Bourdieu is correct with respect to actors' assumption of a "natural stance" in everyday situations, to what extent do these embodied principles remain "beyond the grasp of consciousness" in an extraordinary ritual event like the wedding, which is *about* gender? Even here Bourdieu's insight is to some extent borne out, for the startled reactions to my queries about the logic of the girls' bodily movements suggests that I was bumping up against the boundaries of the unthinkable. At the same time, the very panache with which a young man drapes his jacket over his shoulder in *saltanat* style and the very thoughtfulness with which the bride assumes a pose of modest dignity in her walk to the church testify to a practical awareness of the power and manipulability of the bodily insignia of gender. In framing the wedding as a custom "of this place," a framing made more visible by the presence of the ethnographer and her camera, Sohoians make their own actions and relations objects of more than usually conscious and discursive elaboration, though here the discourse is not exclusively verbal. They are reflexive about their performances, even though the self-consciousness this entails is never unmediated and the understandings thus generated are always ideologically laden.

An individual's commitment to a particular gender order—whether or not its underlying principles are "beyond the grasp of consciousness"—is not a simply intellectual matter. It is therefore important to ask what are the means by which ideology, as a complex of ideas, takes such tenacious hold on the ways individuals experience the world, physically and emotionally, as well as intellectually. In discussing coffee drinking, I suggested that a locally hegemonic ideology of gender is reproduced in the pleasurable yet also obligatory practices of everyday sociability—that gender is not just naturalized but deeply and sensuously linked with those pleasures and obligations. The poses and gestures of wedding celebrations, too, are not simply performances of manhood or womanhood. Because these poses and gestures are also, at the same time, embodied ways of moving, feeling, and communicating explicitly marked as "Sohoian," they link particular ways of organizing gender and sexuality with "this place" and thus to issues of local identity and local allegiances.

It is one of this book's central arguments that dance-events can be read as an embodied discourse on the moral relations between the individual and some larger collectivity, whether this be the *parea*, the town, or "society"—*o kosmos*—itself. The texts in this chapter articulate this theme while repeatedly alluding to the specific collectivity of Sohos and to its Sohoian idiom. Kiki's narrative, shifting fluidly between a unique and a collective subject, is a meditation on her own location within a collectivity, with its collective histories, traditions, and sensibilities, a meditation that acknowledges that in becoming a bride in the Sohoian way, she both embodies and signifies—becomes a sign for—that collectivity. The men at Sofulis' *kafenio*, too, gesturally lampooning the inept dancer, quipping that such a man is condemned to dance "like some kind of animal," insist that a man's very humanity is contingent on his social knowledge: here, on an embodied knowledge of the dance as a collective Sohoian form. Even the configurations of *kefi*, body, and spirits in the *patinadha*—in which the question, "What is the proper relationship between a man and his fellows?" is corporeally posed—interrogate a Sohoian reality, and both ask and answer in a Sohoian bodily idiom.

If Sohoian voices and bodies can be read to articulate themes of social experience at this somewhat abstract level, this should not obscure the intense immediacy and particularity of this social world to the wedding celebrant. Neighbors are treated, companions teased and taunted, sweethearts noticed, and enemies avoided. The "homeland" or *patridha*, the *idea* of the Sohoian collectivity, though only explicitly and nostalgically marked in the songs of departure and exile, is perpetually announced. Nor should it be forgotten that celebrants are posing and dancing these social relations in the midst of a spectacle that is aesthetically vivid and sensuously compelling, at times overwhelming. The throb of the *dauli* and piercing yet dolorous wails of the *zurnadhes* palpably envelop the celebrants as they move through the streets or dance in a courtyard; the eardrums ring, the body buzzes, ouzo is hot on the tongue. The *zurnadhes'* tunes, whose words everybody knows yet which come to carry vividly private meanings, and the *dauli's* rhythms, which pulsate through the bodies of all who stand near, impossible to resist, are in the *patinadha's* exuberant *karsilamas* dances and, especially, in the circle dances translated into rhythmically stepping bodies, a chain of bodies moving to sounds and steps both monotonous and hypnotic, moving as if this collection of bodies were a single body. Indeed, participating in the dance can provoke that sense of recognition—which though not inevitable is still by no means rare—that one is morally part of, just as one is now corporeally merged with, a larger collectivity, a recognition that, as a profoundly visceral knowledge, carries the force of absolute conviction.

It is this experience in its totality that is being saluted in the familiar pronouncements that Greek dance is "the embodiment of the Greek spirit" or "an expression of communal values" and that, when asserted in the highly simplistic and intensely ideologized terms of romantic nationalism and aesthetic (or even Durkheimian) idealism, is for a critical reader all too easy to dismiss. Yet this experience must be acknowledged and respected in any analysis hoping to account for its power. For this task, Jameson's brilliant and controversial work (1981) on the interpretation of literary and cultural production is suggestive. In one part of his rich and complicated argument he distinguishes two basic interpretive strategies within literary criticism: the predominant "allegorical" strategy, which seeks to reveal the "real" or "fundamental" meaning of a text by translating it to another level more abstract or encompassing; and a second, conventional Marxist strategy of demystification, which views cultural texts as "superstructures" functioning as instruments of class domination, legitimation, and social mystification. Although Jameson is unequivocal that only a Marxist analysis can be interpretively adequate, he regards the conventional Marxist strategy of "negative hermeneutics" as incomplete because it constitutes only one of two necessary analytical steps. He recalls Ricoeur's emphasis on the dual nature of the hermeneutic process, necessarily understood both "as the manifestation and restoration of a meaning . . . a message, a proclamation" and "as a demystification, as a reduction of illusion" (Ricoeur 1970:27, cited in Jameson 1981:284). Jameson argues further that a "positive hermeneutics" would have to acknowledge the utopian aspect of ideology, its ability to express collective impulses and desires even while articulating the privileges of some groups over others (Jameson 1981:289).

The Sohoian wedding celebration is, in Jameson's terms, a cultural production that can be seen as "a symbolic affirmation of a specific historical and class form of collective unity" (1981:291). Although a negative hermeneutics enables us to note the various relations of inequality—between male and female, host and guest, groom's and bride's kin, Sohoians and Gypsies—embodied and celebrated, a positive hermeneutics compels us to take seriously how these ideas and relations are enshrined in an event that is itself a manifestation of the townspeople's love and loyalty toward, pride in, and fascination with that Sohoian collectivity. In the conventionalized poses of celebration, these two dimensions of ideology—the iniquitous elements of social inequality and the utopian elements of social affiliation—are tangibly bound together on the topography of the body, a binding together that occurs within an event that is vivid, intoxicating, engrossing. It is this fusion of an embodied configuration of gender relations with "Sohoian" modes of being that makes these relations at once so powerful and so difficult to contest.

CHAPTER FIVE

The Orchestration of Association in
Formal Evening Dances

> To analyse the ideological aspects of symbolic orders . . . is to
> examine how structures of signification are mobilised to legit-
> imate the sectional interests of hegemonic groups.
>
> —Anthony Giddens, *Central Problems in Social Theory*

SOHOIANS' attachment to their traditions is not unambivalent. Elaborate, densely symbolic, and redolent with memories of family and
place, the wedding celebrations also hold for some the taint of backwardness. I recall the caustic tone with which one bride's aunt, ruefully
eyeing the exquisite trousseau hung on the walls that I was admiring
and photographing, inquired: "Do you have such stupid customs in
America?" And one soon-to-be married bride insisted that, were it not
for the ridicule her parents risked if they failed to marry her off properly in the Sohoian way, she would marry "without *daulia* and all that
stuff." This edgy disaffection may be a protest to the curious ethnographer: "Don't think we're just colorful peasant folk!" But it bespeaks,
too, a larger relation of symbolic domination between West and East.

In this regard the formal evening dance, or *horoesperidha*, offers
many contrasts to the wedding celebration. A very different set of
symbols is used to legitimize a particular social order. Sponsored by
local civic associations, *horoesperidhes* adopt a self-consciously "European" idiom. In them, Sohoians celebrate *not* the collectivities of kin,
church, and community but secular alliances within Sohos based on
age, class, and political identities and interests. *Horoesperidhes* are not
concerned with gender in any explicit sense. Nonetheless, they are organized structurally in response to local ideas about males and females
as social actors, and they involve gendered practices.

The annual *horoesperidha* is a major—sometimes *the* major—social
event of many civic associations. Most are held on a Saturday or Sunday night during Apokries, the pre-Lenten Carnival season, in one of
the marketplace's two *kendra*, which are rented for the occasion. Although these events can also be fund-raisers, Sohoians emphasize their
social, rather than their economic, functions. Those who organize *horoesperidhes* intend them to promote and at the same time to symbolize
solidarity and a sense of belonging among the celebrants (Moore and

Myerhoff 1977:10). They organize the activities of eating, drinking, talking, and dancing in a way that encourages the build-up of high spirits, or *kefi*, and prevents conflict, or at least manages it. The towns-people believe that within the dance context it is from men, rather than from women, that threats to this solidarity may arise.

Sohoians recognize that the dance-event is not only a site for collective pleasures but one where individuals compete for social recognition and prestige. And with an acutely "practical consciousness" (Giddens 1979) of their own gender codes, they recognize that it is men who are likely to be the ones competing most loudly. They know that men, whether as individuals or as protagonists of a group, are always liable to act on the dance floor in ways that threaten to "ruin the celebration" (*halnai to ghlendi*). Consequently, the *horoesperidha* is organized in such a way that the typical opportunities for male competition—particularly *parangelia*, the practice whereby individual males order dances from the musicians—are foreclosed. The organizers redirect male competition for prestige into other activities. In boisterous dancing, in the sartorial display of self and of female dependents, and in donating and bidding for consumer goods in the lottery, men compete, as Loizos has said, "to be as unequal as possible" (1975:85), but their competitive gestures enhance, rather than destroy, the sponsoring association's wealth and reputation.

By presenting themselves and the event they have organized as oriented, in a rational and disinterested way, to the collective good, those in charge attempt to control the process of social ordering and to suppress "illicit" manifestations of competition from within the group. This is crucial, because such associations, though ostensibly civic and politically neutral, are often riven by political factions competing for control of the leadership positions. One source of challenge to the ordained unity comes from the ruling faction's political opponents, who may have reasons to wish to ruin the event. Competition and conflict in the dance may therefore have a political, instead of, or in addition to, an individualistic tenor. By laying out certain ground rules of interaction, controlling who can participate and structuring the temporal flow, the organizers attempt to prevent such conflicts from emerging.

Too much order, however, is inimical to the event's success. Celebrants judge *horoesperidhes* not only on the basis of the numbers of celebrants attending, the quality of the music, and the amount of money earned for the treasury but on the basis of the *kefi* that develops over the course of the evening. Inasmuch as *kefi* is seen as an index of the degree of sociability achieved, abundant *kefi* is taken as a vindication of the ruling faction's moral leadership and its ability to ensure a "good time for everybody." Consequently, it is in the leadership's interests to encourage celebrants, especially men, to act as "revelers" (*ghlen-dzedhes*). In Turner's (1969) terms, the event is considered successful only if there is a gradual movement from hierarchy to equality, from structure to *communitas*. The organizers who initially invoked order, therefore, must attempt to orchestrate the socially necessary disorder. This can be problematic, for as the event progresses and as the initial formality subsides while *kefi* builds, the potential for illicit expressions of male competition also increases.

In this chapter I examine the symbols, structures, and convention-alized practices characteristic of *horoesperidhes*, which are oriented to-ward creating conviviality while restraining male disruption. In the next chapter I examine the strategies men use to manipulate or chal-lenge the rules for other ends.

THE CATEGORY OF HOROESPERIDHA

The *horoesperidha* means simply "evening dance," but the word has something of the overtones of the English expression "formal ball," connoting a grandeur that is also somewhat anachronistic. Originally a social event of polite, urban Athenian society, *horoesperidhes* were in-troduced in Sohos during the 1940s. Unlike today's *horoesperidhes*, those of the past were usually individual entrepreneurial ventures. They were held on a Saturday or Sunday night in the cavernous to-bacco workshop-warehouses that had fallen into disuse after the war, and at one *kendro* on the town's outskirts. Musical groups—*daulia*, the Vlach *tzazi* ensemble, or an *orhistra*—were brought in by the entrepre-neur, but "gifted" by the men from each table as the celebrants from the table got up to dance. Dances such as the fox-trot, tango and waltz as well as *kalamatianos*, were popular.

Although the *horoesperidha* is now one of the commonest types of dance-events in Sohos, the townspeople were perplexed at my interest in them. They do not see them as falling in the provenance of the eth-nographer-cum-*laoghrafos* because, unlike wedding dances, they are not considered "customs" (*ethima* or *adetia*) or a manifestation of "tra-dition" (*paradhosi*).[1] Such sentiments again emphasize how Sohoians, who have had direct contact with Greek folklorists and foreign re-searchers, have incorporated into their own distinctions about their cultural life the bias of folklorists and anthropologists, who have his-torically concentrated on the "traditional" (*paradhosiaka*) and "indige-nous" ("of this place," *dopika, tu topu*) aspects of Greek culture. Indeed,

---

[1] *Adetia* (sing., *adet'*) is a Turkish term for "customs" or "ways." It is used as a syno-nym for *ethima* or *ethimata*.

though I could easily negotiate a quite comprehensible role for myself as *laoghrafos* at events Sohoians themselves defined as traditional, I encountered more difficulties in gaining access to and researching the *horoesperidhes*. My research strategies had to be flexible responses to the contingencies of each social situation.

Between 1983 and 1985 I attended eight *horoesperidhes*. In most cases I attended as a celebrant, a member of a group, or *parea*, and in these instances I was bound by the same obligation to participate in the collective interaction as any other member. My companions, who normally indulged my ubiquitous stenopad and pen, became exasperated when I tried to scribble notes during the *horoesperidha*. "You're always writing!" they accused. "What are you writing?" They teased me for taking work too seriously: "Put your work away now, it's time for having fun!" The *horoesperidha* was, they insisted, an occasion for entertainment, a place to forget the troubles of the workaday world.[2]

Yet even in these cases it was not necessary to abandon all my media and recording equipment. It was considered perfectly understandable for me to take photographs. In fact, because it is during such occasions that Sohoians like to be photographed, as a "remembrance" (*enthimio*) and commemoration of the *parea* joined together at that moment, they often jokingly—but insistently—approached me as a sort of official photographer. They jovially demanded that I photograph their table as they assumed conventional poses of camaraderie: two men, linked at the elbow, quaffing glasses of wine, or a table of married couples clasping wine glasses, all held together in the table's center in a stylized toast, as they smiled broadly for the camera (see figure 15). Frequently, men cajoled me to photograph them as they danced.

I always participated as a dancer in these events, not only because I enjoy dancing but because not to have done so would have been interpreted as highly unsociable and standoffish behavior. Yet on some occasions, I also stressed my role as researcher. After my video equipment arrived in March 1984, I videotaped portions of two *horoesperidhes* with the enthusiastic cooperation of the celebrants, who greatly enjoyed displaying their *kefi* to the camera. This practice of videotaping was not totally unfamiliar to the townspeople or even exclusively associated with foreign researchers like myself. During the period of my research it was becoming fashionable among urban Greeks to hire a photographer to videotape events such as weddings and baptisms, or even for a member of the family who owned or rented video equipment to assume this role. The Sohos town hall itself

---

[2] In one *horoesperidha*, sponsored by the Sohos Youth Association, I also participated as a musician, as a flutist in an ensemble with two boys playing bouzouki and guitar.

15. Celebrants at the Businesspeople's Association dance pose for a
photograph that will record the moment of *parea*.

had a video camera, though this was used only to record the Carnival
festivities. Although my videotaping practices were not, therefore, entirely novel, they did set me apart from the other celebrants in a quite
visible way. In the crowded conditions of the dance floor, moreover,
the videotaping process was at times physically awkward. The bright
spotlight required at evening events was distracting for the dancers and
the intense jostling and unpredictable movement dangerous for the
fragile equipment. For such reasons, I found it impossible to videotape
entire events. Instead, I recorded portions.

Many celebrants regarded my video work as essentially a process of
making a high-tech souvenir, a kind of home movie. But in at least
one case it had clear connotations of "spying." The only occasion when
my request to videotape was denied involved the *horoesperidha* of the
conservative New Democracy party's local office. Apparently, noting
my friendships with outspoken supporters of the Left (though I also
had friends among supporters of the Right), its organizers feared a too
public video airing of their event afterward to a less than sympathetic
audience.

These polarities—of conviviality and conflict, of freedom and obligation, of forgetting and remembering, of inclusion and exclusion—
that I encountered in my practical work as ethnographer are also pervasive themes in the event as a whole. Their particular manifestations
in this kind of event can be grasped by examining the category of the

horoesperidha, first in its symbolic nuances and second in its sociological dimensions within the Sohoian social world.

Symbolic Codes

The Sohoian *horoesperidha* explicitly excludes many symbols of Sohos. Instead, it incorporates European symbols and practices that are intended to give it a sophisticated ambience. The civic associations' adoption of Europeanness as an authoritative code is telling: it exemplifies the political domination of Greece by the West and the cultural hegemony that has accompanied it. This hegemony is also one of gender and class, for the *horoesperidha* celebrates a patriarchal, petty-bourgeois conception of male and female persons (Mosse 1985:1–22). Adopting this code of Europeanness, Sohoians in these dance-events stress their identity as civilized (*politismeni*) townspeople, as inhabitants of a *komopoli,* and at the same time eschew the harsher (*sklira*), wilder (*agria*), and more dramatic aspects of the celebratory aesthetic of more traditional events. This is especially true in the early phases of the event, when Europeanness is equated with civility, respectability, and order (see ibid.:181–91).

The conceptual opposition between formal dances and local, traditional dance-events is inscribed in the term *horoesperidha* itself. Its appeal over the simpler *horos* derives, no doubt, from the fact that it is official-sounding rather than "country bumpkin" (*horiatika*) speech.[3] It incorporates a purist form of "evening" (*esperis*), a word one dictionary defines as "soirée," a nuance suggesting that an "outside" culture—here, what is thought to be French—provides the model of sociability.[4]

Nonlocal and "European" ways (*ta evropaika*) of celebrating are manifested in other symbolic codes, as well: in music, dance, in the forms of social groupings, and in the stage management of the flow of the event. Thus, whereas other formal celebratory occasions (Carnival, the *paniyiri,* weddings) require *daulia,* the civic association hires an "orchestra" (*orhistra*) or an "ensemble" (*sygrotima*), but never *daulia.* There is a certain range of stylistic variation among ensembles; what they share in common is a contrast—visual, aural, aesthetic—to the Gypsy *daulia.*

The ensembles hired are rarely famous, even locally. There is no

[3] Ironically, to sophisticated urban Greeks of the younger generation today, the term seems embarrassingly old-fashioned.

[4] For the definition of *esperis* as "soirée," see Divry (1979:515). Interestingly, though Sohoians used *horoesperidha* freely in conversation, in its written form it tended to be used by associations with a right-wing (and therefore, oriented toward the West) identification. Left-wing associations tended, in their more folksy fashion, to call these occasions "our dance" (*o horos mas*) or the "annual dance" (*etisios horos*).

concern to hire "big names" for this type of event, and the musicians' names (either individually or as a group) appear neither on the invitations nor in any way on the musical instruments they play. As in the *patinadha*, the musicians, themselves "instruments" of a sort, tend to be viewed "instrumentally." Yet the ensemble often embodies some features of the sponsoring association's image of itself. Two examples suffice. The ruling PA.SO.K. party characteristically presents itself as a progressive party, led by bright, blue-jeaned intellectuals with a "common touch," supported by Greek youth, and dedicated—as their campaign slogan has promised—to "Change." Predictably, in the 1985 PA.SO.K. *horoesperidha* three young men, with (to my eye) an unmistakable air of casual, intellectual sophistication, dressed in jeans and sweaters, accompanied the dancing on bouzouki, electric guitar, and snare drums. They played a good deal of "New Wave" (Nea Kima, not to be confused with the later punk Western European style), a vaguely left-wing, alternative music that emerged in the 1960s among composers like Theodorakis, Hadzidhakis, and Savvopoulos. The PA.SO.K. "theme songs," such as "Good Morning, Sun" (referring to the party's logo, a huge green sun dawning) and "The Road," both popularized by Manos Loizos, are examples of this tradition. These Nea Kima songs were interspersed with popular songs (*laika*) and popularized island folk songs (*nisiotika*) that were good for dancing.

By contrast, the somewhat larger ensemble hired by the Businesspeople's Association for their *horoesperidha* included the Greek clarinet (*clarino*), two electric pianos, bouzouki, snare drums, and a vocalist. The orchestra marked its professional status by wearing white tuxedos. However, in addition to *laika*, and at least one standard tune for each of the ballroom dances (the tango was, for example, synonymous with "Hernando's Hideaway"), they also played an occasional "folk" tune (*dhimotiko*). In these, the *clarino* was the lead instrument. Among Sohoians the *clarino* is seen as a musical instrument of the Vlachs and of the Sarakatsani. Both groups are, on the whole, politically conservative.[5] Significantly, the *horoesperidhes* of the civic associations with a predominantly conservative constituency (the New Democracy local office, the Businesspeople's Association, Orpheus) all had ensembles that included *clarino*; they were also the only events that included what Sohoians see as a Vlach dance, the *tsamikos*.

These distinctions aside, both ensembles shared musical material in common, especially in their emphasis on Greek popular and popularized island songs. The *daulia* also have an eclectic repertoire; but unlike

---

[5] The Sarakatsani, studied by Campbell (1964), have traditionally been Royalists.

the *daulia*, these hired ensembles never played (and most likely did not know) "local" songs.

Horoesperidhes are the only kind of dance-event to include what Sohoians call "European dances" (*evropaiki hori*). In the early phases of the event, the musicians intersperse the group dances with ballroom dances such as the tango, waltz, fox-trot, and occasionally the polka. Although these are less popular and draw smaller crowds of dancers than dances such as *kalamatianos* (a circle dance) and *karsilamas* (a face-to-face dance),[6] they are considered essential and are taken quite seriously. These European couple dances typically involve married or, less often, engaged couples.[7] As such, they provide a dancing embodiment of the core social unit within the event: the husband and wife.

The model of kinship emphasized in this event, the patriarchal nuclear family, has a definite petty-bourgeois quality. It is composed of the male "head of the family" (*nikokiris* or *ikoyenyarhis*) who is taking out his wife, "the lady" (*i kiria*), and sometimes one or two of his children, for a good time (see figure 16). Unlike the wedding celebration, for instance, in which kin relations are stressed, the emphasis here is upon the nuclear family as an autonomous economic, social, and political unit.

This family is hierarchically organized. The partnership between husband and wife may be stressed, but the husband's authority is never really questioned. Indeed, the economic and social dependence of wives upon their husbands is expressed in many conventional ways during the event. One important aspect of a female celebrant's self-presentation in this context is the way she literally embodies tokens or symbols of her household's affluence through the clothing and jewelry she wears. The practice of displaying family finery upon girls' and women's bodies, whose primary forum for display is the dance space, is deeply rooted in traditional culture throughout Greece.[8] The sumptuous costumes, made of silks, linens, intricate embroideries, and delicately fashioned brass, silver, or gold, traditionally worn by Greek women at ceremonial occasions, testify to this, as does the image of the beautiful and richly adorned young woman that recurs frequently in folk songs (see Caraveli 1982). In the *horoesperidha*, however, modern apparel, rather than elaborate traditional garb, is used to convey claims to wealth.

---

[6] *Karsilamas* is by definition a face-to-face partner dance, but in the *horoesperidha* it may be performed by groups of three or more dancers, on a crowded dance floor.

[7] In contrast to the Western European practice, men do not exchange female partners on the dance floor through the custom of "cutting in."

[8] On festive occasions in Karpathos, for example, unmarried girls wear (in addition to their other finery) necklaces of gold coins.

16. The patriarchal unit is highlighted in most *horoesperidhes*. Two "heads of household" (*ikoyenyarhes*), a green grocer and a news agent, and their wives share a table at the Businesspeople's Association dance.

The importance of such display in asserting class-based prestige and superiority is discussed, albeit cynically, by a fifty-five-year-old laborer and leftist, Dinjo, as he warned me what to expect at the Businesspeople's Association dance:

> Democrats,[9] the [common] people, they know how to have a good time. The others—the rich, the rightists—they just want to make their wives like shop windows, to be "first." To wear "the best" dress, the most expensive boots. They say they are the superior ones [*o protos kosmos*]. But what have they got that we haven't got? My wife has everything for the house, there's nothing she doesn't have, all women have these things [i.e., household appliances]. But she's not supposed to talk to these people. They're up there in the stratosphere. They've kept this old way of thinking—"we're the ones who count," "we're from important families"—yet they're still uneducated! If you want to approach them, you've got to put on airs.

Dinjo's skepticism notwithstanding, this code is widely shared throughout the community. Though one is likely to see the most ex-

[9] Many Sohoians who support left-wing parties have reappropriated the term "democrat" (*dhimokratis*) from the right-wing opposition New Democracy party and use "democrat" to refer to "ordinary" people like themselves, because they feel that the word more accurately expresses their political goals (egalitarianism, participation, opposition to privilege). Note that Dinjo, a supporter of PA.SO.K., follows the word "democrat" with the synonym "the people" (*o laos*), one of PA.SO.K.'s slogans.

pensive clothes in associations dominated by the wealthier townspeople, I noticed that Katina, a devoted socialist and from a rather poor family, arrived at the PA.SO.K. fund-raising *horoesperidha* in a mink jacket. Although this gesture was not sufficient to convince anybody that the family was well-off, it was a way of intimating that her husband, who works as a night watchman for the ladies' garment factory, is able, at least, to ensure that his wife comes finely clad to a dance.

In contrast to the married couple in their prime, who associate with other married couples (usually, friends rather than kin) in a *parea*, the young and the old are not prominent in *horoesperidhes*. Younger children under ten years old, who might attend a wedding feast held during the same hours, never come to these events. With its smoke and noise, it is considered an inappropriate place for children and also for pregnant women, "because of the child." Adolescents sometimes attend, either accompanied by their parents or as members of the association's youth group or its dance troupe. *Parees* of male youths—who do not necessarily have any formal connection with the sponsoring association—usually attend, though analogous groups of female adolescents (not chaperoned by a male) are totally absent. Unmarried adult males or females may sometimes attach themselves to a *parea* of married couples, and a group of engaged couples may attend together. A mixed-sex *parea* of unmarried persons not romantically involved with each other is a more unusual phenomenon.

Elderly people (*i yeri*), those who are receiving pensions and those whose married children now economically support them, rarely attend. Yet gender distinctions are not irrelevant. An elderly man attending with his friends is typically indulged as an honored guest; the attendance of an elderly woman is considered much more anomalous.

Indeed, the category of person considered most "out of place" (Douglas 1966) is the *fustanu*, the older woman who wears the high-waisted, ankle-length smock, the emblem of women from Sohos and one other large town in the area, Nigrita. Though all women used to adopt this dress upon marriage, they do so no longer, and today all the *fustanuses* are fifty or older. Hence, these women connote femaleness, old age, and old-fashioned tradition. The women themselves consider the spectacle of a *fustanu* in a *horoesperidha* to be decidedly strange. One that I queried implied that it would be undignified for a person of her age to attend this sort of event, even though she might quite properly dance in public at a wedding: "What business has a *fustanu* at the *horoesperidha*? It is for young people." Another explained her absence in terms of grandmotherly duty: "I stay home with the children!" A third woman anticipated the mockery she would face: "Me, go? A *fustanu*? They'd all laugh at me!"

The fur-coated matron who attends with her husband and the elderly *fustanu* who stays home with the children embody two opposing orientations—two ideologies—that coexist in Sohos: the extroverted, European, Hellenic orientation, and a more introverted, culturally syncretistic local orientation (Bourdieu 1977; Herzfeld 1982a, 1987b; Leigh Fermor 1966:96–147). As Herzfeld has pointed out (1987b:95–112), the "clothing" (as gerund and noun) of a "body of people" becomes both the guise and disguise of its ideology.

Sociological Dimensions

Because the *horoesperidha* is in the Sohoian context specifically associated with local civic associations, approaching it merely as an abstract symbolic form cannot fully plumb its social meanings. One must also attend to the social dynamics within and among the associations that use it. In the years between 1983 and 1985, a number of associations sponsored at least one *horoesperidha*: the local offices of the two largest national political parties, PA.SO.K. and New Democracy; the town's two "cultural, educational, and folkloric associations," Orpheus and the Sohos Youth Association; the Soccer Association; the Businesspeople's Association; and the Sohoian Migrants' Association (for Sohoians now settled in Thessaloniki). Though other civic associations exist, it is around these that community social life revolves.[10]

Three features of these civic associations are relevant here. The first is that, with one important exception, all of the civic associations are controlled exclusively by adult men—as would be expected in a community like Sohos, where until recently, men had assumed virtually all official public roles in communal life. The second feature, not unrelated to the first, is that these associations, though ostensibly "civic" and thus exempt from activities in the political realm (see Gramsci 1971), tend to become "politicized" (in the strict sense of national party politics, *kommatopiimena*). They tend, that is, to become the object of struggle between factions who vie for control of the governing board. In this community, New Democracy rightists and PA.SO.K. leftists are the main contenders.

This political polarization is most clearly evident in the town's two cultural, educational, and folkloric associations. Orpheus, established in 1978, was initially formed with the help of Grekos, then the mayor,

[10] Other associations include parent-teacher associations, farmers' and forestry workers' cooperative associations, and at the end of my fieldwork, a third cultural association. Cultural associations have a long history in this community. The first, the Association of Ancient Ossa, was established in November 1914, just after Ottoman authorities relinquished the town and it was integrated into the Greek state (Kutsimanis 1974:237). Its goals included the general education of all its compatriots and the establishment of a library, meeting room, gymnasium, and night school.

to assist in the preservation of local traditions, especially Carnival, and in the organization of local festivities, such as Carnival and the *paniyiri*. It was conceived also as an institution that could apply for funds from various ministries, particularly the Ministry of Culture and the Greek Tourist Organization, to "improve" the local Carnival. Within two years of its founding, however, the rightists who had taken control of the governing board, and Grekos, the initial patron, had quarreled. With Greece under the Conservative government of Karamanlis, Orpheus became more and more seen to be in the pocket of the local right wing. Resentful members of the Left complained the Orpheus leadership "ate" (that is, stole; see Herzfeld 1985a:40) the funds given to them for cultural projects.

When I arrived in Sohos, Orpheus was run by middle-aged, right-wing males. The local office of the New Democracy party was next door to Orpheus' storefront office, and men talking politics in the late afternoons seemed as easily to gather in one as in the other. The second association, the Sohos Youth Association, was established in 1981, and had held its first elections for the association's officers in the fall of 1982, just a few months before my fieldwork began. The individuals who formed the core of this group were mostly young women who had been school friends or who had worked together in one of the ladies' garment workshops, plus a few male classmates, cousins, and friends. All the leadership positions were held by young women. The president, Dimitra, had been active in the local PA.SO.K. organization and had strong ties with Grekos.

The establishment of the second association was controversial from the start. Three young women representing this group of young people, who were predominantly, but not exclusively, affiliated with the Left, initially approached Orpheus and asked to become members. Knowing where most of them stood politically, the Orpheus leadership had been ambivalent. Some members insisted that the applicants must be permitted to join; others attempted to block them. In the ensuing stalemate, the young people decided to set up their own new association.

Over my first year of fieldwork, I watched this politically mixed group go through a process of politicization (*kommatopiisi*) in which the left-wing leadership, a coalition of PA.SO.K. and Communist party members, began to squeeze out those with right-wing or independent positions. It was not entirely without reason that many townspeople viewed Orpheus and the Sohos Youth Association (which Orpheus members pointedly referred to as the "anti-association," or *antisylloghos*) as cultural wings of the Right and Left, respectively.

Nevertheless, and this is the third feature, this politicization must be both denied and asserted by the civic association's ruling faction (Cowan 1986a). It must be denied because the ideology—and the ensuing rhetoric—of such associations uses the altruistic language of collectivity, of the town as a united social entity with common, shared interests. The legitimacy of the ruling group relies on being able to appear to use their leadership position, and the association's resources, for the good of all rather than in pursuit of sectarian interests. Politicization must be asserted, however, because the ruling faction's power depends, in part, on effectively showing that it is a force to be reckoned with and that it can provide social benefits and individual favors to those who lend it their support.

That the question of who will be included and who excluded in the *horoesperidha* becomes a problem is a reflection of this paradox. On the one hand, a "collective" celebration requires a collectivity to validate it. Thus those who have organized a *horoesperidha* gloat with satisfaction at the mere thickness of the celebrating crowd. This abundance— of bodies, food, drink, noise—attests to the association's power. It is also a prerequisite for *kefi*, which, if it successfully develops, will be cited as validating that power.

On the other hand, a *horoesperidha* is not a completely open event. Some individuals boycott the celebration. Others are kept out. Sohoians may find the nonparticipation of those who are "too old," "too young," or of the "wrong" gender unremarkable. But they are keenly aware how much the "right" or "wrong" political or class affiliation matters in whether one attends or stays away, is welcomed or is barred.

Individuals who attend a *horoesperidha* are normally members of the organization, invited dignitaries, or (ideally) friendly nonmembers who by their presence indicate their support for it.[11] Those who could attend such an event, but do not, are considered by their absence to be making a statement of nonsupport. An individual who fails to attend may justify his or her absence for reasons of family responsibilities, illness, mourning, or economic hardship.[12] These are "acceptable" excuses. But if such excuses are not forthcoming or are unconvincing, they will be dismissed as *merely* excuses (*dhikeoloyies*). Instead, people will divine a political or personal motive.

Thus, when the mayor Evangelidhis, after having received an "hon-

[11] Thus, certain shopkeepers often insisted to me that they wanted good relations with everyone, because they needed customers, and that to demonstrate this, they would attend the celebrations of all the different organizations.

[12] The prohibitions against celebration when there is illness, a recent death, or some moral or physical anomaly in the family are much stronger for women than for men. Men abstain from celebratory events, especially when in mourning, but for a much shorter period than women. For detailed discussions of the gender dimensions of Greek mourning practices, see Auerbach 1984; Caraveli-Chaves 1980; Danforth 1982.

orary [complimentary] invitation" (*timitiki prosklisis*), failed to attend the Migrants' Association *horoesperidha* in Thessaloniki, the executive board complained bitterly in an article that subsequently appeared in the Sohos' bimonthly newspaper. They suggested, in tones of deep indignation, that he had political motives for abstaining. Given that the newly elected board was now dominated by supporters of his rival and enemy, Grekos, now the PA.SO.K. member of parliament, the accusation was at least plausible. But whatever the actual reasons for Evangelidhis' absence, the board exploited it for all it was worth. Protesting their own disinterestedness, as ruling factions typically and expertly do, they launched a thinly veiled political attack by insisting that in such events, and in their association generally, personal and political interests had no place.

Conversely, the association may at times wish to discourage the attendance of certain individuals. I was surprised to notice that *horoesperidhes* were not advertised on posters in shop windows or in the local, bimonthly newspaper (which members of the Sohos Youth Association put together), even though many were fund-raising ventures.[13] News of the forthcoming dance was spread solely by word of mouth. Significantly, too, one had to acquire not a "ticket" (*isitirio*) but an "invitation" (*prosklisis*). The ambiguity of the term "invitation" here is important. I was given an invitation to my first *horoesperidha*, that of the Sohos Youth Association, by its president, Dimitra; but I was not always offered an invitation to such events. I was never certain whether this was a deliberate exclusion or out of conviction that the event lacked the "folkloric interest" that would attract me. Indeed, when inquiring about how I might be able to acquire and pay for an invitation, I sometimes encountered disconcerting evasion. In hindsight, I believe that in a few cases I was being discouraged from attending, much as certain townspeople were.

When, for example, I learned of the impending dance of the Businesspeople's Association (Silloghos Epanghelmation) in February 1984, I starting asking around among my friends in the marketplace in hopes that I might find a *parea* to join. I inquired in the *kafenio* of Triandafillos Sofulis, former mayor and Communist party (KKE) member, whether anyone there planned to attend. Triandafillos and his customers were unenthusiastic, and they explained their own rebuff. Triandafillos, himself a member of the Businesspeople's Association, remarked that not until that morning—the day of the dance—had anyone bothered to tell him about it. Whoever had informed him had

---

[13] The only exception to this was the Sohoian Migrants' Association, whose celebration was held in Thessaloniki.

denied that "invitations" were necessary. Triandafillos was skeptical; he was sure they existed. He took this man's "evasion" as a sign that he, Triandafillos, would not really be welcome: "Those guys, the big ones, they're doing it *büz-büzé*!" An insiders' affair, in other words; the Turkish term he used might translate as "all puckered together." And he further predicted: "The atmosphere will be a bit heavy. Constricted [*sfihto*]. It won't have *kefi*. They've never put their hands in their pockets before, that's why they're rich." Triandafillos' adjectives are revealing; they convey weight and constriction in a context ideally associated with release. Verbs ordinarily used to describe dancing and celebration in Sohos include those of "bursting out" (*kseskazo, ksespazo*), "taking out" (*ksevghazo, vghazo ekso*), and "throwing out [worries]" (*rihno ekso*) (see also Auerbach 1984; Caraveli 1985; Danforth 1978, 1979a).[14] Here, he maintains, such release will be choked off. The adjective *sfihto*, "constricted," alludes not only to an emotional or spiritual state but also to being "tight" with money. In Sohos, as elsewhere in Greece (see, for example, Campbell 1964:284), the accusation of stinginess (*tsinghunia*) is a serious one. Triandafillos implies that such men hoard wealth, that they refuse to partake in the usual systems of reciprocity. Such a man is incapable of becoming the generous, "open-fisted" man, the *kuvardas* (Papataxiarchis n.d.).

A second man chimed in: "If you don't have an invitation, they tell you all the seats are taken," intimating that the people of this association ignore the moral values of the table, where a mere lack of chairs cannot justify exclusion. Normally, as the proverb says, "At the table, there's room for all but one—Satan himself!" He added that the event would really be "political," implying (though he did not feel the need to spell this out) that it was to be a right-wing event. This linkage was based on class criteria, that those "of the market" (*tis aghoras*), as capitalists (*kapitalistes*), naturally supported the fiscally conservative Right and were against PA.SO.K.'s socialist policies. Triandafillos as a member of the Communist party, was, of course, an exception among the association's members, but in his view this only proved the point. Why else was he being singled out for exclusion?

Finally, a third man described the subtlety and indirectness through which such rejection would be communicated: "It's like going to a wedding without being invited. You feel cold. They don't throw you out, but they don't pay any attention to you." Coldness is symbolically associated with social isolation, ultimately with death (Caraveli-Chaves 1980; Danforth 1982). Interestingly, this man portrays a "living death," where the unwanted individual is tolerated but ignored,

---

[14] Many of these verbs use the prefix *kse*, "to exit," "to go out of."

made invisible, denied his social significance, and thus humiliated (Campbell 1964). His last phrase is of key importance: it could, more literally, be translated as "they don't give you any significance/meaning [*dhen se dhinun simasia*]." This is intriguing in light of Herzfeld's (1985a) discussion of meaning (*simasia*) and manhood; but here, the Sohoian speaker sees a person's "meaning" not as stemming from his performative adeptness but more as a fixed condition.

Yet the situation is not really quite so fixed as he implies. A man who perceives that others refuse to "give him meaning" understands this as an assault on his self-regard, his *eghoismos*. And he may respond with disruptive acts. These acts, to be explored in Chapter 6, constitute dramatic and sometimes foolhardy attempts to force this recognition.

THE BUSINESSPEOPLE'S ASSOCIATION DANCE

Evening came, and my attempts to find a *parea* with whom I could attend the Businesspeople's Association dance had come to nothing. Yet I felt obliged to go. Filled with the anxiety that I might miss something important for my research, but at the same time dreading the prospect of entering where I had not been invited, I tried one last alternative. I dressed up (or so I thought) and stopped at the home of a friend, Maria, who along with her husband ran a dry-cleaning shop in the market. As businesspeople, Maria and Yannis often attended such events. But they were not going out tonight. They had been out several times in the past few weeks and "had to economize." But she encouraged me to go ahead, even without a *parea*. "We are, more or less, hospitable to foreigners. They'll invite you to sit down with them."

I left about nine o'clock, and arrived at the *kendro* Vendetta, where I hung around the door, reluctant and embarrassed to enter alone. The windows were fogged over and the curtains drawn, but the muffled cadences of the amplified electronic piano could be heard. Finally, sheepishly, I opened the door. Squinting through the haze of cigarette smoke, I searched for the faces of friends with whom I could comfortably spend the rest of the evening. I knew that many would beckon me to sit down, but that some would do so out of hospitality rather than friendship. I thus tried to scan faces while remaining noncommittal; were I to allow my gaze to rest on another's, I would be unable to refuse an invitation to sit with them without causing offense. At the table near the door sat Toula, a member of the Orpheus Association's executive board and proprieter of a carpet shop, a young single woman of twenty-six whom I had been trying to get to know. She invited me to sit with them, and I accepted.

The room yawned before us, barren and concrete, a forlorn wood-stove in one corner hardly denting the chill. Because it was the Carnival season the restaurant was decorated with multicolored paper streamers, and garish plastic masks grinned in disembodied glee from the wall. On the table, rolls of streamers lay, waiting to be thrown. The restaurant was crowded with tables that surrounded a dance floor (*pista*) on three sides. On the fourth side was an orchestra, consisting of a vocalist and four musicians who were playing a bouzouki, a clarinet, two electric pianos, and snare drums. When I entered the orchestra was playing a tango, and several couples were dancing. Others were still eating, and the young men working as waiters moved quickly back and forth, gingerly balancing plates of food and bottles of wine.

In the first half hour, especially, but throughout the evening, I found that as I looked around the room many people were waiting to catch my eye, to greet me with a subtle nod or a smile, or—if quite far away—with a wave. A number of men came to the table to shake my hand, welcoming me, and then went on to other tables to greet others. Women stayed seated, primly composed, like immobile fixtures anchoring the table and marking it as their *parea*'s space. Their husbands, meanwhile, leaned forward toward the male visitors, and then stood up, pumped hands, and slapped shoulders in greeting, shouting to friends on the other side or even getting up and circulating around the hall.

Most married women wore clothes that were both expensive and matronly: cashmere sweaters and narrow skirts, or somewhat dated knee-length formal dresses made of silky synthetics. Some had fur coats draped across their shoulders. Few wore more than a touch of make-up, but none lacked jewelry, usually gold. Many had their hair freshly permed or at least stiffly coiffed. Only the young doctor's Athenian wife wore a low-neck, stylish dress, and only one young Sohoian woman, a hairdresser, wore fashionable trousers. All wore new-looking high-heeled shoes. Except for Panayotis, the left-wing electrician, who defiantly appeared in a colorful sweater, the men wore their best suits. It was the most formal dress affair I had ever witnessed, and I felt positively shabby in my skirt, sweater, and leather boots.

The orchestra kept up a steady stream of tunes, mostly waltzes, with some tangos, punctuated by *kalamatiani*. Toula and her friend Vasso (aged seventeen), who sat with their two families and did not have male escorts, waited impatiently for the circling line dances. When the music for a *kalamatianos* began, Toula arose swiftly, pulling me and Vasso along, and moved onto the dance floor. There, waiting until a female friend in the dance line moved in front of her, Toula reached for her hand. The friend let go of the hand of the dancer on her right and let us join in. We thus went round and round as more and more people joined the dance line until it coiled tightly, densely. Sometimes, as new groups joined the dance floor, the single line became a ragged, interlacing coil with several leaders, cheerfully out of step with each other but all moving round a shared center. As we moved, I watched individuals raise their eyebrows or nod ever so slightly in greeting to each other and also to me. The orchestra played not a single tune but a continuous medley of popular tunes in the same meter; a single *kalamatianos* could last for twenty minutes or even more.

At the beginning of every *kalamatianos* (or of another line dance, such as a *tsamikos* or a *hasaposervikos*) a brief scene was repeated over and over: a group of four or five people, usually in their twenties, stood on the floor, amiably jostling each other as they negotiated who would lead the dance. A young woman pushed to the position of first dancer would decline, shaking her head and giggling in embarrassment while the others playfully but insistently coaxed her, "Come on! *Ela!* Why not?" And she would gleefully retreat, pulling one of the other young women to the front, who in turn would laughingly protest and pull someone else forward. These scenes lasted less than a minute and invariably ended when one of their male companions took the lead and started the dance.

Once the dance had started, anyone was free to join the dance line. In this early point in the evening, however, female dancers, especially married women, often feigned reluctance to get up from their tables, refusing entreaties made by men and women alike. Among those dancing, the position of leader changed often. That person kept the lead position for only a minute or two, then pulled another dancer, often the second dancer, to take his or her place. Women brought to the first position seldom declined (though they let themselves be coaxed several times before accepting) and took the lead, smiling, the younger ones with exuberance, the older ones with more dignity and control, eschewing deep, low bends, and performing instead bouncy, delicate steps. A female leader ordinarily beckoned another female friend or relative to take her place. In this way, ten, even fifteen, people might serially take the lead and then pass it on, in a single fifteen- to twenty-minute dance. Individuals did not gift the orchestra, and dancing was open to all tables simultaneously, rather than taking turns.

While the dancing was going on, several young men circulated among the tables, energetically coaxing the celebrants to buy lottery tickets, priced at 100 drachmas each. Men normally bought tickets for wives, daughters, and any otherwise unaccompanied female friends in

the *parea*, but I bought my own set of five tickets (*lahia*). At about
11:30 P.M., the orchestra stopped for a break, and the lottery began.
Mihalis, a youthful, attractive, fortyish bachelor, an administrator for
the Electricity Board who lived in Thessaloniki but who returned
weekends to Sohos, moved to the center, microphone in hand, assuming the suave persona of a nightclub entertainer. He announced that he
would begin the lottery by auctioning off the unsold tickets. Seven or
eight sets of fifty tickets were auctioned off among jeers and laughter
for amounts ranging from 4,000 to 7,000 drachmas.

The auctioning was playful. Men teased as they submitted bids:
"3,000!" Petronis shouted, "3,001!" called Nassos, and in the next
round, "4,500!" shouted Katsareas, "4,501!" cried Nassos. Finally,
with all tickets auctioned off, and all the stubs collected in a plastic bag,
Mihalis asked the president of the organization to draw the first winning number. Mihalis held up the prize, an ornately painted amphora
of ouzo—the kind seen in airport duty-free shops—shrouded in stiff
plastic and a large blue bow, a gift that had been, as he explained,
"kindly donated by Letsios' sweet shop." The president, theatrically
averting his gaze from the bag of ticket stubs, plunged his hand in and
drew one out. Four men looked over his shoulder as he read out the
number. Laughter, comments, and applause filled the room. And so
on with about twenty-five gifts, each donated by a small local business
and including such items as a pair of women's shoes, Metaxas cognac,
a round of cheese from the local cheese factory, a quartz watch, and
various objects for the house (ashtrays, sets of dishes, a salad tray). Last
of all, the grand prizes were announced, along with their value: a
woman's formal dress (15,000 drachmas) and an automobile tire
(25,000 drachmas).

With the lottery over, the atmosphere was looser. The orchestra's
next number was not a group dance but a *zeibekiko*. Although characteristically a brooding sort of dance, this particular performance was
buoyant. Dimitros, a massive fifty-five-year-old butcher who prided
himself as a dancer, leapt up, ran to the center of the dance floor, and
performed a joyful, expansive dance. Men from several tables made
their way to the dance floor to kneel at his feet and clap in rhythm. He
danced for two minutes or so, and then his brother's wife, Angela,
entered his space. As she began to dance, he gave way and clapped for
her. Then followed Hatzu, the news agent, and then Marina Tsilim-
boni, an in-marrying bride from Nigrita. Soloists gave way genially as
each new dancer arrived.

The next dance was a *tsifte teli*, a belly dance, played at a quick
tempo. As the music started, Vasso pleaded with Toula to dance with
her. Toula refused, insisting she "didn't know how." But I admitted

knowing how, and Vasso pulled me up and dragged me to the center, where in the midst of moving bodies we could not be seen by the celebrants watching from the periphery. She danced expressively and expertly. Several men approached me, full of smiles. The father of the trousered hairdresser tried to pull me toward him to make me his partner. A second, Hatzu, from whom I bought newspapers, playfully grabbed my hands and twirled me around. Vasso noted this small detail and gigglingly reported it to our table when we returned. By the end of this dance, there were thirty men and three women (including the two of us) on the dance floor.

From this point on, the orchestra performed no more waltzes or tangos. Instead, they played quick-tempo, face-to-face dances in 2/4 meter (which some danced as a simple *karsilamas*, and others—exaggerating pelvic movements and undulating shoulders—as more explicitly erotic *tsifte telia*), *kalamatiani*, and even *yanka*, a Greek-style "bunny hop."[15] As male and female celebrants jammed the dance floor, small groups of five or six danced at the edges of the room, in the aisles and in spaces between tables. Two young men climbed on top of their tables, fondling crepe-paper streamers and parodying the postures of sexual intercourse in a raucous belly dance as the were urged on by the whistling and clapping of their *parea* (see figure 17). Slightly tipsy men came up to me or gestured insistently from across the room, each demanding that I photograph him with his *parea*. When I left with my table at half past one, the dancing was still going strong.

Ground Rules

Each *horoesperidha*—the Businesspeople's Association dance being only one example—is a unique event. What happens within it depends largely on which organization sponsors it and which individuals and groups happen to attend. Nonetheless, as a genre of dance-event the *horoesperidha* has a characteristic organization of space, time, and activities. In certain respects, the *horoesperidha* incorporates meanings and practices of convivial sociability common to Sohoian dance-events generally. Yet because the *horoesperidha* is not a random gathering of groups of townspeople but an activity to some degree stage-managed by an association whose prestige is at stake, the customary convivial practices may be consciously altered by the organizers' interventions. The spatial arrangements of persons, groups, and objects, and the temporal flow (the ordering, pacing, and timing of activities) are managed

---

[15] According to Michael Herzfeld (pers. comm.), this dance is originally from Finland.

17. A youth dances a belly dance on a table top in the final ecstatic hour of the Businesspeople's Association dance.

so as to order the celebrants' experience. Though the outcome is in the final analysis indeterminate (Moore, in Moore and Myerhoff 1977:219), the event is typically organized to move from an initial emphasis on formality, constraint, and hierarchy to an atmosphere of informality, excess, disorder, and lack of hierarchy, in other words, of "antistructure" (Turner 1969).

The major activities of the Sohoian *hθroesperidha* occur in two sites: at the table and on the dance floor. These sites are conceptual as well as physical. It is important to describe the meanings and practices associated with each site more generally before considering how these meanings and practices are manipulated in the *horoesperidha*.

With its members seated around it, facing inward, creating a closed circle, the table is the physical representation, the symbol, of the *parea*.

The *parea* is situationally defined as all of those who share this table. New members may, over time, join the table in (theoretically) unlimited numbers: already seated members cheerfully squeeze together—two celebrants often precariously sharing a single uncomfortable straight-backed wooden chair—rather than reject a latecomer. The *parea* may be composed of individuals who know each other well—kin, affines, coworkers, neighbors, friends, or some combination of these categories. Or it may be a more serendipitously created, *ad hoc* collection of individuals linked to a central core of intimates and gathered together for a specific occasion. Whether or not the *parea* has an existence outside of the situation does not, ideally, matter, because the *parea* is not a passive entity; it must be invented through interaction. "Making company" (*kanume parea*) is, to borrow Giddens' (1976) phrase, a skilled social production. The table is therefore not just the physical representation of an already constituted group, but the site where the group actively constitutes itself.[16] This is achieved through particular practices, which have a clear logic and etiquette.

The major "objective"—if it may be so called—of the table as a social unit is "being together." It is, in Simmel's terms, sociability itself (1971a). The practices of the table—ways of eating, drinking, talking, dancing—emphasize, as they help to create, this collectivity. These practices, through which sociable pleasures are constructed, are also regarded as "obligations" (*ipohreosis*), because an individual is obliged to subordinate his or her individual needs and pleasures for the group as a whole. Hunger, thirst, physical discomfort, and boredom should be cheerfully borne for the sake of the *parea*. A person suffering some private grief or anxiety often comes along with the group anyway, out of a sense of obligation or in the hope of being able to "get out of him/herself" (*na ksefigho*) or to "forget" (*na ksehaso*). Though this person's participation may be subdued, she or he is expected to participate in the toasts (even if drinking little), to eat something, to dance a few dances. Such a celebrant is not expected to pretend an attitude of gaiety but is, rather, expected quietly to witness (and ideally, to get pleasure or comfort from) other people's *kefi*. In any case, the celebrant should not "spoil the celebration." Individual distinctions among people should be used to *enhance* the collective pleasure: a person good at jokes or storytelling, a singer who knows many songs, a skillful or humorous dancer, or a musician (I, for example, was often urged to bring my flute, to accompany the group singing) can "give *kefi* to everyone" (*dhini kefi s'olus*).

[16] Caraveli, similarly, stresses the constitutive qualities of collective celebratory actions. She describes the Karpathiot "*glendi*" as a "community born in performance" (1985).

The practices of commensality reiterate this collective orientation. A *parea* eating together typically orders not individual portions for each member but a variety (*pikilia*) of meats, fish, cheese, and salads (and later, sliced fruit on a platter), which are placed in great profusion in the center of the table. Each member has a fork, but no individual plate. Each person spears a morsel, chews it slowly, then puts down the fork. The table must be (and appear to be) bounteous; empty platters and bottles are often left on the table, rather than cleared away, which enhances this effect. Individual members may urge each other to "eat! eat!" Here, inverting the symbolism of the household (where women feed others), men feed women and all *kseni*, regardless of the latters' gender (see Herzfeld 1985a: 130). Even so, an individual member, no matter how hungry, would be "ashamed" (*drepete*) to eat ravenously or to appear greedy. Though large quantities of food may, in the end, be eaten, consumption is a slow, drawn-out process of nibbling.

The *parea* also drinks together, usually wine, which is served in very small glass tumblers. (Women, as noted earlier, tend to dilute their wine with soda water or soda pop.) Whoever refills the glasses always refills others within reach before his or her own (males often take this prerogative).[17] Before the first quaffing of wine, celebrants lift their glasses toward the center, clinking them together, and utter conventionalized toasts such as "To our health [*stin iya mas*]!" or "To life [*eviva*]!" Throughout the evening, especially after a refilling of glasses, any member (and particularly the person pouring) can initiate another toast. Frequently, this is done in a lull in the conversation, or when the person toasting perceives that conversation has become too dispersed into small separate units. The celebrant initiating the toast stamps his (or rarely, her) tumbler down and then lifts it, saying, "So, to our health [*Aide, ya mas*]!" or even just "So!" letting the ensuing gesture of raising the tumbler up toward the center silently complete the meaning. The other members are obliged to repeat his words, or at least his gesture, in unison. This practice, which visually and physically reaffirms the collectivity, may also be initiated after a song or an entertaining exchange of jokes or banter. Wine, like food, may be consumed in great quantities (especially by men), but it is always consumed in this collective manner.

As they imbibe, so do they pay. Though Sohoians may buy rounds of drinks for each other in the *kafenio*, the norm when eating out is to divide costs of food and drink equally among all celebrants, a practice

---

[17] It is proper to "fill" these tumblers about halfway. An empty glass is a signal that one wishes more.

called *refene*. In all-male *parees* and in mixed *parees* like the one with
whom I often socialized, which were not composed of "couples," each
celebrant, male or female, generally pays an equal amount. When couples or family units are involved, the male head of household pays.

There are normative ways of talking when gathered around a table,
as well. Regardless of the subject matter (and this can include almost
anything, except "personal" issues), talk should be a collective affair.
This does not mean that everyone participates, for often only a few
individuals exchange words while others listen, occasionally making
cryptic or sly comments about this main exchange. It does mean, however, that the table should not break up into separate conversational
dyads or triads, except momentarily. Certain forms of talk are preferred over others. In situations such as the *horoesperidha*, or when a
parea spontaneously goes out to a *taverna*, people often engage in a
form of talk that rhetorically invokes and marks the separation of this
site from everyday worries and that marks, also, the playful, nonseri-
ous quality of the interaction. This is *kalaburi*, a joking banter that includes stories, jokes, wordplays (puns and double entendres, which are
often sexual), and playful innuendo. *Kalaburi* may include gestural
horseplay (touching, teasing, slapping), as well.[18]

Kalaburi is believed to facilitate the collective *kefi* most appropriate
in this sort of situation, a state of being where one is "without
thoughts" (*horis skepsis*) or, in other words, "without worries." By
contrast, other forms of talk—serious discussion (*sizitisi*) or discussion
of "personal" things (*ta prosopika*, a phrase that often implies "personal
differences" or quarrels), idle but intimate neighborly talk (*muhabet*),
gossip (*kotsombolia*), and the wide-ranging but sometimes testy conversation of the *kafenio* (*kuvenda*)—are all considered inappropriate and
disruptive in this context. Talk should be both collective and recreational, and *kalaburi*, associated with laughter and forgetting one's worries, is ideal. While watching various dance-events I often noticed that
those at a table not engaged in *kalaburi* might simply sit silently, rather
than attempt polite group conversation or break into separate conversational dyads. The presence of musicians allows another mode of collective communication to take place, as well. Celebrants know by heart
most of the popular tunes played by the orchestra and often sing along,
both at the table and while dancing (see figure 18).

The table is the social unit for dancing. In what Sohoians regard as
the customary dance situation when mixed (rather than all-male) *parees*

[18] The degree of this gestural horseplay depends on the youth and the character of the
parea, of course. A *parea* of friends of both sexes or young married couples tends to be
more rambunctious than a middle-aged group. Young men may sometimes pinch,
tickle, or try to embarrass their female compatriots, who may hit back in jesting protest.

18. My *parea*, which includes active members of the Sohos Youth Association, enthusiastically claps and sings along with the orchestra at the 1985 PA.SO.K. *horoesperidha*.

are involved, the dance floor is not open to all tables all of the time. Musicians who have received no special requests will certainly play tunes to which any and all may get up to dance. But in a situation organized by *parangelia*,[19] a man from one table can negotiate directly with the musicians to order a song on behalf of the table. The musicians assign him a place in the order (*sira*) of those patrons waiting to dance, normally on the basis of "first come, first served." When "his" song is being played, only this man and his table have the right to use the dance floor. This "right" is also an obligation for those sitting at the table, who are generally expected to participate. Although those who are dancing may beckon others to join them, for the duration of the song the dance floor belongs to them.

The forms of association and practices of the table in the *horoesperidha* have many similarities with, but also a few deviations from, this standard form. The *parea* is typically composed of married couples. Tables may seat as few as four people (usually two couples) but more

[19] The placement of the accent when pronouncing the word *parangelia* marks a subtle distinction between two nuances of meaning. *Parangelia* pronounced with the accent on the penultimate syllable is the general term for "ordering" or "requesting" something, used in dance-events as well as in other contexts. Its more colloquial form, however, in which the accent is placed on the last syllable, is (or, at least, was originally) associated with the male practice of ordering the male solo dance, *zeibekiko*, by members of a specific urban subculture whose social center was the seedy urban nightclub, as will be discussed in Chapter 6.

typically accommodate eight to twelve. At these larger tables, partners in a couple do not necessarily sit side by side. Women may congregate together on one side of the table while men sit on the other, though the seating arrangement is rarely as segregated by gender as one finds in, for example, Sohoian name-day celebrations. Thus, though the patriarchal unit is stressed, the couple is symbolically oriented *outward*, toward the table. These couples associate together as "friends" (*fili*). Such individuals are usually about the same age, and they may be related as cousins or in-laws. By describing the *parea* as composed of "friends," however, Sohoians emphasize the voluntaristic, rather than obligatory, quality of this "being together."

The inward orientation of the table, however, is mitigated somewhat by the fact that all celebrants share a common identity as members or supporters of the sponsoring association. Indeed, there is intense interaction among tables, both verbal and nonverbal. Though the table remains a collective unit socially and economically, even early in the event there are intimations that a more comprehensive collectivity will be constructed.

What most strongly distinguishes the *horoesperidha* from many other dance-events,[20] however, is the relationship between the table and the dance floor. In these other dance-events, the dance floor is monopolized successively by separate tables; a *parea* that is seated and watching another *parea* dance cannot but view this through the prism of its own exclusion from the dancing. Being denied the chance to dance, or having one's place in the ordering usurped, is a grave insult, and people often tell stories of fighting that erupts "because of the dance." Since the object of the *horoesperidha* is to provide a good time for everyone and thus to enhance the sponsoring association's prestige, the organizers often attempt to restructure what happens on the dance floor. They change the "ground rules" in order to make the dance floor a site where unity is forged rather than threatened. Most notably this occurs by prohibiting the practice of *parangelia*, but it also involves using the dance floor for the performance of small rituals of solidarity through which the organizers attempt to orchestrate association.

RITUALS OF SOLIDARITY

Although the invitation usually indicates a starting time for the *horoesperidha*, celebrants are concerned not about being late but about find-

[20] For instance, the dancing that occurs in local *kendra* on Sunday and Monday nights at the climax of Carnival (when mixed *parees*, rather than all-male cohorts, fill these establishments); dancing that occurs on the evenings of the summer *paniyiri*, in Sohos and in surrounding villages; or dancing that occurs at commercial *kendra* and *bouzoukia*.

ing a table. Celebrants straggle in; most arrive in the first hour, but a few trickle in over the course of the evening. As they arrive they are seated at tables by waiters, and from here they wait—sometimes for quite a while—for the waiter to take their order. During this time people chat, look around to see who else has come, and greet one another. There is an intensity of visual communication in the din and clamor of the hall from the moment celebrants gather. All are watching and being watched.

Despite all this activity, people say that things have not really started yet. The musicians are still arranging their amplifiers and tuning up their instruments. Each table, after waiting to order food and drink, begins to eat when their platters arrive. Commensality is centered on the table, not the whole group.[21] The separate tables do not feast in unison but are served as they arrive.

Once a reasonable crowd has not only arrived but has also been served dinner, the musicians begin to play dance songs. At this early stage, most celebrants treat this as background music. Even after they have finished eating, they seem reluctant to go up to the dance floor. The musicians may play a *kalamatianos* for several minutes before a *parea* ventures onto the dance floor, and a waltz or a tango lures only a few couples up to dance. At this early stage the atmosphere is often stilted, hesitant, expectant.

Opening Words

In the initial moments of the *horoesperidha*, group identity is declaimed in formal ways. These opening rituals stress relations of hierarchy. They stress orderliness and articulate social orderings within the collectivity of celebrants and the larger society. Distinctions among members on the basis of political status, organizational power, and gender are articulated openly.

This is evident in the evening's first "performative utterance" (Austin 1975): the welcome. Each *horoesperidha* has a master of ceremonies, usually male.[22] The emcee is typically a member of the sponsoring association, though he need not hold any formal position or play an active role in its affairs. He is typically of youthful middle age, good-looking, and smartly dressed. He should "know how to speak"; in other words, he must, by turns, be authoritative, genial, and clever.[23]

---

[21] In contrast to formal banquets familiar in American or Western European culture, where everyone is served simultaneously.

[22] The one exception, predictably, was a young "mistress of ceremonies" in the dance sponsored by the female-led Sohos Youth Association.

[23] The male emcee perhaps embodies, in an institutional way, male control of speech in public contexts. Because of the ambivalent nuances put upon female talkativeness—which can be interpreted as sexually loose and socially disruptive (see du Boulay

The emcee stands in the center of the dance floor and, holding a microphone, opens his speech by welcoming the celebrants. Out of courtesy, the invited dignitaries are acknowledged first. A typical opening speech would begin with the words, "Honorable Minister(s) of Parliament, Honorable Mayor, Honorable Chief of Police, Dearest Members and Friends, good evening and we welcome you to our dance." The decision about which names to include in the welcome is crucial and is usually made carefully beforehand by the insiders in control of the association.

The ordering of the names is also meaningful. It enunciates a hierarchy of status. In most cases, the order of names is a matter of convention, a nicety of ceremonial etiquette, lending a sense of grandness and formality to the occasion. Duly noted, it arouses little comment. Because this hierarchy is not unambiguously fixed in reality, however, the emcee's ordering of honors in the welcome speech can occasionally precipitate "misunderstandings" (*pareksighisis*).

After the greeting, there are often speeches. The PA.SO.K. and New Democracy–sponsored dances predictably have a host of speeches by both local activists and regional party officials; speeches at gatherings of other organizations tend to be much fewer and briefer. Speeches usually emphasize the goals of the organization, list what has been accomplished that year, describe what the executive board envisions as its goals for the future, and call upon the assembled group for continued help and support. Although those delivering such speeches may try to create a sense of solidarity wholly through reference to the group's activity and identity, they may in some cases (as in the events organized by political parties) try to stimulate this through highlighting antagonisms and differences with competing groups. Thus the PA.SO.K. speeches enthusiastically praised the success of government policies and repeatedly emphasized that these were expressions of the "will of the people" (*i thelisi tu lau*); the speeches of the New Democracy *horoesperidha*, in contrast, promoted solidarity by attacking and ridiculing these same policies.

Opening Dances

The welcome and the speeches formally declaim what the association stands for. The verbal highlighting of social distinctions is fundamen-

---

1974:201–229; Hirschon 1978:84–86; Lakoff 1975)—public speaking can be more difficult, and more embarrassing, for a woman. However, not all public speaking is the same. The dignity and decorum required in formal speeches poses few problems, and the young women that I observed delivering such formal greetings and speeches did this without any sign of embarrassment. It is the genial, jokey tone appropriate at later moments (for example, in the lottery) that young women find compromising, and avoid.

tal to this discourse; the presence of dignitaries, even as guests, lends authority and prestige to the group, and their absence can provoke enormous bitterness and accusations of intentional sabotage. Group identity is also articulated formally yet nonverbally through dancing. In the *horoesperidhes* of Orpheus and the Sohos Youth Association, it is always the children's folk-dance troupe, whose performance starts off the evening, that choreographically announces the association's vitality. The carefully memorized formations and endearing stumbles of these brightly costumed children, as they perform a medley of Greek mainland dances to the accompaniment of taped music or to the orchestra's amplified drums, *clarino*, and electric piano, seem indisputable bodily evidence that the association's cultural, educational, and folkloric objectives are being fulfilled.

But being a theatrical spectacle rather than a participatory form, such a performance cannot by itself initiate the evening of social dancing. Rather, the first dance that follows the welcoming speech "opens the dance" (*anighi to horo*). The phrase is noteworthy. More than just a poetic way to convey "beginning," the verb *anighi* evokes auspicious beginnings (for example, a new bride "opens her house," and the season of spring, *aniksi*, literally means "opening"; see also Hirschon 1978:76–79). The term *horos*, too, is intentionally ambiguous; though it certainly refers to the dance-event as a whole, "opening" is graphically—and again nonverbally—achieved through an actual dance.

Distinguished guests may be invited to open the dance by leading the first dance. Thus, in the 1984 Migrants' Association dance, the president invited the two local members of parliament, Grekos from PA.SO.K. and Rouhas from New Democracy, to open the dance. Although these two were political rivals, relations between them were respectful, if not warm. As the musicians struck up a *kalamatianos*, Grekos insisted that Rouhas take the lead first. After an appropriate interval, Rouhas passed the lead to Grekos. As they danced, members of the board and then other celebrants gradually left their tables and joined the line of dancers.

The organizers' subsequent representation of this incident exemplifies the use of hierarchical distinctions ("distinguished" guests) to proclaim unity. The Migrants' Association executive board, reporting this *horoesperidha* in a newspaper account, described the celebrants' "common spirit and fellowship confirmed by the presence of our two MPs." The rivals' cooperative dance, deftly maneuvered by the board, was meant to demonstrate the "irrelevance" of political differences in this context. Indeed, the executive board used precisely this example of bipartisan cooperation when castigating Mayor Evangelidhis for refusing to attend.

When invited dignitaries are not present, however, there is often no explicit invitation of particular individuals to join this first dance. Rather, those who consider themselves "important" in the association spontaneously join or are urged to join by others. Participation equals a claim to be recognized and honored.

The "first dance" of the 1985 Orpheus *horoesperidha* was an instructive and somewhat unusual case in which the informal, rather than formal, leadership publicly presented themselves to the assembled celebrants. The children's dance troupe had left the floor, and the emcee thanked them, then welcomed those who had braved the snow to join the celebration and wished them a good time ("*kali dhiaskedhasi*"). For some moments people milled around, talking to the musicians. Suddenly, without announcement, the tune for the first dance began: a *kalamatianos*. Three men from the executive board entered the dance space and began dancing. Within a few minutes, eight men had joined the line of dancers. All of them were powerful in Orpheus, either as officers and members of the board or behind the scenes. These eight men (and one eight-year-old boy, who amused everybody by imitating the stereotypically male gestures of the others) led the line in turn, each accepting applause from the audience as he moved into the first position.

Two principles of exclusion appear to be at work here: gender and political affiliation. No woman took part in this dance, despite the fact that three of the seven positions on the Orpheus executive board were held by young women: that of secretary (held by Eleni, then eighteen) and two positions on the board (Toula, twenty-six, and Rena, thirty-five, the only one of the three who was married). Because she was in mourning for her father's recent death, Rena was not present. But the other two were. Were these two young women excluded from this first, honorary dance or did they choose not to participate? The point is a fine one.

When, standing with Toula as the men were dancing, I asked her why she did not join them, she admitted to feeling too "embarrassed" (*drepome*) to do so. Although such reluctance to put oneself forward may not be entirely gender specific, the sentiment is surely intensified for female Sohoians, who learn throughout their lives the dangers of appearing to take the initiative too readily, especially when among men. Under the circumstances, one might have expected the men dancing, who could reasonably anticipate such shyness from young women, to invite, coax forward, or otherwise recognize Toula and Eleni, but they did not. They did, however, "pull in" a young man, the bright and dynamic leader of the New Democracy youth group, as he walked past their little circle on the dance floor. This performance seemed to present the same conclusions that had been drawn by Orpheus' rivals about the dynamics of gender and power in that association. Dimitra, the president of the rival association, was always skeptical that her female counterparts had any real power in Orpheus: "What do they do? They see these women as cleaning ladies," she once remarked acidly, implying that the "old men" continued to make all important decisions.

It is possible, too, to read this dance line in terms of political affiliation. The line included all three male members of the executive board present that night. But it also included men who were involved in only a minor way, if at all, in the public activities of Orpheus. Among these were the young leader of the New Democracy youth group and several middle-aged men active and influential in the New Democracy party's local affairs. Contrary to the usual rhetoric of political neutrality, this performance seemed to celebrate the identification of the political with the nonpolitical sphere.

Dancing "All Together"

The dance is opened by a small group of individuals symbolically set apart from the rest of the celebrants on the basis of their age, gender, political status, or organizational position. They dance before the others in both a temporal and a spatial sense. They not only take precedence, they are given it. But now, having established the hierarchial social ordering that legitimizes the association, the organizers turn their attention to orchestrating association in another way: by emphasizing an egalitarian ethic of collective participation, making sure that *kefi* is generated and quarrels are avoided. In order to do this, they must attempt to restructure the customary power dynamics and pattern of social relations of the dance.

One of the ways they do this is by intervening in the economic relationship between dancer and musicians. As discussed earlier, musicians ordinarily rely on "gifts of chance" (*tihera*) as remuneration for their playing. In the system of *parangelia* that results, individual patrons (representing themselves or their tables) are placed in a relationship of competition for the orchestra's songs and for the right to dance them on the dance floor. In the *horoesperidhes*, however, the orchestra is usually hired by the sponsoring association. The relatively high fee that the association pays takes into account the fact that the musicians will not be able to rely substantially on *tihera*.[24] The organizers then

---

[24] The Businesspeople's Association paid the orchestra 50,000 drachmas for the evening.

feel free to discourage *parangelia* and to expect the musicians' cooperation. Once the dance has been opened, the emcee invites everybody to join the dance.[25]

A second way that the organizers may attempt to manage things is by encouraging particular sorts of dances and discouraging others. Kiki, whose husband, Stavros, was president of the Soccer Association and involved in organizing its *horoesperidha*, was discussing with me her concern that the fights that had blighted the association's *horoesperidha* in past years not be repeated. She argued that by emphasizing "European" dances, conflicts occurring "because of the dance" could be minimized. Interestingly, Kiki explained that by *evropaiki*, she meant not just the "shake," tango, fox-trot and waltz but also *kalamatianos*. She was contrasting this category to *zeibekiko*, over which fights were reputedly rampant. She claimed that Stavros had agreed to pay the musicians a higher fee in exchange for refraining to play *zeibekiko*.

That the arrangement worked fairly successfully is illustrated by this account from Kostas, a member of my *parea* during the 1984 Soccer Association *horoesperidha*. We both agreed that this dance had been exceptionally exciting and "had a lot of *kefi* [*ihe poli kefi*]," but I asked him to try to explain what had made it so good:

> The *kefi* was excellent [*ihe kalo kefi*] because the orchestra was just right [*sosti*], real professionals, they chose and ordered the songs well [*ihan kali sira*]. They played "light" songs [*elafra*] when we were eating, and later they played a good combination of songs.
>
> Also, there was no *parangelia*. Somebody, some young guy, went up to the orchestra and asked for a *zeibekiko*, and the musician said, "Haven't you even a little bit of shame?" You see, that is an individual dance. Whereas we were all together. As much as we bumped into each other—it was a small space, after all—there was no quarrel. But in *zeibekiko*, if you come into the middle, there are blows! A fight! Sure! The guy would say, "You cut me off!"

Kiki's emphasis on *evropaiki* and her rejection of *zeibekiko* articulate the symbolic opposition relevant in defining the *horoesperidha*, but the distinction is too static to explain the change in the forms and dynamics of dancing over the course of the evening. For there is a shift, as the hours pass, from a mixture of group and couple (that is, European)

---

[25] Judging from the comments of various individuals, it seems that sponsoring associations have not always tried to discourage *parangelia* in their *horoesperidhes*. A young woman, Magda, commented of the New Democracy event that "this year, anybody who wanted to got up to dance"; likewise, Kiki remarked of the Businesspeople's dance that though she had "expected to see lots of money fall" (that is, "gifts") and "quarrels," she had been pleasantly surprised at how well the participants had gotten along.

19. As *kefi* builds, the dance floor becomes crowded. Celebrants at the 1985 PA.SO.K. *horoesperidha* dance face-to-face dances, arms raised in the conventional posture of spirited *kefi*.

dances, to wholly group dances. As the repertoire changes, the tempo usually increases. As the *kefi* builds, the central dance floor becomes more crowded (see figure 19); small groups of dancers also spill out to the sides and form small clusters at the periphery. Many of the tables are empty, and the dancing is decentered; indeed, it is as if the whole *kendro*—the area not just in the center of the tables but also surrounding and encompassing them—becomes a dance floor. The dancing of both males and females becomes looser and more buoyant, but male gestures are particularly exaggerated. Sometimes tables even *become* dance floors. Men climb on top of tables, calling attention to themselves (using, perhaps, the height of tables to assert a kind of higher status, now that the celebration has so "democratically" spread out). But now it is wild flamboyance, not civilized restraint, that marks distinctions among men.

Such antics may demonstrate a man's ability to distinguish himself as a good *ghlendzes* and to give *kefi* to the collective. But they may also be a way for men to express friendship publicly. At the 1985 Orpheus *horoesperidha*, two middle-aged businessmen—a barber and a tobacco chemical salesman—responded to my video camera by climbing onto a table top. There they performed an acrobatic face-to-face dance, with the tobacco chemical salesman leaping up and wrapping his legs around the barber's waist and leaning backward, as the latter waved his hands in the air, eyes closed, smiling. When the dance ended, the barber turned to his partner, kissed him on the cheek, and with one arm round the other's shoulder, turned dramatically to make a broad, smiling gesture of greeting to the camera.

These men were friends and fellow businessmen, people "of the market." Dramatizing their friendship, their skill and sense of humor as dancers, and the good time they were having, this playful dance enhanced the drama of the *horoesperidha* as a whole, even as it was used, competitively, to draw special attention (the crowd's as well as the video camera's) to themselves.

The Lottery

The lottery (*lahio*) is the climax of the event. If the event has been successful, the celebrants are no longer hesitant and self-conscious. They are in a state of heightened excitement, lubricated with wine, their bodies warmed up by hours of dancing and vibrating from the amplified music. When the music stops, the celebrants return to their tables, perhaps circuitously, pausing to talk to friends at another table. They may talk excitedly to each other, laugh, or perhaps just watch the scenes about them. There is a feeling of disorder, mixing, the absence of a center. But stepping onto the dance floor, the emcee once again draws attention back to the middle. The din of laughter and talk, though unceasing, nonetheless subsides somewhat.

In contrast to the ordered, ceremonious quality of the opening of the dance, the lottery is playful, boisterous, full of inside jokes and innuendo. The emcee, who spoke formally at first, now assumes an affable, even joking persona,[26] and the celebrants, no longer merely spectators, engage him (and each other) in a rowdy dialogue.

Although the organizers elsewhere may have tried to promote unity among celebrants, competitive male display in the auction is sanctioned and encouraged because it can be directed to benefit the association. Situated on the dance floor, the auction replaces the dance as the arena in which men compete for attention before the collected audience of celebrants. As the emcee offers up for auction packets of unsold tickets, male celebrants call out their bids. With each bid, the emcee repeats both the amount and the name of the bidder: "Eighteen hundred, Mr. Tourloumis!"

Men compete not only by showing that they have money and are

---

[26] In one event, the Migrants' Association dance, the emcee—while waiting for the unsold tickets to be collected together for the auction—launched into a humorous monologue in the style of a stand-up comedian.

willing to part with it but through wit and style. Sometimes men accompany their verbal bids with a humorous running commentary about the bidding process. I several times observed two young men, friendly rivals, shout out bids in jocular belligerence, playing with the timing. Initially they bid in rapid alternation, one remaining silent until the emcee appeared to be ending the bidding, whereupon, at the last moment, that young man topped the bid. In this repartee, timing is of the essence (Bourdieu 1977:6–7). Similarly, a table of youths will sometimes tease one of their fellows, especially if he is reputed to be tight with money (a *tsigunis*) or even merely shy, by bidding in his name. Shouting to the emcee, "Two thousand from Liolios!" and again, after an opposing bid, "Three thousand from Liolios!" they point theatrically at their unfortunate mate, and burst into laughter.

Commentary may also be more quietly ironical. I have described how Nassos, at the Businesspeople's Dance, showed his amused disdain for the competitive bidding—but also his wit—by adding one drachma to every bid called out. As each bid is proffered, there are remarks, laughter, exclamations, and nonverbal commentary—hoots and whistles for a dramatic leap in the bid, rolled eyes for a small increment. Friends call out to the current bidder, goading him to bid more.

With the remaining tickets auctioned off, the emcee begins the lottery. He usually, as Mihalis did at the Businesspeople's Association dance, chooses another person to draw the winning ticket stubs: if not the president of the association, then an especially boisterous celebrant pulled up from one of the tables near the dance floor, or perhaps even a child. Before each drawing, the emcee holds up for all to see the object that will be drawn for, praising it and naming the individual who donated it. For the more expensive objects, he also frequently mentions how much they are worth. The excited celebrants endure with impatience the perusal and rechecking of the winning ticket by at least three people, and they strain to hear the winning number. If one individual, perhaps someone who has bought a large number of tickets during the auction, wins more than once or twice, there will be playful jeers and joking accusations of cheating. However, although an aura of suspense surrounds the announcement of the winners, the emphasis is equally on the contributor of the object.

Like the bidder's bid, the giver's gift publicly asserts magnanimity and self-importance (Mauss 1967). The objects are not called "prizes" but rather "gifts" (*dhora*) or "contributions" (*prosfores*). Most of these are donated by local merchants from their stocks of merchandise, but occasionally they are purchased, then contributed, by donors. The richness and abundance of the lottery items are a testimony to the sponsoring association's prestige and the degree of its local support. It is one of the things people comment about afterward as a mark of a successful event.

At several *horoesperidhes* a list had been compiled of all the contributions and distributed to each table before the lottery began. In some cases the list included not only the objects to be given away in the lottery but also cash contributions. The organizers of the 1985 *horoesperidha* of the local New Democracy branch—the *horoesperidha* reputed to have offered that year's richest lottery—produced a "list of contributions" (*kataloghos prosforon*) containing fifty-five items. Each entry included the name of the individual contributor and/or the business, the object contributed, and, for the first ten items, its value. Forty-seven of these entries were objects given away in the lottery; the final eight indicated cash contributions ranging from 500 to 10,000 drachmas.

The objects given away in such lotteries constitute a bewildering hodge-podge of items, representing as they do the different occupations of their mostly entrepreneurial contributors. Not unlike the donations at the Businesspeople's Association *horoesperidha*, the New Democracy list included, among other things, a goat (from several brothers whose livelihood was shepherding), a carton of cigarettes, an elaborate light fixture, an acrylic blanket, and a bottle of Old Spice cologne. For the most part, items are luxury goods and decorative objects, many destined for public display in the formal *saloni* or used to hold sweets (crystal dishes, a serving tray), savories (a platter for dried nuts and seeds), or liqueurs (a set of Italian glasses) in offerings of hospitality.

The most expensive items, the top prizes, are another indication of the extent to which ideas about gender are involved in the display of status through consumer goods. The top prizes invariably include a combination of expensive women's clothing (ideally, a status symbol such as a fur coat) and, for men, automobile accoutrements (automobiles, which—unlike the more utilitarian trucks—are still a luxury item among Sohoians and are owned and driven almost exclusively by men). The top three prizes in the Orpheus lottery were a fur coat, a lady's dress, and a one-year insurance policy for the driver of an automobile. The Businesspeople's two top prizes and the top ten prizes in the much grander New Democracy lottery of 1985 were remarkably similar.[27]

[27] The top ten New Democracy prizes and their values were listed as follows: (1) one fur coat (60,000 drachmas); (2) two Fulda automobile tires (50,000 drachmas); (3) two Victor automobile tires (8,000 drachmas); (4) one electric kitchen stove (38,000 drachmas); (5) one imitation fur coat (17,000 drachmas); (6) four inner-tubes with pump

The lottery thus has carnivalesque yet contradictory features: equality and hierarchy are juxtaposed. During the auction of unsold tickets, nominally (situationally) equal men jovially and raucously compete to outbid each other. Although their words and gestures mark individual distinctions in economic resources, wit, and style, these also enable the collective treasury to be enriched. In the drawing, the wealth of the donor is juxtaposed to the luck of the recipient. The "gifts" are an index to the socioeconomic position of the donors in the everyday world, but the recipients acquire these tokens of wealth and status entirely by chance, by the luck of the draw. The lottery transforms potentially divisive distinctions into collective resources. This is symbolized by the act of redistribution. As the newspaper account of the Migrants' Association dance explained, "rich gifts, donations of local enterprises and of Sohoian businesspeople, were offered to everybody!"

Keeping Order through Orderly Disorder

Although it is about "having fun," the *horoesperidha* is a highly structured event. It has clearly defined codes of dress, music, dancing, and consumption. More than any other dance-event, it draws upon a "European" aesthetic and celebrates a patriarchal, petty-bourgeois morality. The primary unit is the married couple, seen as patriarchal head of the family and the lady of the house. Voluntaristic ties between these supposedly autonomous couples are emphasized over those based on kinship.

Stage-managed by the organizers and those who help, the event has an ordered, theatrical quality. The emcee officially running the show from the center relies on the somehow less noticeable men who stand at the edges and move around the crowd, helping out and keeping an eye on things.

Although the *horoesperidha* celebrates the association and the fact of association itself, marking the distinction between "us" and "them," internal distinctions are not wholly eschewed. Hierarchical social ordering occurs, but not in the unpredictable and potentially violent context of *parangelia*; social ordering is instead presumed and invoked in more orderly ways. Yet as the event proceeds, disorder is encouraged. An event is judged successful to the extent that it achieves dis–order (that is, "being all together") without becoming disorderly.

(8,000 drachmas); (7) two Dunlop automobile tires; (8) one container of 20–50 motor oil (6,000 drachmas); (9) two automobile air filters (5,000 drachmas); (10) one container of Bardahl motor oil (5,000 drachmas).

CHAPTER SIX

Male Prestige and the Eruption of Conflict

I light my cigarette and the rain puts it out
I knock on the door I love and it doesn't open.
I see fancy cars passing on the avenue
and I know you're laughing at my pain.

—"In Piraeus It's Cloudy," *Zeibekiko* by Mitsakis

ALTHOUGH it is meant to appear spontaneous and natural, the buoyant conviviality of *horoesperidhes* is a tenuous achievement.[1] Organizers attempt to orchestrate association, and thereby legitimize a particular social order, by reformulating the ground rules and prescribing an etiquette and normative set of practices. But without the celebrants' cooperation, they cannot be successful. Getting women to accept this etiquette and set of practices is relatively easy. The mechanisms of gossip that penalize female nonconformity, the valorization of the wifely role, and the very enjoyment a woman may feel in going out all combine to inhibit women, married or unmarried, from challenging the social order of the *horoesperidha*. Getting men to accept it, however, is more difficult, because the pressures on men are more contradictory.

Both organizers and celebrants actively encourage men to act cooperatively. In their words and in the ways they organize space, time, and activities, the organizers do not merely invite but literally exhort all celebrants to create unity ("to be all together"), fun, and high spirits. They attempt to make celebrants feel obliged to create a "good time" and simultaneously to feel embarrassed and ashamed to ruin it. Men's boisterous, attention-getting behaviors are not only tolerated but encouraged; and when men become good revelers they express and conform to, rather than contravene, Sohoian ideals of collective sociability (see figure 20).

Most of the time men do, indeed, act cooperatively in these events. They do so for a variety of reasons. Men, like women, value "good company" (*kali parea*) and a "good party" (*kalo ghlendi*). They enjoy the pleasures of sociability: eating and drinking, recreational talk, laughter, dancing. Young men, though their style is rowdier (norma-

[1] The song in the epigraph was first recorded in 1960. The translation is by Butterworth and Schneider (1975).

20. Respectable excess: the pose of the reveler at the *horoesperidha*. Sohos' news agent, having come into his *kefi*, insists that I photograph him.

tively so), cooperate because they enjoy the opportunity to socialize and dance. Married men, in addition, want to show themselves as capable and respectable providers, to take out (and be seen to take out) their wives and families. In attending the event, observing its formalities of greeting and etiquette, and belonging to a *parea*, a married man, especially, shows himself as a sociable person worthy of social recognition and in turn, concerned to maintain good relations with his fellows.

Nonetheless, no one is really surprised when conflict among men is expressed. For despite their rhetoric of solidarity, *horoesperidhes*, no less than other dance-events, are a site for the negotiation of male prestige and of male hierarchy based on prestige (Ortner and Whitehead 1981). In the *horoesperidha*, categories of persons (member versus nonmember, local versus foreigner, young versus old, male versus female, leftist versus rightist) are hierarchically "ordered." Specific males are also formally "ordered." Individual assertions of self-regard by which men attempt to claim—or to improve upon—their position in the ordering are tolerated, even encouraged, as long as they are expressed within the ground rules. Still, certain men have reasons to wish to break these ground rules. These may be men who are less powerful in the context of the event: unmarried youths and men whose faction is not in power, for example. Yet they may also be men who are already extraordinarily powerful and who can therefore defy the rules of ordering with relative impunity. For both sorts of men, individual and factional prestige may come only from breaking the rules of ordering or even from attempting to create a new ordering.

ZEIBEKIKO: THE POSES OF DEFIANT MASCULINITY

When a person acts out of *eghoismos*, he or she is seen by Sohoians to be expressing the autonomy of the individual. This individualism is nonetheless socially configured and involves a highly conventionalized posture. One of the most common—indeed, stereotypical—ways this notion of autonomous individualism is expressed in dancing is through the solo dance, *zeibekiko*. *Zeibekiko* is the favorite dance among unmarried youths, and they clamor for it whenever musicians are present.

Those who organize a *horoesperidha*, and many who attend, regard *zeibekiko* as undesirable in that context. Most obviously troublesome is its exclusiveness. One person dancing *zeibekiko* monopolizes the dance floor, and all other celebrants are put into the position of spectators. When the dance order involves a succession of *zeibekika*, the vast majority of celebrants—and virtually all women—are prohibited from dancing.

It is not merely its form as a solo dance that makes *zeibekiko* problematical, however. Its cultural and historical meaning (both in Greek culture more broadly, and within Sohos) as an activity through which *mangia*, a tough, swaggering yet also introspective style of masculinity is performed, also poses difficulties.

The historical evolution and cultural connotations of the *mangas*, the "tough," and the *zeibekiko* as the site par excellence where the *mangas* constitutes himself, are a rich and complicated story. Yet even a cursory account makes clear why the *zeibekiko* might be thought to clash with the official values of the *horoesperidha*. Most fundamentally, the *mangas* is self-consciously antisocial:

A *rebetis* or *mangas* . . . was a person who lived outside the accepted standards of the traditional Greek society, and who showed contempt for the establishment in all its forms: he didn't marry, for example, and wouldn't walk arm-in-arm with his girlfriend; he didn't wear a collar and tie and refused to carry an umbrella, smoked hashish, bitterly hated the police, and considered going to jail a mark of honor. (Petropoulos, in Butterworth and Schneider 1975:11)

The *mangas*, understood as a specific ideological construction of male personhood, emerged out of the experience of once-affluent Greek refugees of Asia Minor who, after the 1922 "Catastrophe" and compulsory exchange of minority populations, were forced to flee their homes and resettle in Greece. Impoverished, disenfranchised, the *mangas* lived by petty crime and occasional labor. He repudiated the values of both the peasant communities and the urban middle class who, in turn, despised him.[2] But within his own marginalized subculture, the *mangas* became a potent image of masculinity. A complex ethos of being and doing, with moral, social and aesthetic dimensions, developed around him.

A man's *mangia*—the essence of his "self" as *mangas*—was expressed through gestures both subtle and aggressive:

[He] wore a fedora hat pushed far back on his head, or so far forward that he had to tilt his head back to see. The hat had a black band to show mourning for his victims. He carried a knife or a revolver in his belt and in his hand a cane made of hard cherry wood which he could use as a weapon in fights. He wore his jacket with only the left arm in the sleeve so that he could flip it round the forearm as a shield against his opponent's knife or cane. He walked with a subtly arrogant swagger, left shoulder hunched slightly forward to keep his jacket on, often playing a *komboloi* (worry beads), and swinging only his right hand. (Petropoulos, in Butterworth and Schneider 1975:12–13)

Other men acknowledged a man's *mangia* by the quiet, respectful distance they kept from him.

The image and experience of the *mangas* was rendered most profoundly in the songs of the *rebetika*, a musical tradition that developed in Aegean port cities and that came, after 1922, to be associated with the underclass of refugees from Asia Minor, sailors, and petty thieves (Butterworth and Schneider 1975; Holst 1977; Petropoulos 1972). According to the accounts of musicians and other *rebetes*, before the pop-

---

[2] Campbell reports that the Sarakatsani considered the *mangas* an unambiguously negative character, cunning and untrustworthy (1964: 283).

ularization of the *rebetika* tradition in the 1950s, *zeibekiko* was a controlled, intense, and introspective solo dance. Its almost intimate quality presupposed the inviolacy of the dance space, of the *mangas'* person. Petrides' eloquent description of a "typical" *zeibekiko* of this period not only conveys a feeling of the context in which it was performed but also articulates the value of "dancing for himself" that remains important, though in a different way, to Sohoian youths forty years later:

> Envision a small smoke-filled room late at night, the neighborhood hangout, a dozen or more *manges* and perhaps some of their women seated at tables around a small space for dancing. At one end of the room, or at one of the tables, are seated the musicians, apparently tuning their instruments: a *bouzouki*, a guitar, and a *baglamas*. The aimless strumming and picking gradually leads into something more recognizable—a *taxim*, an arrhythmic instrumental introduction which draws the *manges'* attention. They try to follow the course of the improvised melody in their minds, murmuring satisfaction at an unexpected turn, or disappointment at the insufficient development of a theme. Gradually the *taxim* builds to a climax and the tension mounts as the rhythm of the *zeybekiko* is introduced. Now one of the *manges* pushes back his chair and gets up. Putting his lit cigarette between his lips, eyes on the floor, body tense and slightly crouched, arms loosely out to the sides, he begins to move slowly, deliberately around some fixed imaginary point on the floor. Snapping his fingers to the rhythm, he elaborates his steps, occasionally doubling a step or holding a step for two beats, always circling round the point on the floor which is the unwavering focal center of his intense concentration, now and then breaking the heavy tension of the dance with explosive outbursts of energy as in sudden leaps, hops, turns, squats. No one else gets up to dance; it would be an insult and a trespass on his impending emotional release. Oddly enough, this moment may come at any time, and he may decide to sit down again in the middle of the song; he is satisfied, he is released. No one cheers, no one claps. Perhaps another *mangas* who was able to project himself into the dancer's mood has a carafe of wine quietly sent to the man's table. But nothing more. The man danced for himself. (Petrides in Butterworth and Schneider 1975:28–29)

The social and political nuances of *rebetika*—and therefore of *zeibekiko*, as its most characteristic dance—have changed many times over the last eighty years. A musical and dance tradition previously known only within a small urban subculture, it developed new musical forms and new contexts of performance after the Second World War. In the 1950s, for the first time, certain versions of the *rebetika*—for example, the songs of Vassilis Tsitsanis, some with romantically "Oriental" lyrics and melodies—became popular among middle-class audiences who attended the relatively respectable nightclubs (*kendra*). Additionally, a genre referred to as "popular" music (literally, "music of the people or folk," *laika*, which is nonetheless distinguished from "folk music," *dhimotika*, of rural origin) developed out of *rebetika*. Though highly commercialized, this music retained much of the *rebetika*'s rough yet soulful quality and its classic themes of poverty, despair, loneliness, and unrequited love.[3] *Laika* was (and continues to be) popular among the working classes and, in particular, among the predominantly male immigrant workers who left the devastation and high unemployment of postwar Greece to work in the factories of northern Europe and Australia. In a somewhat slicker guise, it became the music of the nightclubs (*bouzoukia* or *kendra*) that catered to the urban nouveau riche. But although music inspired by *rebetika* was becoming more and more widespread, the establishment—from the conservative postwar Greek state to the Communist party—continued to view *rebetika* songs themselves as contemptible and immoral. It was not until the dictatorship of 1967–1974, when certain *rebetika* songs, though officially banned, were used as vehicles to express criticism of and resistance to the regime,[4] and then afterward, with the Greeks' postdictatorship aversion to U.S. influence and the concurrent interest in Greece's "roots" (a slogan of the eventually victorious PA.SO.K. party) that a flourishing, though largely purist, revival of the *rebetika* occurred.

Rebetika songs, including *zeibekika*, have been heard in Sohos since the wartime era of the 1940s. The songs of Stellios Kazantzidhis, a gifted interpreter of *rebetika* and *laika* who started recording in the 1950s, are still enormously popular among the townspeople. Men of late middle age remember listening in their youth to phonograph recordings of Kazantizidhis' *zeibekika* in the local *kafenia*, and sometimes dancing to them. Some who suffered during the war and others who spent years as immigrant workers in Germany respond with special intensity to the pathos of these songs. They describe how just listening to the words and music makes them ache to dance *zeibekiko*, a dance in which all their pain and sorrow can be physically expressed.

[3] Especially its "heavy" style (*vari laika*), which contrasts with the much "lighter" style (*elafra*).

[4] One song, still extremely popular, was Kaldaras' "Night Is Fallen without a Moon," which describes a man in a prison cell who is unable to sleep. It was originally written in 1947 about a political prisoner of the Greek Civil War; during the dictatorship, its performance was understood to allude to the plight of political detainees in the prison cells and torture rooms of the regime.

The young men who clamor for *zeibekika* in the *horoesperidhes* have inherited and are manipulating this complex, embodied rhetoric of masculinity.[5] Like their fathers, and like the dancer Petrides described, Sohoian youths that I spoke to describe the *zeibekiko* performance as an introspective, psychologically private act: "I dance for myself, not for others." Its motivation and its rationale are said to emerge from the dancer's private world of desire and memory. "When you dance," Grigoris explains, "you dance either from anxiety [*stenahoria*] or from enthusiasm [*enthusiasmos*]." Through *zeibekiko*, such sentiments are given bodily shape. He continues: "A desire, a past long gone, something upsets you, and you put it in your body. You're in love, crazy with love, and you don't understand a thing that's happening!" The dancer expresses his sentiments through the "breaking" movements of his body. Simultaneously, his friends, who crouch in a circle around him, clapping, often break plates and bottles at his feet. This practice of "breaking" (*spasimo*) both echoes and commemorates, in a conventionalized and public way, the dancer's imputed inner state (see figure 21).

Yet however much the dancer dances "for himself," he only does so in a public setting. This stylized choreographic articulation of the lone self is always posed to a watching audience, and it is those youthful male peers who witness and, by their supporting gestures, validate his performance. As a public performance of the "inner" self, *zeibekiko* is externally directed; it is both a form of and a forum for display (*epidhiksi*).

People say that young men dance *zeibekika* "to show themselves, to show their *mangia*." Showing *mangia* here alludes not only to the body language of the dancer, the conventionalized poses of defiant, atomistic individuality: the cap pulled low, the half-closed eyes, the cigarette dangling from the lips, the rolled-up sleeves, and the brittle movements of the body. It alludes, as well, to the social practices of the dance floor as they are organized by *mangia*. Here the dancer does not merely "separate" himself by his improvisations while remaining part of the line of dancers. He dances alone, and that is what matters most of all. As one youth explained quite simply, "The significance of *zeibekiko* is that you dance alone." Only the one who has ordered the song has the right to the dance floor, and he gives it up to another dancer when and if he chooses. The tense, testy quality of *zeibekiko* is thus a central part of its choreographic rhetoric. Dancing in front of the other celebrants, he also—figuratively and sometimes actually—dances *against* them. Sohoians are therefore distressed but not entirely sur-

---

[5] I explore this dance more extensively in Cowan 1989.

21. *Zeibekiko* is performed to *daulia* accompaniment in the street in front of a local restaurant on the final night of the summer *paniyiri*. Though buoyantly acrobatic rather than brooding, this performance maintains the convention of the solo dancer flanked by a crouching, clapping admirer.

prised when a youth, believing that someone has physically transgressed his dance space, reacts with anger.

Because it is seen as an especially volatile dance, *zeibekiko* does not feature prominently in *horoesperidhes*. Organizers do everything they can to discourage requests for *zeibekika* and to discourage the musicians from obliging them when they are put forward. For the most part, it is only very late in the evening, after the lottery, when the event is breaking up and the *parees* of the middle-aged couples who dominated it are gradually leaving for home, that this vigilance is relaxed and young men's *zeibekika* performances begin to emerge. As celebrants trickle out and as the proprietor and waiters clear the tables and sweep the floor, the several *parees* of young men who linger begin to order *zeibekika* from the musicians, treating the rented hall like, and in a sense transforming it into, a provincial nightclub (*bouzoukia*).

The meanings of *zeibekiko* are not wholly fixed, of course. Within particular performances, the meanings of *zeibekiko* can be manipulated. But this presupposes that celebrants will recognize "a pre-existent stratum of meaning" (Karp 1988:3) that the dancer is altering or playing with. At the Businesspeople's Association dance I attended, the authoritative yet buoyant performance, jovial good humor, and theatrically broad gestures of Dimitros, the butcher, took the pathos, power, and performed isolation of the dance and turned it outward to include all the celebrants. Both the artistry of the performance and its timing, just after the playful competitiveness of the lottery, gave the dance its sense of exhilaration.

The scene I videotaped at the end of the 1985 Orpheus *horoesperi-dha*—the description of which opens the Introduction—suggests further semantic possibilities. Not only can the meanings of *zeibekiko* be manipulated in performance, as Dimitros' gregarious rendition shows, but the performance itself may on occasion constitute a critical, multi-layered commentary on the unfolding social interaction. The video records Lakis, the young vice-president of Orpheus, a respectable businessman and householder, performing in an informally created dance space a *zeibekiko* that explicitly parodies the "serious" performances occurring at the same moment on the central dance floor. By framing the performance as a kind of choreographic joke, Lakis refers to, yet distances himself from, such performances. Analyses inspired by Bakhtin (1984) often stress that humor and irony are the stategies of the oppressed to subvert the order of the powerful; here, however, the reverse has occurred. A member of the ruling faction in Orpheus appropriates this form to "show himself" and, at the same time, through ostensible self-mockery, to poke fun at the intensely serious performance occurring across the room. This "inside joke" is hugely enjoyed by his own group of friends watching him. The way Lakis plays with the camera's (and implicitly, my) gaze is another noteworthy dimension of his performance. He acknowledges the camera by performing for it but also by confronting it with the seductive intensity of his own gaze. In this moment, in which a woman observes and videotapes a male subject, the usual gender positions in practices of surveillance are reversed, yet Lakis' answering gaze expresses a bold confidence indicative of his position as a socially powerful male. If his performance is already "framed" as a choreographic joke, it is doubly "framed" by the video's eye, and Lakis plays with the logical, aesthetic and sexual tensions set up by these multiple frames to communicate a number of things, both to others watching and about the unfolding interaction.

Although the meanings of *zeibekiko* may be skillfully manipulated in particular performances, the more typical "serious" renditions of the dance are seen by many as "inappropriate" within the *horoesperidha*. What is it about *zeibekiko* that renders it so "undesirable" to those in charge? First, at a practical level, its character as a solo dance impedes the construction of collective *kefi*, which is based on dancing "all together." In group dances, bodies crowd and bump together "without quarrel," but in the solo *zeibekiko*, the male dancer whose space is transgressed will say, as Kostas reported, "You cut me off!" *Zeibekika* provide a pretext for young men's exhibitionistic displays of *mangia* and for the fights that are its quintessential manifestation.

At a second, symbolic level, *zeibekiko* is associated with a plethora of images: the Orient, the criminal underworld, the nightclubs of the urban nouveau riche and the shabbier "dog's dens" (*skiladhika*) of the poor and working classes, and the rough, morally flawed side of the Sohoian (indeed, Greek) character. This persona of the *zeibekiko* dancer clashes with the upwardly mobile, respectably bourgeois European persona emphasized in the *horoesperidha*. And though *zeibekiko* is danced by affluent businessmen, not just by poorer farmers and laborers, it is only a confident performance by a member of the former group, like that of Dimitros at the Businesspeople's dance, that can convincingly resurrect it from its working-class connotations, at least in the context of the *horoesperidha*.

Similarly, as a choreographic embodiment of defiant masculinity, *zeibekiko* challenges the dominant model of masculinity, that of the patriarch (*ikoyenyarhis*), in this context.[6] *Zeibekiko* celebrates the isolated individual, at once self-absorbed, tortured by love and anxiety, and acutely self-conscious; it presents the man without family responsibilities, a man for whom women exist only as obsessions and children not at all. Such nuances are inappropriate for married men who attend with their wives and, occasionally, their children. The prestige of these men relies on being recognized as capable providers for their dependents and on cultivating friendly relations with other men with whom they must interact, daily, as neighbors, customers, allies. In this context, being a *ghlendzes* often involves an exaggerated display of affection and camaraderie with specific other men, rather than hostility. Through his self-presentation as a sociable person, a reveler but not a "spendthrift" (*spatalis*), in other words, as one whose generosity is tempered by prudence, a married man demands that he be recognized and given significance (*simasia*) in the community. The performance of *zeibekiko*, in this context, implicitly challenges the right and ability of the *ikoyenyarhis* to organize public pleasure for the public good.

FACTIONS AND FIGHTING

The contradictory pressures on men to cooperate and to compete in the *horoesperidha* are not matters of individualism alone. Unlike most women in this community, men are engaged in political activity—

---

[6] This is, of course, less true in the case of a *horoesperidha* like that of the Soccer Association, where unmarried men form the majority of participants and where the person or the image of the *ikoyenyarhis* is not very prominent.

perpetual discussion, if not always organized action—as part of their everyday lives, and political issues tend to find their way into dance-events. Thus men do not compete in the *horoesperidha* solely as individuals, whether "legitimately," through the channels set by the organizers, or "illegitimately," through *zeibekika*. They also compete as members of collectivities, specifically, as supporters of political groups against opposing groups. The rhetoric about politics employed by those in charge of a *horoesperidha* depends very much on the specific character of the relations among the association's political factions at that particular moment.

Political rivalry is most visible in the *horoesperidhes* of associations in which the political domination of one faction over another is either newly emergent or is unstable and contested. In such circumstances, the organizers attempt to disclaim political interests and to suppress politically inflammatory acts that call into question the association's official neutrality.

The leadership of the Soccer Association used a rhetorical strategy of "disclaiming the political" in their *horoesperidha* of 1985. In the fall 1984 elections, a majority of those elected to the association's executive board were PA.SO.K supporters. A few weeks before the Soccer Association *horoesperidha* in February 1985, a member who was an activist in the New Democracy Youth organization was suspended from the Soccer Association for a minor infraction; his supporters claimed that the real reasons had been "political." They complained that the association was becoming too politicized, and some left the club in protest. When the 1985 *horoesperidha* was poorly attended, in stark contrast to the wildly successful event of the previous year, each side came up with its own excuses. Opponents of the present board pointed to the "politically motivated" suspension as having provoked a right-wing boycott. Supporters found another explanation: that a significant number of members did not attend because they were in mourning. A middle-aged woman who had one son and several nephews in the club had some days before died after a long struggle with cancer.

During the poorly attended dance, the association's president, Stavros, had to choose between sanctioning a "provocative" gesture asserting the symbolic dominance of his own party within the association, and censuring (and thus preventing) it in the interests of maintaining at least an appearance of harmony. This story was told to me, several days later, by my host and friend Katina, who was present at the table.

Traveling from Athens, Grekos arrived at the Soccer Association *horoesperidha* at about midnight. He was immediately seated with three of his staunchest political supporters—Mihalis, night watchman at the

ladies' garment factory; Stavros, secretary of the town hall and Soccer
Association president; and Yannis, owner of a record shop—and their
wives. The three men argued loudly over who would have the privilege of paying for Grekos' dinner. Later, Yannis, whose record shop is
the hangout (*steki*) for local PA.SO.K. activists, jumped up from the table, announcing he was going to order the song of EAM-ELAS partisans,
"On Top of the High Mountains," from the musicians.[7] As Yannis got
up from the table, Stavros followed behind, alternately pleading and
scolding, trying to convince him to stop, insisting that this was inappropriate here and could easily precipitate a fight. Yannis requested the
song; but the musicians, noticing the disagreement, claimed (implau-
sibly but diplomatically) that they "did not know it." The two men
returned to their table.

Though Yannis and Stavros shared political loyalties to Grekos,
their different positions in this context shaped their responses. Yannis'
grandiose gesture, made on Grekos' behalf, performed his sense of obligation and his loyalty to his powerful political patron, but it also constituted a dramatic claim to their collective superiority as members of
PA.SO.K. It was a gesture of pride and bravado, asserting collective *eghoismos*. Stavros, as president, had to balance the quest to maintain real
political control with the obligation not to "give [the opposition] the
right" to protest or even resign from the association on the grounds
that it no longer looked after the interests of all members. Stavros'
political loyalties were tempered, moreover, by his life-long passion
for soccer and his desire that this association remain viable.

Sometimes, however, an influential man can manipulate the conventions of obligation boldly to assert his own power and get his own way,
a strategy of self-advertisement I call "declaiming the politician." He
may do this in such a way that, whatever their own agenda, the leadership of the association find that they are not in a position to refuse
him.

In a *horoesperidha* in the early years of Orpheus' existence when, as
the town's sole cultural association, Orpheus was vehemently insisting

[7] This Civil War song, set to the island tune "Samiotissa" (Girl from Samos), celebrates the valor of the Greek Resistance (EAM/ELAS partisans) against the Germans and
the Greek right-wing collaborators. Much sung by those on the Left, its Civil War connotations make it particularly irritating to the local right wing. The first of its many
verses proclaims:

> On top of the high mountains,
> Partisans and young fighters,
> Struggle for freedom
> Battling the fascists!
>   Oh, Sweet Greece!
>   People's democracy!

on its political neutrality, Adonis Letsios, the leader of the right-wing faction in the town council, stood up to dance. He handed a check for a large sum to the Orpheus president, as a contribution to the association. He then requested that the orchestra play the *tsamikos*, "Grivas, the King Wants You," a song identified with the extreme right.[8] The man reporting this story to me, who had recently become an officer on the Orpheus executive board, explained, "Well, we couldn't tell him to sit down, could we? He put us in a difficult position." Although it severely compromised the publicly apolitical posture of the association, Letsios was permitted to have his dance.

The contradictory ways a defiant act of this sort by an influential person may be regarded by other celebrants is indicated by a discussion I witnessed after the 1983 Sohos Youth Association *horoesperidha*. Grekos had been offended when in the welcoming speech, greetings had been offered first to his rival, the mayor Evangelidhis, and only then to him. He had reacted by ordering a *kalamatianos* to the tune of "On Top of the High Mountains." A few days afterward, I was present when three association members argued about the appropriateness of Grekos' request. Kyriaki and her husband, Thomas, who had helped to found the association and wanted it to remain politically nonaligned, argued that Grekos' act had been churlish and provocative, and thus completely inappropriate for a festive occasion, and that it had merely bolstered public perceptions that the association was PA.SO.K.-controlled.[9] Vivi, though not herself a very active member, was the young Salonikan wife of a local man who had recently become quite active in the association and who supported Grekos politically. Vivi would not accept the assessment of Kyriaki and Thomas. She did not explicitly reject the contention that Grekos had individual political motives, but she justified his act on other grounds. "He had the right to order whatever he wanted," she insisted, "We are not all one."

Kyriaki and Thomas, on the one hand, and Vivi, on the other, disagreed strongly about the legitimacy of Grekos' act. Their very different assessments were grounded in their very different positions and interests within the association. Each side called upon a different norm, however, to justify its interpretation: Kyriaki and Thomas to

---

[8] Grivas was a royalist leader of "X," an ultra-right organization that during the Greek Civil War fought against partisans of the Greek Resistance, who were regarded as "communists."

[9] Within this group, this couple came—over time—to be labeled "anti-PA.SO.K.," and they were subtly and gradually pushed out of their previously active participation in the association's decisions and affairs. About a year after the above discussion, they left the association altogether.

the ideal of cooperation and "being all together," and Vivi to the first dancer's "right" to choose his own song.

Symbolic enunciations of political dominance are less ambiguous in civic associations in which the controlling faction's power is well entrenched; and the political affiliation of the dominant faction may be openly declaimed. Such was the case during the 1985 Orpheus *horoesperidha*. Since the founding of Sohos' second cultural association in 1981, certain individuals who were dissatisfied with the Orpheus leadership had defected to the new association; others, disgusted with the politicization process in general, had dropped out altogether. In the period of my fieldwork, Orpheus remained comfortably under right-wing control; no competing faction emerged to challenge its hegemony.

As discussed in the previous chapter, this state of affairs was demonstrated in the performance of the opening dance, where not only the ruling male elite of elected officers and activists but also powerful friends active in local New Democracy politics joined in a *kalamatianos*. It is reasonable to suggest that most who witnessed this dance, and who smilingly applauded as each man, in turn, took the first position as leader of the dance, considered this institutional conflation of Orpheus and New Democracy a quite obvious and, moreover, an unproblematical fact. To a large extent, this link had become naturalized. In any case, whether or not all of those who witnessed this dance fully approved of its symbolic message, no one openly contested it.

Finally, the fact that *horoesperidhes* are typically held during the Carnival season creates further possibilities for male strategies of disordering, strategies that stress even more dramatically the collective, rather than individualistic, component of defiance. For during this period, not only is anarchic and unpredictable behavior expected, but those who engage in it are customarily masked. Sometimes a *parea* of masqueraders in masks and costumes (*maskaradhes*) or one or two masked *karnavalia*, with goatskins and bells—celebrants who have been wandering from house to house, or from one public establishment to another, to feast, sing, and dance—enters without invitation into the *horoesperidha*. Often, they come "for a lark" (*ya plaka*), clowning at the edges or peaceably joining a line dance in the central space, and then, after a few minutes, leaving to continue their peregrinations. Those in charge of the *horoesperidha* seldom bar these interlopers altogether, for that is considered rude, and besides, their antics can contribute to the laughter and *kefi*; but they watch them warily.

Occasionally, a *karnavali* rushes into the dance space, leaping and clanging his (it is assumed) bells. This gesture may amuse but also may annoy the celebrants, especially those who are dancing. I found that

although some dancers interpreted such a gesture as a contextually inappropriate but wholly "traditional" expression of drunken, prankish
kefi, many others described it very differently, as a politically motivated act of "sabotage" (*sabotaz*).

Celebrants who witness such an act may consider it as directed
against the association as a collective body. Thus when a group of *karnavalia* entered the 1985 New Democracy dance, some of the celebrants became angry. Afterward they complained bitterly that the
group must surely have been members of the Left who had tried to
interfere with their opponents' collective merrymaking. But sometimes a celebrant will see such an action as a more specifically personal
affront. During the 1983 *horoesperidha* of the Sohos Youth Association
Evangelidhis was leading a dance when a *karnavali* tried to join. On
bad terms with Dimitra, the association's president, Evangelidhis,
later accused her of "sending the *karnavali* in to ruin his dance," an
accusation Dimitra dismissed as "ridiculous."

In a specific instance, of course, whether masked celebrants intend
to disrupt a dance and whether they intend to do so on the basis of
political motives (and even whether they are, in fact, members of a
hostile political faction) are intentions that are rarely possible to ascer-
tain with any surety. But at the least hint of any trouble, masked celebrants are immediately accused of having such intentions by other celebrants who witness their actions. And the quickness with which such
accusations are made testifies to the widespread conviction that it is
political differences that divide the community most profoundly, and
that male disruptiveness on the dance floor is likely to arise from and
express the antagonisms and conflicting interests of these political
groups. Indeed, the fact that this explanation—of political motivation—is seen as so much more plausible than other explanations for
male disruption helps to perpetuate the situation it explains. It practically guarantees that dance-events like *horoesperidhes* will continue to
be important sites for expressions of endemic political conflict.

DISORDERLY CONDUCT AND REORDERING

As these examples demonstrate, certain males in any given *horoesperidha* may have reasons to wish to challenge the event's social order and
may use the dance as a means to do this. Young men in their teens and
twenties, who are subordinated within the male hierarchy on the basis
of their age, are one category of person notorious for such gestures.
Lacking the economic resources and social status of married men, and
therefore situationally subordinated to them symbolically and practically, youths may try to redefine the situation and usurp the spotlight.

Typically, they do this by attempting to bargain with the musicians to play *zeibekika*. If they are successful, they achieve a double coup: they assert their defiant prowess, first, by claiming the redolent meanings attached to the dance itself, and second, by having gotten away with this violation of the rules, despite the best efforts of those in charge.

Such a youth, as the musician quoted by Kostas in chapter 5 remarked, may be lacking "even a little bit of shame," but though lack of shame in a young man is, in one sense, a flaw (cf. Peristiany 1966:181), it is also a sign of spirited *eghoismos*. Thus, while Sohoians (not least the girls, whose opportunity to dance is spoiled by these occasionally violent confrontations) complain of such disorderly conduct among male youths, this opprobrium may be mixed with indulgence and even rueful admiration. A boy who stretches or breaks such rules, and perhaps even gets involved in quarrels, may be labeled *zoiros* ("lively, wild, willful") or a *dzanabetiko pedhi* ("perverse, stubborn boy"), but these are not wholly negative labels for a youth. Much like the Cretan shepherds Herzfeld describes (1985a), whose rule breaking is accepted and praised to the extent that its performance is deemed successful, the Sohoian youth receives this admiration especially if his antics are funny or entertaining. Young males execute such performances for the celebrants in general, to be sure, but one suspects that they do it as much for their peers. In front of them and against them, they take turns dancing out their defiant masculinity.

Other incidents, as we have seen, involve men acting as representatives or supporters of a political faction. Some disruptions involve politically powerful men who are also "symbols" of their party. Letsios broke the implicit rule against *parangelia* in a coolly arrogant move. Having submitted a large donation, he no doubt anticipated that no one would dare to block his request. This confident gesture of political authority resembles the matter-of-fact way that the local right-wingers who act "behind the scene" in Orpheus took their places to "open the dance" at that association's *horoesperidha* several years later. Grekos' request, by contrast, was reactive. His facial expressions showed (and people later said) that he had "taken offense" (*pareksighithike*). His request for the partisan song appeared calculated to assert his precedence, and that of his party, in the association, to contradict the precedence of his rival, Mayor Evangelidhis, enunciated in the welcoming speech. It seemed calculated, as well, to provoke and humiliate this rival by playing a theme song of the party that had, during the elections, abandoned him and forced him to run as an independent. Whether aggressive or defensive, these expressions of *eghoismos* represent claims both for the individual man and for the collectivity, his political party.

Less powerful individuals may also make such gestures. Yannis tried

to order a political song on Grekos' behalf. Although, had he suc-
ceeded, he would have gained prestige himself, the gesture was primarily an assertion of PA.SO.K.'s collective power in that group. That
men may act as protagonists of a political faction even without the
promise of individual recognition is exemplified by the case of the
masked celebrants. Those who disrupt the *horoesperidha* for political
reasons are effective saboteurs only as long as their masks stay in place.
Although such men might privately relish upsetting their political enemies and might gain approval and prestige from their own *parea* or
faction for their boldness, their disruptive gesture is best seen as truly
made on behalf of a larger collectivity: the political party.

I have described the acts of men who might have reasons to challenge the social order and social ordering from the point of view of
these reasons. It is, of course, impossible to know what such a man is
thinking and what his motives for a particular set of actions are. But it
is possible to report what other people *say* they are. The explanations
here have incorporated the public logic of such acts, the ways they are
socially constructed in Sohos. The public discourse that surrounds instances of disruption, whether the instigators are weak or powerful,
indicates that Sohoians interpret individual acts of disorderliness both
in terms of what they perceive as "natural" masculine proclivities for
conflict and in terms of the specific interests they perceive particular
men to have as political actors and as members of the community.

CHAPTER SEVEN

Ambivalent Pleasures: Dance as a Problem for Women

> A woman must continually watch herself. She is almost continually accompanied by her own image of herself. . . . She has to survey everything she is and everything she does because how she appears to others, and ultimately how she appears to men, is of crucial importance for what is normally thought of as the success of her life.
>
> —John Berger, *Ways of Seeing*

THE SOHOIAN female celebrant's attitudes toward dancing, and her experiences of it, are shaped by the socially constructed meanings of female selves and bodies, and by her practical position(s) as a female person within the specific social relations of her everyday life. Given the patriarchal character of the world she inhabits, the female celebrant encounters the dance as a pleasure but also as a problem. Dancing is for her an often ambivalent experience, as it is for her male counterparts. But because the patriarchally ordered relations impinge differently upon male and female members of this community, it is ambivalent in a distinctly gender-specific way.

When men convivially join and contentiously confront each other in the site of dancing, they explore the ambiguities of their experience *as men* in the Sohoian social world. Here, convivial and cooperative male fellowship is always potentially threatened by competitive assertions of "difference," by claims to priority grounded in distinctions of age, social status, political affiliation, and individual character.[1] Though "good company" is highly valued, a male dancer's willingness to participate in the collective fellowship is contingent on, as townspeople say, "being given meaning" by his fellows, on being acknowledged as socially "significant." He claims his *right* to be acknowledged as so-

---

[1] Not all assertions of "difference" are deemed unacceptable, nor do they necessarily cause disruptions. Men within a *parea* may show deference and respect to a fellow celebrant who is older or who is more powerful, as long as they are also "given significance." But maintaining the fiction of equality among celebrants seems generally to be important. Recall that a table of Grekos' staunchest political supporters argued over who would have the privilege to pay for his dinner (perhaps treating him as a "guest" to be honored was also a strategy for reciprocating the favors of this powerful politician, and thus balancing the relationship), and that one of them, Yannis, undertook a provocative gesture on behalf of his "friend" (not his "patron").

cially significant; much male dancing is concerned with the negotiation of such claims. Inasmuch as the forms and limits of male dancing are organized through the dual requisites of defiance and conformity in masculine *eghoismos*, the criticism directed to a man who defies "the rules" of the collectivity (a defiance that usually assumes a conventional form) is often balanced by grudging admiration. Likewise, a "misunderstanding over the dance" (*pareksighisi ya to horo*) among men, though in one sense the moment of breakdown, exemplifies with especial starkness the tensions always inherent in this process of negotiation.

Consequently, celebrants "read" the sexual qualities of male dancing in particular ways. A man's dancing can be sexual, and it can be provocative, but it is rarely provocative *because* it is sexual. However explicitly (in a sexual sense) men dance, and however they frame these performances (as serious, parody, irony, burlesque), a man's performance of sexuality is not seen as a comment merely on itself. Rather, the poses a man assumes in the dance, whether they enact bodily control or the stylized performance of its absence (as in somatic representations of intoxication), are seen to allude primarily to this negotiation of power and prestige among men.

The pleasures as well as the problems of the female dancer are quite different. They are linked to the fact that her sexual expressivity, though a central and valued element within the dance-event, is also a central issue for her fellow Sohoians in defining what sort of a girl or woman she is. They are linked, too, to the fragility of the dance as a framed event and to its ambiguities as a site set apart from, yet embedded within, the social relations of everyday life. Although the question of how the dynamics of power within gender relations shape female experience in dance-events is a complex one, it may be opened up by examining some accounts made by and about female dancers.

Both the indigenous discourse and the discourse of non-Greeks about Greek dance implicitly presume a male subject. Just as female bodily practices are stylistically muted, so are female verbal articulations about their experiences in dance-events, in Ardener's (1975) sense, conceptually muted. The first task, therefore, must be that of giving voice to otherwise silenced, perhaps inchoate, female experiences of the dance process (dance and the problem *of* women) by drawing together fragmentary linguistic, paralinguistic, and gestural evidence with several longer narrative accounts. I pursue this exercise, however, not simply to balance the picture, to hint at the contours of social and sensuous experience of those who "hold up half the sky." In exploring how specific ideas and relations of gender impinge upon how girls and women present and experience their bodies in dance-

events, this exercise is also a critique. For these distinctive verbal accounts by girls and women do not merely indicate different voices and
alternative conceptions, just as their distinctively gendered postures
and gestures do not merely indicate different historical bodies and alternative bodily orientations. They are also, emphatically, positioned
utterances and positioned gestures that—however artfully, playfully,
even subversively—articulate women's collective position within
asymmetrical gender relations. They articulate how the female dancer's subjectivity (in all its senses) is constructed both on and off the
dance floor, and they suggest that her pleasures are contingent, in ways
that a man's pleasures are not, on the ways her bodily actions are read
by others (dance as a problem *for* women).

Dance is a problem for women because in the dance site, Sohoians'
ambivalent attitudes about female sexuality as both pleasurable and
threatening are juxtaposed. In dance-events the female individual as
celebrant and dancer is invited to act in ways she would not in public
contexts of everyday life. Far from being asked to deny her sexuality,[2]
in this context she is encouraged to display her beauty, energy, skill,
sensuality, and even seductiveness (see Caraveli 1982:142–43).[3] She is
encouraged, one might say, to "make a spectacle of herself." Moreover, she is invited to take a carefree attitude: to laugh, to forget, to
escape from ordinary worries, to let go and enjoy herself (see Karp
1980:105), acts that involve release and loosening of self-control.

But if aesthetic expressions of female sexuality are an essential and
valued aspect of dance events, they also can be viewed with suspicion.
A female dancer may find herself criticized for failing to maintain self-
control and for drawing "undue" attention to herself. Calling upon
either of two incompatible canons of behavior—one stressing release,
another stressing control—Sohoians can easily read a woman's bodily
presentation in diametrically opposed ways, as expressing either
"good" or "bad" sexuality. From the female dancer's point of view,
the normative injunctions she faces—"Let go!" and "Uphold your position!"—are incompatible. Although she may experience this logical
paradox as a double bind (Bateson 1972b:271–78; Laing 1969:144–48),
its effects are not merely formal; rather, they reverberate into and complicate her social, emotional, and sensual responses as well as her
bodily acts.

As those who analyze human movement often remind us, bodily
signs are inherently ambiguous. What differentiates a "legitimately"

[2] As, for instance, Campbell (1964:287) suggests is true among the Sarakatsani and as
Peristiany (1966:182) describes among the highland Cypriots.
[3] The form and expressions of this will vary according to the category of dance-event
and the kind of dances being performed within them.

sensual and pleasing gesture from one that "goes too far" is only in a limited sense something that Sohoians can agree upon; though it is, to be sure, partially a question of knowing the "code," it is not entirely so (but see Caraveli 1985:264), because such interpretations always involve imputations about the dancer's intentions. Those watching a female dancer will interpret not only how she danced but why. The problem for a woman is that she is invited and even obliged to act in ways that, if misinterpreted, can have severely negative consequences for her. Because the same gesture can be either praised or condemned, she can neither predict nor control what people will say about it. Under such conditions, the pleasures of the dance are often ambivalent.

DANCE AS PLEASURE

Both male and female members of this community look forward to the sensual and social delights of feasting, dancing, and socializing that dance-events promise. Yet the relative confinement of girls' and women's everyday lives often serves to intensify their anticipation of the event. Whether they work outside the house or not, married women's lives are dictated by their domestic responsibilities—housework, child care, and the emotional support of family members—and as the discussion of coffee drinking suggested, neither they nor their daughters have the opportunities taken for granted by their menfolk to go out in the evenings, to socialize and to escape, if briefly, the problems of the house. A woman's moral and practical preoccupation with her house and family, moreover, can create a sense of isolation, while the incessant and repetitive nature of her daily tasks can perpetuate a sense of monotony, a sense that every day is the same. Although a girl's domestic duties are lighter, and she often has more time to spend relaxing with her cousins and school friends, she, too, is expected not to wander too far from home. Girls and women consequently regard a dance-event as a valued break in the daily routine, as a chance to get out of the house and to socialize with friends.

Many girls and women told me that they loved to dance and that they looked forward with excitement to situations where they would have opportunities to dance (see also Danforth 1979a:160–61). From the age of six or seven, young girls in Sohos join children's dance troupes, organized by the school and by the two local folklore associations, the most advanced dance troupe being composed of young people up to about eighteen or nineteen years old. Girls are enthusiastic participants in such troupes. They usually outnumber the boys and sometimes take on male roles (including wearing male apparel) in the dancing when there are not enough boys.⁴ Through participation in a dance troupe a girl learns dancing skills and confidence, and she also gets a chance to travel to festivals in a safe, chaperoned and friendly context.⁵

For a woman beyond school age, opportunities to dance are restricted to occasions of social dancing: weddings in which she is closely related to the bride or groom, *horoesperidhes* of the associations her family supports, celebrations at Carnival and the summer *paniyiri*, perhaps an occasional visit with her fiancé or husband and a few other couples to a *kendro* in Thessaloniki or in the surrounding area. These rarely add up to more than a half-dozen occasions a year, and as the years go by and a woman finds herself in mourning for the illness or death of family members, they become even fewer (see Auerbach 1984). This paucity of opportunity—a stark contrast with men's easy access to public sites of sociability, both quotidian and festive—can make women's anticipation of dancing vivid and intense, especially if the event is an important one. Thus, as I, the three married daughters of my elderly landlady, and several female neighbors sat in the courtyard peeling potatoes for the wedding *ghlendi* of Eleftheria (the eldest sister's daughter), the women, in their late forties and early fifties, spoke with animation of the evening's upcoming festivities. "Are we going to dance tonight, Yanna [*tha horepsume apopse, Yanna*]?" the bride's aunt demanded, giggling and buoyant as she waved her arms over her head and snapped her fingers. Then she grabbed one of her sisters and led her through a few rounds of *kalamatianos* as her female companions hooted and clapped.

That evening Eleftheria's mother and aunts seemed to have a wonderful time. They danced often and enthusiastically, initially in circle dances led by their husbands and sons, but later in the evening without the men, in jubilant face-to-face *karsilamadhes*. Indeed, it was this trio of dynamic sisters who dominated the celebration and the dancing. The bride's mother, Sofia, was an especially dominant and expressive performer. A widow of many years, she had during the preparations expressed great anxiety about this wedding of her only child. She had lamented the heavy burden of bearing the responsibilities alone, and the tightness and fear that gripped her stomach and chest. Several

⁴ Interestingly, I never saw a girl who had assumed a male role take the first position in a circle dance during a public performance.

⁵ After I left Sohos in 1985, the day center for the elderly (KAPI) organized a male dance troupe, and some months later, a female dance troupe. These troupes now perform occasionally at festivals in the area. This phenomenon has interesting implications concerning the incorporation of the elderly (in addition to children) into the folklorization process and warrants further examination.

22. Sofia dances a radiant *zeibekiko* at the Saturday evening celebration for the wedding of her only child, Eleftheria.

hours into the *ghlendi*, however, her face shining with joy and release, she danced a powerful solo *zeibekiko*. It was an exceptional moment; I seldom saw a woman, especially a middle-aged woman, dance a *zeibekiko* in Sohos. Yet Sofia's radiant and confident performance seemed an especially apt rendering of her cathartic release (see figure 22).

After such dance-events, women who have celebrated together talk about the experience with delight. Often employing conventional phrases, they review the different activities they shared: "We had a lovely time! Didn't we have a lovely time? We ate, we danced, we laughed, we enjoyed ourselves—we had a *really* lovely time!"

Yet such a straightforward account of female pleasures oversimplifies what occurs. How girls and women enjoy themselves as dancers is entangled in complex ways with how and whether others enjoy *them* as dancers. Townspeople expect female celebrants to present themselves in pleasing ways. Every female celebrant's clothing, hairstyle, makeup, jewelry, and demeanor is critically scrutinized; indeed, I found women to be even sharper critics than men in this regard. A woman is also expected to please the spectators by dancing in particular ways. The adjectives people use to describe a skillful female dancer show that female sensuality—as an expression of life and energy—is considered an essential element of "beautiful" female dancing.

Townspeople say that it is only when she takes the lead position in the circle dance that a female dancer really "shows" (*fenete*). And when she does, spectators closely watch her bodily presentation. Ideally, they say, the young unmarried dancer—whom they expect to dance most vivaciously because she has a legitimate interest in attracting young men—should be "tall" (*psili*), "slim" (*lepti*), "[well]-appearing" (*emfanisimi*, a general evaluation based on personal beauty, clothes, and bearing), and "well-dressed" (*me to kalo to disimo*). In her movements, she should be "open" (*anihti*), "buoyant" (*petahti*), and "confident" (*na ehi tharros*). She should execute improvisations with originality (*kati dhiaforetiko*) and with spirit and confidence (*me aerata*).[6] She should "differentiate" herself (*kapos na dhiaferi*) in these ways if, I was told, "she wants a man to notice her!" An exceptional female dancer may become known as a *meraklu* (female "master"), one who, as an elderly grandmother put it, "has swagger" (*ehi çalim*, a Turkish word for "airs"). It is in the quicker-tempo dances, which young people prefer, that these qualities are particularly evident. Significantly, although her movements are expected to be "more delicate" (*pio leptes*) and "more restrained" (*pio mazemenes*) in relation to those of her male counterparts, these positive evaluations hardly describe modest, self-effacing maidens hiding their sexuality.

Married women may also (in some dance contexts) join in on fast-tempo dances and perform with verve and liveliness, but generally, as these women get older, their style of dancing is expected to become more serious and less playful.[7] Older women tend to use walking, rather than springing, steps when they dance. In Sohos one often sees married women dancing in the stereotypical "matron's" style when leading a *kalamatianos*; that is, a sedate syncopated walk comprised of small steps, a rigid torso, and a proud but fixed facial expression. Townspeople say that older women—particularly the *fustanuses* in their Sunday-best jackets and woolen smocks—are the most impressive performers in the grand, slow-tempo *sighanos*, where improvisation is

---

[6] *Kolpa* ("tricks"), *skertza* ("flirtations"), and *fighures* ("embellishments") are vaguely defined and contextually relevant, rather than fixed, gestures or signs. They might include ways of holding or waving a handkerchief, of waving the hands, of twirling around, or of adding extra steps, bounces, or unexpected pauses. Wearing an article of clothing with a certain flair or originality can also be labeled a *kolpo*.

[7] Auerbach, working in an Epirot village, notes a similar expectation that adult women will show more restraint in celebratory situations (1984:140).

23. With gravity and grace, the bride's aunt leads a *sighanos* in the street in front of the bride's house when, at Sunday noon, the groom's party arrives with *daulia*.

centered (for female "first" dancers) not on subtle body movements or footwork but on the manipulations of the kerchief held in the hands. In this dance, the weightier, more serious qualities appreciated in an older woman are presented in a stylized form; this is the dance for the tall (*psili*), full-figured (*evsomi*) woman, the *dardana* (*i dardana yineka*; from the Italian, meaning a large ship). Such performances, though stressing control, weight, and bodily rigidity, do not necessarily lack sensuality. I saw a breathtaking performance by a stout, modestly attired, and rather homely fifty-year-old woman in a *kafenio* on the eve of Clean Monday of Carnival. Placed in the first position by her husband, rigidly holding a white handkerchief in her right hand, she began a *sighanos*, and was transformed from an unremarkable matron into a powerful presence. All eyes fixed on her as she danced a *sighanos* that combined the qualities of gravity, grace, and a controlled yet undeniable sensual power (see figure 23).

Sohoians take pleasure in watching these female dancers, but they are valued not only as persons "good to watch" but as persons "good to be with." Sotiris remarked appreciatively of his thirty-five-year-old wife, "It isn't that Maria has the most beautiful steps—you could say that her sister, Popi, dances better—but Maria is so cheerful [*efthimi*], so enthusiastic, she encourages you, she gives you *kefi*." People enjoy a female celebrant who is eager (*prothimi*), open (*anihti*), and jovial (*yelasti*). A "closed type" (*klistos haraktiras*), whether male or female, cannot give *kefi* to the group. Though to call a woman a *ghlendzu* (the female counterpart of a *ghlendzes*; see Auerbach 1984) is an ambiguous compliment at best, a woman who is funny (*ehi plaka*) can be considered a great asset to the *parea*. I heard Varvara, a thirty-five-year-old woman known for her zany sense of humor, described with affection by her husband's best friend with the words, "in a *parea* she is a 'mother'[*stin parea ine manna*]." In this context, the term "mother" was meant to indicate a person especially skilled and accomplished at something (here, at *parea*-making), and to suggest that through her ability to make people laugh, Varvara nurtured that sense of togetherness, just as a mother is expected to do within the family context.

Yet the expectation that a woman be an accommodating member of the group can be exploited. Female celebrants, especially wives, are expected to suffer indignities quietly from belligerent or overly drunk husbands or other male members of the *parea* to a degree that men would not tolerate if they were the object of the unwanted attention. I was told of a scene in which a man, stubbornly insistent from an excess of ouzo, wanted to dance a *tsifte teli* with his wife, but his wife refused. So he persuaded another single woman in the *parea* to accompany him. "When a man comes into *kefi*, he doesn't care whom he dances with. He just wants to dance!" twenty-two-year-old Vicki explained. The stubbornness covertly encouraged in men has repercussions for the women they are with. Although not confronting him directly, thus sparing both him and herself the public humiliation that can follow when a wife criticizes her husband publicly (Danforth 1979b), the wife let her displeasure be known through her bodily gestures: "There wasn't a big scene, she couldn't say anything, but she 'put on a face' about it."

NOTES ON THE FRAME

What and how females dance depends to a large extent, of course, on the situation. Certain categorical distinctions constitute a common code shared by males and females, and appear "obvious." As I noted earlier, Sohoians distinguish between formal and informal dance contexts, and the kinds of dances appropriate to each. Thus, my question to Kiki about what dances they would perform when "dancing the bride" in the church courtyard, after the wedding ceremony, provoked the ironic, even scornful retort: "What is she going to dance? *Tsifte teli? Zebekia?* At that moment, only *kalamatianos* is appropriate, and another [line] dance, the *sighanos*, an old dance." Sohoians also distinguish phases within a category of event. They take it for granted not only that one performs different dances (and/or different styles of the same dances) at a *horoesperidha* than in the churchyard, but that one dances different dances (and/or different styles of the same dances) at the beginning of the *horoesperidha* than at the end, and in the *patinadha* than in the churchyard.

However, within the context of these generalizations about category, several points need to be made. The first is that, although the Sohoian category of the dance-event (or phase within the event) may include assumptions about which dances and which dance styles are appropriate, this is at least potentially negotiable. Thus, in the Businesspeople's *horoesperidha*, the butcher Dimitros was able to transform the *zeibekiko* from a divisive to a group-enhancing dance through his performance. Sofia's performance, likewise, turned the *zeibekiko* into a vehicle of catharsis, of joy, empowerment, and release.[8]

At the same time, negotiation carries risks. It is equally possible that Dimitros' dance, however skillfully performed, could have provoked a misunderstanding. Whatever its humor and style, another celebrant could have become irritated or taken offense. Sofia's dance, too, could have been misunderstood. A querulous guest need only, over coffee the next day, have murmured meaningfully to her neighbor, "You should have seen Sofia dancing *zeibekiko!*" and for her neighbor to query, "Sofia the widow?" The second point, then, is that the attempt to negotiate can fail

The third point is that such failures have consequences. Although the dance-event as a framed event is ideologically set apart, this frame is permeable. Just as the everyday social relations enter inside the frame and affect what happens there, so can the consequences of activities inside the frame spill out into everyday life.

What female celebrants do within dance-events and how their actions are interpreted depends to an extent on how the situation is defined—what type of dance-event is thought to be occurring at a given moment. But though both acts and interpretations of those acts are situationally variable, they are not situationally determined. Innovations and negotiations can occur; ambiguities in meaning, likewise, remain. The female dancer acts, but she cannot control how those acts will be interpreted by others. Although the potential gulf between pri-

---

[8] Danforth (1979a) describes a similar situation for female Anastanaridhes.

vate intention and public meanings is a feature of all communicative acts, the conventional meanings and dynamics of misunderstanding within the context of the dance-event involve and affect the male and female dancer in fundamentally different ways.

DANCE AS A PROBLEM

Though many girls told me they loved to dance, some added the significant qualification, "but not as the first dancer!" Why not? "Because everyone watches the first dancer!" This answer is instructive, for some of the ways in which dance is a problem for women are highlighted by the ambiguities of being the first dancer.

Some people insist that how an individual feels about being "first" in the dance is not a question of gender at all; rather, it is considered to be "in the person" (*ston anthropo*). They say that if some girls are shy, others "want always to be first." Likewise, they say that though many men compete over who will take the dance or be the first to lead, some men actually dislike being first, at least in certain types of dances. Indeed, some men admitted to avoiding joining the dance line of a dance they did not know well. They said that they feared making a mistake (*sfarma*) and being subjected to social ridicule (*yinome rezili*). Certainly, in a society where personal reputation depends on how one is "seen," both males and females may fear (while, often, also desiring) exposure. But there are gendered nuances to this fear; explanations alluding only to individual differences are not entirely adequate. Girls' expressions of ambivalence at dancing "first" need to be approached as "positioned utterances," which articulate a specifically gendered experience. The female dancer's experience of herself as an embodied self and, moreover, an embodied self on display to a watching audience is inevitably affected by both the cultural representations and meanings of the female body and the institutionalized surveillance of women (as both images and persons) within everyday life.

Ideas about the female body in Sohos draw upon representations of sexuality within the various ideological currents that constitute "common sense." Among these are the patriarchal tradition of Greek Orthodoxy, bourgeois notions of respectability rooted in Enlightenment philosophy, and the advertising practices of the capitalist culture of consumption. Although distinct historically, these ideologies share certain tendencies. They tend to collapse the distinction between the female person and the female body, and they also tend to sexualize that body. The female body is seen as the "*locus* of sexuality" (de Lauretis 1984:37). Yet the Sohoian female's experience of her embodied self is shaped not only by the propositional resonances of these ideological representations of the female body. Feminist scholars, in particular, have shown that both the content of images of women as bodies and the practices of "seeing" women as bodies are implicated in the construction of female subjectivity. Identifying the female body as the primary object of the male "gaze," they have enunciated the gender implications of Foucault's insight that the practice of seeing and being seen entails a power relation, that observation, or "surveillance," is a mode of domination and possession.

Girls are constantly watched in Sohos in ways in which their male counterparts are not (see also Handman 1983:115–18).[9] This surveillance, a mode for controlling female sexuality, arises from and is rationalized in terms of the patriarchal system. The (mostly unstated) goal of this surveillance is to "protect" girls from sexual encounters. Ironically, on an everyday basis, it is married women, much more than their male relatives, who are directly engaged in exercising this control over unmarried girls. Women thus act as agents of the control of females on behalf of men, with married women collectively keeping younger ones in line. For instance, a married woman commonly greets a girl or a pair of girls walking down the road not with a "good day" but with the implicitly suspicious question, "Where are you going?"

Girls often complain that the watchfulness of married women is intrusive and annoying. But they describe and react to the male gaze quite differently. Men's surveillance acknowledges, rather than merely chastises, a girl's sexuality, yet this acknowledgment can be ambiguous. Though a girl may find it exciting to be seen by a man she finds attractive, male surveillance can also be experienced as aggressive and even violating. Girls often remarked to me that they "feared" (*fovame*) entering spaces dominated by men. Although this may partially represent a claim to virtue, it is also more than this. I witnessed a number of occasions when a girl entering such a space expressed acute discomfort and embarrassment. One evening I returned home from an outing with three unmarried girls (aged twenty-two to thirty). We were all absolutely famished and entered a *suvlaki* grill to buy a sandwich. So intense was the embarrassment of my companions that "all those men are watching us [*oli i andres, mas kitazun*]," that we left as soon as

---

[9] I did not find that the evil eye figured very importantly in discourse about the dance; yet it is not, perhaps, insignificant that one of the girls who most vigorously claimed to dislike dancing "first" also claimed herself to be quite vulnerable to "being eyed [*to matiasma*]." In addition to being an attractive young woman, she is also a twin; Sohoians believe that pretty girls and twins—both "exceptional" beings—are objects of admiration and thus of (possibly unconscious) envy. She described being "eyed" as a sudden clumsiness, followed by total paralysis. Interestingly, this girl explained her dread of being first to stem from the fear of "making a mistake."

possible, preferring to eat our sandwiches on the street in the pouring rain.

The adjectives I discussed earlier suggest that, in contrast to everyday life, the dance space is a site where girls' open expressions of their sexuality—beauty, energy, skill, and "feminine wiles"—are appreciated and encouraged. However, girls sometimes feel that the permission—indeed, the injunction—to make a spectacle of themselves, to set themselves apart, is contradictory. For instance, when I asked Vicki how a girl should dance when in the first position, she described how a girl is expected to transcend her embarrassment in order to make an impression (*na kani endiposi*):

> She should dance with confidence, she shouldn't be shy or embarrassed [*me aerata, na mi drepese*]. With many tricks [*me kolpa*], with little movements [*me kunimata*]. If you're embarrassed, you don't do anything! You want to make an impression, to show something, to differentiate yourself a little. But not too much. If she does, they will say she's "crazy," that she's dancing in a "frenzied" way.

A girl is equally vulnerable to criticism for timidity or lack of skill. Of a girl who goes to the first position in line but cannot give a convincing performance, a middle-aged unmarried woman explained, "People would say, 'What's she dancing there for, since she doesn't know what she's doing?' Afterward, people laugh. There's talk."

The difficulties a girl faces with the injunctions Vicki describes become clearer when we examine the gendered nuances of the evaluative language more deeply. Like the movements themselves, the words used to describe them are ambiguous: the same adjectives that praise a girl can also vilify her. Significantly, the adjectives used by Vicki and others to praise a female dancer have darker undertones. They are often used to describe euphemistically the behavior of what are considered sexually wanton females: *aerata*, "confidence," can mean "effrontery," "impudence," and a kind of erotic boldness. Similarly, *tharros*, "courage," can indicate "brazenness"; and a girl who is *petahti*, "leaping" or "lively," may be sexually "uncontrollable."

The words for improvisation are especially double-edged. In the dance context, *kolpa* can be any kind of "trick" or embellishment which draws attention to the dancer; but female *kolpa* tend to be seen as literally "seductive" tricks. An older man noting, with obvious admiration, the way a young woman in the middle of a dance line wore her jaunty red cap cocked slightly off-center, remarked, "*That's* a *kolpo*! She's doing that so that 'somebody' will see!" *Kolpa* are closely associated with the notion of *poniria* (deceitful cleverness, cunning, a quality Greeks both publicly condemn and secretly admire), which has in many contexts sexual nuances. But although male *kolpa* may have

sexual nuances, female *kolpa* seem to have them practically by definition. A man who "makes *kolpa*," a *kolpadhoros*, is cunning and manipulative; a woman, a *kolpadhora*, is cunning and manipulative in a specifically sexual sense. *Kunimata*, likewise, meaning "little movements,"
when used to describe a female's movements inevitably in part implies
female sexual movements. These adjectives can be used admiringly,
and may even indicate an appreciation of what is perceived as the sensual power and beauty of a dancer's performance. But if her well-co-
ordinated gestures are seen to express a finely controlled sexuality,
overenthusiastic or uncoordinated gestures indicate a corresponding
lack of moral as well as physical control. Thus the judgment that a girl
who makes such gestures with excess zeal has "gone crazy" (*eksali*,
"beside oneself, frenzied") not only connotes lack of skill and self-dis-
cipline but has a clear sexual implication (see Caraveli 1985:264 on *ex-
alo kefi*; Danforth 1979a; du Boulay 1974:116).

A comment by Triandafillos Sofulis, when I asked him why girls in
the *patinadha* eschew the dramatic poses of their male counterparts,
both recognizes the self-censorship a female dancer is required to un-
dertake and articulates the contradictory ways that this is rationalized
within the hegemonic gender ideology:

> A woman restrains herself; a man is unrestrainable. The woman
> holds on to womanly things [*kratai to yinekio*]—she doesn't want to
> fall onto the road, whereas the man falls. The woman becomes like
> a guardian to him. The woman, being the weaker sex, upholds her
> position [*san adhinato meros, kratai tin thesi tis*]. When she comes into
> *kefi*—you want to, but you restrain yourself. You can't show it, you
> hide it, because you'd become degraded. People don't misinterpret
> the man, however [that is, as they misinterpret the woman]. He can
> fall, shout, sit on the ground up to his nose!

A man is unrestrainable, and his excesses may even have to be brought
under control by a solicitous wife, but he is not, on this account, "misunderstood." A woman, though the "weaker sex," is all the more required to show self-control so as not to "degrade" herself.

The problem that dancing expressively poses for girls and women is
partly that what constitutes "too much" is wholly a matter of interpretation. The qualities of enthusiasm, courage, confidence, even initiative encouraged in a girl can be the basis for condemning her performance. Miranda, a friend of Vicki's, expressed the constraints she felt
in this way:

> Some people consider it as *eghoismos* for a woman to go and dance
> "first." So maybe she wants to go first, but she is afraid, embar-
> rassed, about what people will say. "There, see? She just wants to

go first [*theli mono na pai proti*], to be seen, to appear, to 'wiggle' [*na emfanisti, na kunithi*]!" So, she *never* goes first, however much she wants to! Whereas a man doesn't wait til they call him.

Miranda's use of the word *eghoismos* is telling. Sohoians take it for granted that a man who takes the lead acts out of *eghoismos*; though it can be a disruptive act, it need not be so. A man can properly take the initiative, going forward on his own "because he is a man, after all [*ine andras, ya?*]." Yet a girl who does this has reason to fear "what people will say." At a minimum, they can say that she "just" wants to go first. In Miranda's emphasis—as she quotes "what people will say"—on the word "just" lies a moral accusation: it implies that the desire to put herself forward indicates a sexual "forwardness" that is morally reprehensible in women.[10] Therefore, as Miranda expresses it, "however much she wants to," she cannot go first. To do so is to risk being misunderstood.

PAREKSIGHISI AND KEFI FROM A FEMALE PERSPECTIVE

The phenomenon of *pareksighisi* ("misunderstanding," "misinterpreting," or as I have suggested, "mis-explaining") is of central importance in dance contexts. In Sohoian discourse about dance, *pareksighisi* is spoken about in conventionalized ways. Though the potential for *pareksighisi* makes dancing problematical for both males and females, it conventionally involves them in different ways.

People say that dances are always vulnerable to breakdown by a "misunderstanding over/because of the dance." They portray this *pareksighisi* as an open confrontation erupting between at least two protagonists who are, stereotypically, males.[11] It concerns the conflicting claims of those two protagonists (and implicitly, of the male and female members of the group that each represents) over rights to the dance. Misunderstanding concerning a female subject is different, and

[10] Berger describes the hypocrisy involved in such condemnations by taking the case of medieval representations of "Vanity" in painting: "You painted a naked woman because you enjoyed looking at her, you put a mirror in her hand and you called the painting 'Vanity,' thus morally condemning the woman whose nakedness you had depicted for your own pleasure" (1972:51).

[11] This is, in actuality, a matter of a male "subject position," for on rare occasions a woman acting as a protagonist for her group can become involved publicly in such a quarrel. Forty-five-year-old Maria quarreled with her son-in-law (husband of her eldest daughter) when, at the wedding *ghlendi* of her second daughter, "he" (actually he and his kin, Maria's affines) monopolized the dancing so much that other wedding guests, particularly the bilateral kin (*soi*) to Maria's second daughter did not have a chance to dance.

is articulated differently in the discourse about dancing. The differences can be expressed in five propositions.

First, males (and the groups they, respectively, represent) as protagonists[12] "are misunderstood to each other" (*pareksighiunde*) or become *pareksighimeni*, each vis-à-vis the other. A female tends to be "misunderstood" by others: "they misunderstand her" (*tin pareksighun*). In the first expression, which uses a reflexive construction, males participate equally and reciprocally; in the second expression, by contrast, the woman becomes the "object" who is misunderstood.

Second, the grounds for misunderstanding differ for males and females. Misunderstandings among youths or men are assumed to have a personal (an old grudge, a desire to assert *mangia* or *eghoismos*) or political tenor. Misunderstandings involving a girl or woman are assumed to have a sexual tenor.

Third, while a female's actions can thus be interpreted or understood in many ways, they are misinterpreted or misunderstood primarily in one way: sexually. In contrast, however sexually explicit a man's gestures may be, they are not misunderstood in this way: as Sofulis says, "People don't misinterpret the man. He can fall, shout, sit on the ground up to his nose!"

Fourth, a female's actions can be misunderstood in and of themselves, because how she uses her body is fundamental in defining who and what she is. A male's actions are not misunderstood in and of themselves but rather are misunderstood relationally. A male's actions are misunderstood only to the degree that they constitute a specific challenge to specific male others.

Fifth, misunderstandings involving men are, consequently, confrontational virtually by definition, usually in a direct sense. Misunderstanding is a process of accusation and counteraccusation; the opportunity to reply (whether verbally or nonverbally) is built into the form. The active and reciprocal quality of such misunderstanding expressed in language is a characteristic of its actual dynamics. In contrast, when a female is misunderstood there is rarely a direct confrontation. Accusations are not voiced to her directly; rather, they are made about her to others, through commentary (*skholia*) or gossip (*kotsobolia*). She has no opportunity to reply, whether verbally or nonverbally, to "what people say."

---

[12] A situation in which a female protagonist confronts a male is rare. A female can "misunderstand" what another female does, but although the two women can be said to *pareksighiunde*, that is, to be reciprocally "misunderstood to each other," it is not commonly expressed through direct public confrontation. A female celebrant who "misunderstands" another will, rather, tend to express displeasure in more indirect ways, as discussed below.

The gendered conventions of misunderstanding have specific consequences for the female celebrant. She looks forward to the dance not
only as an escape from the physical, social and emotional confinement
of her everyday life, but also as a way of "getting out of" herself. Most
of the verbs that females (like males) use to describe what they look
forward to incorporate the prefix *kse*, a prefix of transformation, of
undoing and escape: "bursting out" (*kseskazo* or *ksespazo*), "getting rid
of [worries]" (*ksedhino*) and "forgetting" (*ksehno*). As a member of a
parea a female celebrant is not only permitted but encouraged to enjoy
herself and this legitimately includes playful, flirtatious expressions of
sexuality as well as expressions of liveliness, enthusiasm, and joy that
enhance the pleasure of the *parea* and the whole group.

But because her actions are always open to misinterpretation, in
ways that are not only beyond her control but potentially beyond her
awareness, the female celebrant is forced to think (that is, "worry,"
skeftete) about how to act. Excess and enthusiasm, though encouraged,
are also the things for which she can be criticized. In a site of release,
she often finds that she must be vigilant about her self-presentation.
She admits that she cannot fully give up inhibitions and enter into the
carefree spirit: "you want to, but you can't." The predicament female
celebrants face is, to some extent, recognized by men, too: Triandafillos Sofulis' statement articulates very clearly the hegemonic sexual
ideology yet also, poignantly, recognizes how, because of it, the female celebrant's engagement in the joyous spontaneity of the moment
is socially constrained. Echoing Miranda's more personal confession,
he notes: "When she comes into *kefi*—you want to, but you restrain
yourself. You can't show it, you hide it, because you'd become de-
graded." For this reason, girls in the *patinadha* balk ("*po po po!*" they
exclaim in mock horror) at the very suggestion that they should become drunk and lie on the ground. For this reason, young women at
horoesperidhes laughingly resist initiating a circle dance while eagerly
accepting the lead when they are pulled up by someone else. For this
reason, Toula claimed "not to know" the *tsifte teli* at the Businesspeople's *horoesperidha*, and Vasso—dying to dance it—found us a place
among the dancers where we could dance more freely, hidden from
the critical eyes of those who were not dancing.

Given such conditions, girls and women tend to talk differently
about *kefi* than do men. Male *kefi*, which involves a situational reor-
dering of the relations between self and collectivity, is typically mediated, both practically and symbolically, by alcoholic spirits; female
kefi, in contrast, is neither achieved through nor conceptualized in
terms of drink (see also Auerbach 1984). Girls and women talk about
kefi as emergent from "being all together." Though men certainly

value "being all together," this ideal state of collectivity is related in contradictory ways to a man's *kefi*. An individual person, whether male or female, can "make *kefi* for [*kani kefi*]" or "give *kefi* to [*dhini kefi stin*]" the group. Indeed, Miranda spoke of her (now deceased) father's constitutive role with the words, "He was a *meraklis!* He would shout, laugh, tell jokes, he was the *kefi* of the *parea* [*itan to kefi tis pareas*]." And a male (like a female) can "come into" *kefi* (*erhete se kefi*) within and through association with the collectivity. But a male can also "do his own thing" (*kani to kefi tu*), that is, take a belligerent or defensive stance against the collectivity in ways that would be self-destructive if done by a female.

Very much to the contrary, "being all together" is a necessary precondition for a female celebrant's realization of *kefi*. A Sohoian female celebrant's engrossment in the moment is contingent upon her confidence that she will not be misunderstood. What and how she dances depends, therefore, not just on the category of event or on ostensibly unambiguous criteria of outside/inside or public/private, as much previous work on gender in Greece would seem to imply, but on much more truly situational features. It depends on her continuous and ongoing assessment of who is present, of the relationships among the celebrants, and of the dynamics of the emerging situation: as girls often said, "it depends on the *parea*."[13] Much as the Teso of Kenya describe successful beer parties as evidence of "much understanding" (Karp 1980:108), female celebrants, especially, regard *kefi* as a state in which everybody is so "all together" that misunderstandings cannot happen.

[13] Caraveli (1985) sensitively discusses the role of such assessments in the structuring of Karpathiot *glendia*, though not in relation to the specific question of gender performance and experience.

CHAPTER EIGHT

Aphrodite's Tables: Breakdown, Blame, and Female Sexuality

> Through a culturally dictated chain of reasoning, women become the moral custodians of male behavior, which they are perceived as instigating and eliciting. Women inherit a substantial task: the management of their own sexual desire and its public expression. . . . As a result, female desire is suspect from its first tingle, questionable until proven safe, and frequently too expensive.
>
> —Carole Vance, *Pleasure and Danger: Exploring Female Sexuality*

A PARTY I attended hosted by Aphrodite, a young woman from Thessaloniki employed as a social worker in Sohos, was not a dance-event on the scale of those already discussed, and it was almost certainly not thought of by those attending as a dance-event (*horos*) per se. Yet this smaller and more intimate gathering, held in Aphrodite's apartment and involving only a small group of people, was not structurally dissimilar to other local festive gatherings I attended: celebrations hosted by young married couples on the husband's name day, for example, often included dancing.

The event's intimate character and its more centralized focus of action and attention make possible a more detailed description and a more extensive account of celebrants' responses here. But the event is worth recounting even more for other reasons. As it unfolded, it became a complex drama, in both of the senses in which Greeks use the word: a "performance" and an "ordeal." Like Turner's (1957, 1974) "social dramas," too, the event dramatizes ideas and tensions that, though always present, tend to remain unspoken until a disturbance forces participants to articulate them (see also Stone 1982:9). Moreover, it is one of the few Sohoian examples I encountered—and is certainly the most striking one I witnessed—of a "breakdown" that the participants believed had been caused by a female celebrant. This party and the varying interpretations it received reveal how conflict, breakdown, and notions of accountability are themselves configured by and expressive of gender relations. At the same time, the existence of conflicting accounts reminds us both of ambiguities in the situation and of the situated nature of interpretation.

Paradoxically, some of the aspects of this situation that made it an ideal case study—its small size and its breakdown—also made me less comfortable than usual about probing into its aftermath. The fact that I was invited as a member of a particular *parea* and not as an anthropologist intensified my reluctance. I couldn't hide behind the so-called objective posture of the *laoghrafos* seeking information. Although my reticence was consistent with being a "good" (that is, polite) acquaintance, it undoubtedly hindered my attempt to be a "good" ethnographer (see also Karp and Kendall 1982). Unable to compose questions about this embarrassing event that did not sound prurient and accusatory, I could never bring myself to question Aphrodite about what she thought had happened and why (indeed, whether) she thought the event had failed. My only clue to her reactions came second hand, through a mutual friend, Stavros. Consequently, in this examination of the construction of bodily meanings through talk, Aphrodite's voice is absent. This silence perhaps underlines (as it also, unfortunately, replicates) the gender dynamics of misunderstanding—for in the social process of "misunderstanding" Aphrodite, she is never really given the chance to answer back.

The Party in Context

Sohoians rarely entertain friends at home. Except for certain ritual occasions (name days, engagements, portions of wedding celebrations and house visiting during Carnival) and informal visits for coffee, the house is not a site for social gatherings. Socializing not linked to ritual events involves "going out"—to the *kafenio*, *kafeteria*, or *zaharoplastio*, to a *taverna* in a neighboring town, or once in a while to a *kendro* in a nearby town or Thessaloniki.

There is, however, a category of event called "making a table" (*kano trapezi*). To "make a table" is to prepare a feast in honor of an individual or an occasion, and though one makes a table at home for many ritual events (for name days, engagements, and at Easter dinner, for example) one may also make a table in special circumstances: to welcome a relative or friend back home from a long absence or to honor a visiting dignitary. In this case, Aphrodite—a foreigner, someone from outside the community—made a table for various people in Sohos with whom she was friendly to reciprocate the hospitality she had received from them. To refer, as does the title of this chapter, to "Aphrodite's tables" draws on the symbolism of the table, but here with a sense of failure and irony. The plural alludes not so much to a physical fact, although it is true that when a large number of guests are involved in a celebration, the literal singularity of the table is not always possible. Rather, it metaphorically states a social fact, echoing the complaints of several celebrants who, as the event progressed, came to see the separate tables as a veritable emblem of disunity.

Aphrodite's party involved only sixteen people. They were linked not only through their friendship with Aphrodite but also through friendship with each other. Some of them were couples or close, even inseparable friends, who spent time together on a regular basis and who were seen by others as constituting a fairly stable *parea*; in the narrative below the inclusion of several individuals within a single paragraph indicates such a grouping. Others were not on such friendly terms. My knowledge of the history of each individual's relationship to every other individual—histories that undoubtedly affected the dynamics of the celebration—was (and is) incomplete, of course, but I knew something about each participant.

Aphrodite, the hostess, was twenty-two, single, with a diploma in social work, and had been recently employed by the town council as a social worker at the newly opened day center for the elderly. Though born in a village in the area around Sohos, she left as a young girl when her parents moved to Thessaloniki. Her affiliation with the region was initially a point in her favor: when—before her appointment—the mayor and the town council were discussing two candidates for the job, the mayor expressed his preference for her over the Athenian-born candidate, remarking of Aphrodite that "she is from our mountains, she knows our ways." Upon her arrival, Aphrodite immediately made an impression upon the townspeople. They found her gregarious, lively, and somewhat flirtatious. Plump and pretty, she dressed much more ostentatiously than most Sohoian girls her age: Dimitra was fond of remarking dryly on the quantities of gold jewelry that Aphrodite habitually wore. Within a few months of her arrival, a story began to circulate that Aphrodite was having an affair with Nikos, a married civil servant with two children. "In her work she is very honorable [*filotimi*]," an older woman who attended the day center remarked to me and her married daughter, "and as a single girl, she can do as she likes. But she has no business in getting in the middle of a family. Some people say if she doesn't leave Sohos willingly, they'll force her to go." By the time of her party in October, that relationship had supposedly ended.

Stavros Karakunelis, age thirty-one, was a tax office accountant. Very active in local affairs, both in his capacity as employee of the local administration and as a result of his leisure-time interests, he was then president of the Soccer Association, a supporter of the Sohos Youth Association, and a respected singer at local *ghlendia*. His wife, Kiki, twenty-six, ran a small family shop in the market and looked after their two small daughters. Because of Stavros' work, they had particularly intense contact with *kseni* who came to Sohos as teachers and civil servants, and they made a special effort to welcome and befriend them. Aphrodite spent a great deal of time socially both with Kiki individually and with Stavros and Kiki as a couple, and usually attended *horoesperidhes* and public functions with them.

Stavrakis, thirty-two, a patrilateral first cousin to Stavros (they share their grandfather's first name), worked for the local post office. His wife, Anna, thirty-two, worked at home as a housewife. Stravrakis and Anna frequently socialized with Stavros and Kiki, attending social events together.

Alekos, twenty-seven, was a primary-school teacher, born and raised in Sohos, and his friend Panayotis, thirty, principal of one of the town's two primary schools, was from another Macedonian village.

Mihalis, thirty-two, the chief of police, had been posted in Sohos for two years, but came from a village in Thrace. Mihalis was well liked in Sohos, and seen as an eligible and highly desirable bachelor. Educated, tactful, with a real respect for the local singing tradition, he was often invited to celebrations by the older men, who enjoyed his company and his very good voice, though he was also appreciated by younger men with such interests, like Stavros.

The party's largest grouping involved members and officers of the Sohos Youth Association. This *parea*, as I have mentioned, was made up of young people between seventeen and thirty-two, mostly unmarried. As well as core members of the association it included some non-Sohoians: young unmarried men and women who worked in the town, primarily as schoolteachers, and myself. The membership shifted over time: newly resident colleagues of the *kseni* schoolteachers joined the group, while a local member might drop out if there were conflicts with another member, sometimes to return several months later. Aphrodite was friendly with a few people in this *parea* but was only peripherally involved in it. On this evening, the *parea* consisted of eight individuals. Dimitra (thirty-two) and Roza (twenty-four), president and secretary, respectively, of the Sohos Youth Association, had both been born and raised in the town. Though both had worked in the past in a ladies' garment workshop, Dimitra had recently gotten a job as clerk in the town hall; Roza, then unemployed, helped out (unpaid) at her aunt's shop and her father's restaurant. Both had left school at sixteen. Yannis (eighteen), son of a local barber, having just completed high school, was apprenticed to an electrician but wanted to be a professional musician. He was accompanied by his close friend, Markos (nineteen), a student in a technical college, son of a post office employee. Tolis (twenty-seven), from Thessaloniki, had just started his first year as a primary-school teacher; Alexandros (thirty), also a primary-school teacher, was a long-time member of the *parea*, having taught for four years in Sohos. Artemis, my flatmate, and I, both twenty-nine, were also part of the group.

On the whole, the celebrants at Aphrodite's party were young and either unmarried or recently married. They included both Sohoians, most of whom were among the town's "educated" (*morfomeni*) and/or were active in the town's voluntary associations, and also young, educated *kseni*. All but one of the Sohoians involved represented (or were children of) the town's middle class—that is, people "of the market" and civil servants.[1]

FIRST IMPRESSIONS

Ethnographic interpretation of an event may be constructed over a period of time. Although the ethnographer's first impressions are critical in suggesting lines of questioning, those that she or he subsequently elicits from others who were present can verify, shift, challenge, or even contradict these original impressions. As my role at Aphrodite's party was primarily that of celebrant and musician, rather than researcher, I did not take any notes during the event, nor did I videotape or take photographs, though I did tape-record some of the singing. The fieldnotes that I wrote the following day, after discussing the event with Artemis, record what I observed, with as much detail as I could muster less than twenty-fours later, and include speculations on their possible significance. They incorporate knowledge about and understandings of the individuals present that I (and where noted, Artemis) had developed over the previous eight months. Some days later, they were followed by other fieldnotes, recording conversations and reports of conversations about that event among people who "witnessed," directly or vicariously, the events of that party.

The textual strategy here is intended to highlight not only the specificity—and multiplicity—of their responses, but also the gradual and dialogical process through which this ethnographic interpretation has been constructed. The textual form itself shows the successive layers of interpretation. Thus the first description of the party is a reproduction of my initial fieldnotes.[2] In the footnotes, I elaborate implicit

[1] Dimitra, daughter of a leftist laborer who died suspiciously in an industrial accident in the early 1950s, was the one exception. Her widowed mother made a marginal living from weaving and occasional production work. Although poor and unmarried, Dimitra's dynamism and intelligence had earned her the respect of many townspeople.

[2] I have edited these slightly, for reasons of style and clarity only. No new information has been added to them; I confine any interpretations about the events recorded, made after the time when the notes were written, to footnotes.

meanings, pose questions, and draw out ambiguities that become significant in the other celebrants' interpretations later on.

Fieldnotes #1: The Day After

Last night, starting about 9 P.M., Aphrodite had a party, attended by Stavros and Kiki, Stavrakis and Anna, Alekos and Panayotis, "my *parea*" (Dimitra, Roza, Yannis, Markos, Alexandros, Tolis, Artemis, me), and later, the chief of police, Mihalis. Kiki had spent the day helping Aphrodite to prepare the food (cheesepies, meatballs, salads), laid out on the table in buffet style. Kiki and her *parasinifadha*, Anna, were helping Aphrodite to serve it to the rest of us.[3] The women served us our food from a table in the kitchen, but once we got our plates, we sat down in the main room, where two medium-sized square tables had been put together in the center, and a small round table was set off to one corner.[4]

At first, Alexandros, Alekos, Panayotis, and Aphrodite sat at the small table, while the rest of us sat around the larger one.[5] We listened to tapes of popular music for a long while, joked and talked as we ate. Yannis had brought his bouzouki, Markos his guitar, and I my flute, but Yannis and Markos (for some reason) seemed reluctant to begin playing.[6] Artemis mentions that Anna asked the boys, twice, in a barbed, joking way, "Why haven't you started playing? Or are you waiting for us to leave?" Artemis says that the boys were, in fact, grumbling about being uncomfortable, not wanting to play until

[3] In Sohos, *sinifadhes* (literally, "co-brides") are women who marry brothers. *Parasinifadhes* ("nearly co-brides") are women who marry patrilateral first cousins, and hence share a surname.

[4] In more traditional celebrations (for example, name day celebrations, wedding feasts) seated guests typically receive from women of the household plates of food, each holding exactly the same items of foods in standardized portions. Alternatively, the table is set with dishes of *mezelikia* (frequently replenished) from which guests "nibble" (*tsimbane*). Both of these modes deemphasize the salience of individual preferences in the celebratory context and emphasize collective consumption. Aphrodite's use of the buffet was quite unusual in the context of Sohoian events as a whole, and it is interesting that her Sohoian friends, Kiki and Anna, intervened to reestablish the serving relationship between host(ess) and guest. Thus, though each guest had some latitude in choosing what food he or she preferred, that guest was still "served" by the hostess or the women helping her.

[5] Aphrodite's failure to provide a single table for all the celebrants, however makeshift, was in retrospect significant, and for some exemplifed the lack of unity of the group. Without this symbolic focus, performative attempts to overcome fragmentation faced an even more difficult battle.

[6] Yannis, Markos, and I often brought our instruments to such gatherings—for example, to Dimitra's name day celebration, to a "table" that my husband and I had made at our house a month before while he was visiting, and to occasional excursions to a taverna for a meal. We accompanied the singing that was usually an important feature of these events.

"they" ("especially Panayotis") left.[7] After an hour, Stavros left, he explained, "to get more wine" and (as others explained to me) to try to find a table so that we could all sit together.[8]

We did eventually begin to play. Finally, singing began in earnest, and not too much later, Stavros returned with Mihalis, the police chief (about 11 P.M.). Both of them were given seats near us, the musicians. Mihalis smiled, amused, when—as they arrived—I pulled out my tape recorder. "Don't I know my work?" I quipped.[9]

I noticed several things about participation here: (a) Stavros dominated the singing, through the power of his voice, through his closed eyes and gestures signifying focused attention to the songs, and through the way he sometimes cut off others after they started a new song when he wanted to begin another, of his own. Others could and did sing along on some songs, however. (b) When starting a new song, the singer did not verbally announce it first, or try from the outset to negotiate an appropriate key with the instruments. Rather, the singer would start off singing and expect the instruments to pick up the tune. With the general racket—conversation, joking, laughter—Yannis usually had trouble discerning the pitch. Consequently, Yannis and Markos often strummed away in two different keys, while the singer continued in a third. A few times, however, Stavros put his hand on Yannis' shoulder to make him stop playing, and a few times, he called out for everybody to stop singing so that the musicians could set the key. (c) Verbal interaction shifted easily between singing and speaking. Aphrodite initiated a heroic song, and was teasingly stopped by Mihalis, who objected, "That's a song for *pallikaria*!"[10] Later, Alekos started a song, whose first line began, "Two green eyes with blue lashes are driving me crazy," when Mihalis quipped, "Whose eyes?" There was a tone of playful, sexual banter, with puns and innuendo.[11] At the same time, while the singing went on, conversations contin-

[7] I do not understand the historical reasons for this tension between the boys and Anna, and between the boys and Panayotis. Artemis' report indicates, however, that certain social tensions already existed among participants that had little to do with the events of that evening.

[8] Whether this was Stavros' intention or not, the explanation was plausible to those who offered it to me during the party. Their explanation indicates a belief that finding a table would be a "reasonable" motive for leaving the party (as is Stavros' own explanation).

[9] Sohoians (especially certain singers) were, by this time, quite accustomed to my activities of tape-recording and note taking during informal singing sessions. Mihalis, who often participated in singing sessions at Sofulis' *kafenio* or at his house, had often been tape-recorded by me. Initially suspicious, he now seemed to enjoy my recording activities, often teasing me about them.

[10] *Pallikari*, as mentioned in Chapter 4, is a term for unmarried youths who are courageous and strong. The valor of such youths is often praised in folk songs.

[11] This is an example of *kalaburi*.

ued.[12] Stavros, especially, would sing loudly, yet at the same time, close his eyes in a stylized performance of introspective reverie.

During a rest break for the musicians, Aphrodite turned on her cassette recorder again and put on dancing music. She urged people to get up and dance, but everybody seemed somewhat reluctant. Stavros then got up and began to dance a *tsifte teli* with Aphrodite. They danced face to face. Stavrakis called out, "[make] all the embellishments, all of them [*ola ta tsakismata, ola, ola*]!"[13] Aphrodite seemed to take this as an encouragement to move right up close to Stavros, playfully shimmying her shoulders and leaning her body toward his.[14] I remember looking around, but I couldn't read hostility in anybody's face at that point. When the dance was over, Stavros sat down, and Aphrodite continued to urge others to dance. After a few minutes, Stavrakis got up and danced a *karsilamas* with Aphrodite. Anna then rose to dance a *zeibekiko*, and then a reserved *tsifte teli* by herself.[15] Aphrodite danced a brief *hasapikos*[16] with Panayotis, then Artemis rose for a waltz with Alekos. Except for one *hasaposervikos*[17] and one *kalamatianos*, which nearly everybody joined in to dance, these four—Stavros, Aphrodite, Stavrakis, and Panayotis—did most of the dancing.

One critical moment of the party was when Stavros got up and performed a *tsifte teli* by himself. Aphrodite, who was standing nearby, picked up a plate from the table and broke it at his feet, then took

[12] This is a common characteristic of Sohoian *ghlendia* and seldom a cause of misunderstandings.

[13] *Tsakismata* are "breaks." In songs, they refer to melodic embellishments, verbal exhortations or phrases, often improvised on the spot (cf. Caraveli 1982); in dances, they refer to gestural embellishments of shoulders, hands, torso, as well as of the legs and feet.

[14] Shouts of greeting and encouragement are standard features of such celebratory interactions (cf. Caraveli 1982). It appears that Aphrodite is being specifically "encouraged" to elaborate her movements in playful, sensuous ways.

[15] Anna's personal motives in dancing are unknown, but she was at least "going through the motions" of participation and of having a good time.

[16] In this dance, the two dancers stand beside each other, facing the same direction, each resting a hand on the other's opposite shoulder, and execute various steps, kicks, squats, and turns. Linked in this way, the two dancers ideally dance in unison; when they do not, the dance tends to break down in choreographic confusion. This dance, like the *zeibekiko*, developed within the *rebetika* subculture, but unlike *zeibekiko*, it expressed the intimate communication between two dancers. Traditionally, "changes in steps were signalled solely by the pressure of the leader's left hand on his partner's right shoulder, and required the partner's close concentration on the leader's step" (Petrides, in Butterworth and Schneider 1975:51). Today, dance routines tend to be memorized. For these reasons *hasapikos* is not commonly seen in dance-events; when it is, its performance usually involves playful, jokey "horsing around" as partners try to sustain more than a few steps in unison. Aphrodite and Panayotis' performance was much like this: several short-lived attempts, punctuated by laughter and teasing horseplay.

[17] *Hasaposervikos* is an open circle dance (found throughout the Balkans) that uses a basic pattern of six steps.

another and broke it.[18] Kiki objected to this, but Aphrodite retorted, "It's only plates. [You've got to] give everything to your man [*dhos' ta ola ston andra su*]."[19] A bit later, during the same dance, Aphrodite went into the kitchen and brought out a stack of plates, and Kiki became agitated, insisting that she put them down.[20] Artemis thinks this is the point when Kiki really started becoming upset. For the last hour of the party (from about midnight to 1 A.M.) Kiki periodically urged Stavros that it was time to go home. Stavros, however, became more and more stubborn the more he drank. During the last hour he resumed singing, with Mihalis. At one point, after singing, Stavros called out, "Now, we on our side have sung, it's your turn, you on that side [of the table]." Stavros made this remark as if in complaint, even though he had previously sometimes cut off the others' attempts to start new songs. Mihalis tried to calm Stavros ("Forget it now, leave it alone!"), as did Panayotis ("Come on, cousin").[21] Kiki retorted crossly, "He just wants to act out his own *kefi*,[22] he to sing and we to listen!" Artemis says that Kiki grumbled, "I'll fix him." A bit later, she got up from her chair, indicating she wanted to leave, but Stavros initiated three more songs.[23] Artemis, who was sitting nearby, heard Markos lean over to Stavros, with Kiki out of hearing distance, and ask him ("seriously, I think," Artemis explained), "Love, what's it worth [*i aghapi, poso aksizi*]?" "A nickel [*mia pendara*]," Stavros replied glumly.[24] Finally, he jumped up to dance, "One more *zeibekiko* and we leave!"

After this the party began to break up. Stavros and Kiki, with Stavrakis and Anna, left first. There was some milling about as we pre-

[18] The practice of breaking objects (*spasimo*) is discussed briefly in Chapter 6. *Spasimo* is typically associated with performances of *zeibekiko*, not *tsifte teli*.

[19] Might this have been taken to imply, "And you, Kiki, don't give everything to Stavros"?

[20] Why? Because she was making a spectacle of herself? Because it's a shame to break a perfectly good stack of dishes? Because Aphrodite was showing too much attention to Kiki's husband? Because she appeared to be chiding Kiki for not giving enough attention to him?

[21] Panayotis and Stavros are not kin. Panayotis probably used this intimate term, "cousin" (*ksadherfe*), to try to assuage Stavros' anger.

[22] A man who has sexual relations with a woman can be said, euphemistically, to *kani to kefi tu* ("enact/make his own *kefi*"; cf. the American expression, "have his fun"). The vehemence of Kiki's complaint suggests that it may not have been just his domination of the singing that angered her.

[23] Keeping others waiting (as in the wedding *patinadha*) is an expression of power (cf. Bourdieu 1977:6–7).

[24] This formulaic expression of the antagonism between men and women in erotic relationships is here an aside, a spontaneous comment shared "secretly" between two men, on the interpersonal dynamics of the moment. It shows not only that tensions between husband and wife, or between other family members, may emerge in celebratory contexts, despite the emphasis placed on the public display of family unity, but also that they are occasionally quite explicitly acknowledged within that context.

pared to leave. Panayotis and Alekos lagged behind, with Aphrodite. Artemis offered to help clean up, but was, after thanks, turned down. The rest of us left together, exchanging meaningful looks and bemused expressions, and walked home without speaking.

This morning, during our discussion, Artemis said she felt that both Stavros and Stavrakis had become somewhat aroused by Aphrodite's movements. "I wouldn't use the word 'provocative' [*proklitikia*], because it wasn't quite that," she said, "but she was going too far. I was surprised. Maybe it's good because she wanted to get it all out, but [pause] you know, in situations like this, you want to let go but you can't."[25] Artemis said she had felt uncomfortable, that it wasn't like being with friends whom she knew well and trusted, and with whom she could feel free to let go without hesitation. "Maybe I am naive, because I have never tried to take someone's husband or boyfriend away."[26] She then noted that in being careful not to appear to "go too far" with a male friend involved with someone else, she would "hide her feelings, put up a wall." She remarked that one of her male friends had complained about this barrier, and that this had hurt her.[27] I told her how careful I try to be here, to be friendly without creating suspicions.

Apropos of this, something I found odd, difficult to understand (but this is not the first time I've encountered it), is the demonstrative "friendship" between Aphrodite and Kiki. They are together often, and Kiki helped Aphrodite prepare the party. Yet I've been told that Kiki has said (*about* Aphrodite, I suspect not *to* her) "if she makes any move on Stavros, I'll gouge out her eyes!"

[Added later the same day.] In the afternoon, Artemis and I were standing on our balcony when Stavros passed by on the street below. We greeted him, "How are things?" "We're not doing well," he answered. "Why is that?" He stopped, half joking (half not): "We've been

[25] Artemis, in her explanation, articulates the dilemma discussed in Chapter 7; indeed, the similarity of her words to those of Triandafillos Sofulis is striking. "Maybe it's good, because she wanted to get it all out" (the invitation to release) *but* "in situations like this, you want to let go but you can't" (the injunction to maintain [self-]control).

[26] Here, Artemis stresses a female celebrant's dilemma in relation to her attempt to manage her relationships with other females in the group. The institutionalized social dependence of a woman upon a man in Sohos, as in other Greek communities, often creates competition and jealousies among women over men.

[27] Artemis is caught in the double bind, too. In making sure she is not misinterpreted by other women as pursuing an already-claimed man within the *parea*, she censors herself to the extent that this male friend accuses her of "putting up a wall." Artemis does not indicate what her female friends say about her actions, but the man's objection is an articulation of a "blame the victim" dynamic. In similar situations (occasionally it happened to me), I heard overly cautious girls labeled "cold" (*kria*), "closed" (*klisti*), and "uptight" (*kompleksihia*).

slandered." My hunch is that Kiki quarreled with him when they left. I wonder what else he could have been referring to?

THE ANATOMY OF MISUNDERSTANDING

Having sensed anxiety and conflict in the air at the party, I recorded in this first set of notes and interpretation whatever examples (from sharp words and ambiguous teasings to nonverbal tugs-of-war) that I had noticed or that Artemis had suggested. But I did not yet have a very clear idea of what other celebrants believed had really gone wrong. Over the next week, I talked to some of the participants about the party. Artemis also reported to me remarks that had come up spontaneously in conversations she had with several others. Some of the statements were uttered by individuals who had not been present but who had heard about the event from someone else. Their remarks illustrate how gossip works in building and breaking reputation in this community. In the second and third sets of fieldnotes, I recorded the statements of all these individuals. Each person diagnoses the situation; each imputes motives, discerns causes, and assigns blame. Both what the speakers note as significant and what they ignore are critical for understanding how "plausible" interpretations—analyses the speakers believe to be reasonable—are constructed.

Fieldnotes #2: Follow-up to Aphrodite's Party

Kyriaki Dhendhros. During a visit to the house of Kyriaki Dhendhros— a regular member of our *parea*, who had not attended the party—I asked her what she had heard from Dimitra and Roza about it. She replied:

> An orgy! Dimitra said she didn't enjoy herself, that it wasn't a relaxed environment, and that she doesn't want to go back ever again. Aphrodite danced in a totally lascivious, vulgar way [*hidhea*].[28] She was kissing Panayotis, even though she has something going with Alekos. When the chief of police came, then, at least, Dimitra and Roza expected her to restrain herself [*na simazepsi ligho*, literally, "to pull herself together a little"], but nothing happened, she didn't correct herself at all.

"Were they critical of the *tsifte teli* in particular, or just the dancing in general?" I asked. "It was the *tsifte teli*," she replied. Kyriaki's husband, Thomas, who was also present, then broke in, saying, "But everybody

---

[28] The term *hidhea* has sexual connotations.

dances *tsifte teli!* Women, men, girls." "Yes," Kyriaki retorted, "but the real, genuine *tsifte teli* is a provocative dance." I remarked that though I had felt very definite tension in the party, I myself would not have interpreted her gestures in such extreme terms. Kyriaki mused that if Aphrodite had not become involved with this married man, people "would not have given such significance [*dhen tha ta dhosane tosi simasia*]" to her movements and her actions. "I might have gone to the party and not noticed anything, either," she laughed. Later Kyriaki mentioned, hinting again at "an orgy," that she had heard that both Alekos and Panayotis had spent the night with Aphrodite.

Kyriaki's story (based on Dimitra's and Roza's reports) portrays Aphrodite's presentation of self as vulgar, sexually wanton, out of control. This is reinforced by portraying the party as a figurative "orgy" followed by an alleged literal "orgy" (two men staying behind with Aphrodite). It is Aphrodite's performance of *tsifte teli* that confirms this. When Thomas objects that "everybody" dances *tsifte teli* (an indisputable fact, even though female performances tend to be more muted than those of men), Kyriaki counters not by disputing Thomas' statement, or even by claiming (as she might have) that what offended people was the "way" Aphrodite performed it. Instead, she alludes to its original, "authentic" (*ghnisio*) meaning as a "provocative dance."[29] Just afterward, however, perhaps in response to my remarks, Kyriaki admits that the construction of meaning is not based solely on Aphrodite's dancing: were it not for her previous adulterous history, people would not have given her actions so much significance. Interpretation is not, in other words, a mere matter of knowing the grammar of body movements: reading the body incorporates a range of social knowledge.

Stavros. I met Stavros in the marketplace a few days later, and over a sandwich, I asked him whether he had enjoyed Aphrodite's party. He replied:

> I didn't have a good time at all. I got drunk and sang more from "nerves" than from *kefi*. That wasn't a *parea*. Those guys were "unrelated, irrelevant" to the group [*afti itan askheti*]. They came out of devious, sexual motives, smart guys who thought they were putting

[29] In 1976, while researching the *tsifte teli* in Athens, I found that many Greeks whom I approached for information expressed uneasiness at my interest, and often tried to dismiss the dance as "Gypsy" or "Turkish"—in other words, as "Other"—and "not really Greek." It is unclear whether Kyriaki's explanation is alluding to the stereotype of the professional Turkish belly dancer or to the claim made by some historians that *tsifte teli* derives from the provocative dance of temple prostitutes in ancient Greece. However, the attempt to assert that the original, "pure" meaning is the "real" meaning is a common legitimating strategy, often used by folklorists in their accounts (cf. Cowan 1988b).

something over on us [*ilthan ya poniria, na mas kanun ksipnio*]. *Kefi* comes from inside, it's spontaneous. It's not something to be faked.

Aphrodite, he explained, had drunk too much: "She didn't realize what was happening." He claimed that though she had become upset when he told her this, she nonetheless thanked him for doing so. (The implication, of course, is that no one else had talked directly to her, an illustration of the indirect accusation via communal talk that characterizes the "misunderstanding" of a woman.) Stavros had expected trouble in any case, once he had learned that Alekos and Panayotis had been invited. Indeed, he said he had not wanted to come, but had given in to Aphrodite's and Kiki's insistence. "Didn't you see how late I came, and how I left to get my harmonica and the wine, and how long I took to return, with Mihalis?"

Stavros blames not Aphrodite (whose flaw, he implies, is not purposive seduction; at most, he sees her errors as naïveté and failure to manage her presentation of self because of too much drink), but the two male teachers. He insists that they did not come for the pleasures of "being together"; he describes them as "unrelated" to the *parea*, making it "not a *parea*." Instead, they perceived the situation instrumentally: they came "for *poniria*," for deceitful, sexual goals. Stavros judges their expressions of *kefi* to have been "faked" for dishonorable purposes. In contrast, his own insistent drinking and singing—his assumption of the conventional postures and practices of "making *kefi*"—were, he says, motivated by "nerves" rather than by spontaneous *kefi*. But, attempting to make this attitude comprehensible to me, and perhaps to himself in light of Kiki's reaction, he explains that it was provoked by his anticipation of disunity.[30] Stavros attends out of "obligation" but leaves when breakdown seems a foregone conclusion. Of the tensions between himself and his wife, Kiki, Stavros says nothing.

Dimitra. Dimitra was slightly impatient, and cryptic, when I tried to elicit what she felt had gone wrong at the party. This was not unusual; she tended to regard with amused skepticism my frequent attempts to get her to spell out the meanings that she thought were perfectly obvious. "It was a *ghlendi*, not a brothel! We weren't together! My heart got tight, it was very upsetting."

I had attended many *ghlendia* and festive outings with Dimitra over the year and had watched her engage in and enjoy flirtatious banter,

[30] To do something "from nerves" (*apo nevra*) is to act out of bottled-up anger, anxiety, worry, or upset. Stavros' explanation may be compared with Grigoris' statement in the discussion of *zeibekiko* that he dances "either from anxiety or from enthusiasm" (see Chapter 6).

raunchy jokes, and dancing. Dimitra's sarcastic reply indicates that she found the erotic interaction here somehow different. Her characterization of the event as a "brothel" certainly implies a criticism of degree: flirtatious behavior had gone "too far." But the comment immediately following, lamenting that "we weren't together," suggests just as strongly a criticism of intention: the (legitimately) playful had become (illegitimately) serious. A collective entertainment had become a pretext for individuals' erotic strivings.

Dimitra's disappointment recalls Simmel's meditation on sociability (1971a). In this "play form of association," being with others is not directed toward objective ends but is, rather, an end in itself. Sociability creates

> an ideal sociological world, for in it—so say the enunciated principles—the pleasure of the individual is always contingent upon the joy of others; here, by definition, no one can have his satisfaction at the cost of contrary experiences on the part of others. (1971a:132)

Dimitra implies that certain celebrants eschewed this collective project of "making *parea*" in favor of individual, and divisive, erotic interests. The tightening of her heart, a sense of emotional constriction that is the antithesis of an expansive, all-embracing *kefi*, metaphorically testifies to this lack of unity.

Fieldnotes #3: Reports from Artemis

Alexandros. Artemis talked with Alexandros about the party. In her paraphrase, she reports his statement:

> It was Alekos who spent the night with Aphrodite, but Panayotis did not leave the party immediately. Indeed, Panayotis took Artemis' offer to help clean up after the party "cunningly" [*to pire ponira*], hoping that the four could have "something going together."[31] After Panayotis left, and only Aphrodite and Alekos were inside, someone came every quarter of an hour and rang the doorbell, then ran away. This person continued this until late into the night. I know who it was, but I'm not going to say who. Too bad for her, but the whole situation was really her fault.

How Alexandros "knows" this information is not clear. Since he lives down the street from Aphrodite, it is not unlikely that he actually heard the doorbell ringing. The attributions of Panayotis' motives may come from something Panayotis said, or may be speculation. Though

[31] Artemis told me she was shocked to hear this.

Alexandros does not here identify Aphrodite's motives, he does say she is to blame.

Yorghos and Mara. Artemis visited another couple, Yorghos, thirty-three, a carpenter, and Mara, twenty-five, a housewife raising two children, who are friends of Stavrakis and Anna. Artemis described the conversation they had about this party: Mara mentioned that she had learned (from Kiki via Anna) that Aphrodite had been frightened by the doorbell-ringing disturbances and had slept every night since then at Stavros and Kiki's house. Mara repeated Anna's statement that "the whole point of the party was for Aphrodite to make a pass at the chief of police!" and also reported Anna's story that she had urged her reluctant husband to dance with Aphrodite, saying, "He didn't want to dance but I said, 'Go on, dance with her!' "

Yorghos reported that Nikos, the married man who had earlier been involved with Aphrodite, had remarked to him, "I'm just waiting for something to happen between Aphrodite and Stavros!" Then Yorghos recalled an exchange he'd had with Aphrodite some weeks before. Aphrodite had commissioned Yorghos to construct a wardrobe for her, and while negotiating the payments, she had said, "Can I give you 2,000 drachmas now and the rest later?" "No," Yorghos had said, "if you don't have the money now I can't do it." He then quipped to Mara and Artemis, "Maybe she's thinking of some other way to pay me." "You'd be lucky, wouldn't you?" teased Mara. "Well, it isn't nice to have the same wife all your life," Yorghos retorted wryly.

Mara's report reveals something of both her own and Anna's perceptions of the event. Mara quotes Anna's disapproving conclusion that for Aphrodite, the "whole point" of the party was not the celebration itself, but rather "to make a pass" at a man. Yet Anna also apparently insisted that at one point in the party, she encouraged her husband to dance a *karsilamas*, a face-to-face couple dance, with Aphrodite. Perhaps Anna had encouraged her husband to dance, and later got up herself to dance, in an attempt to deflect the spark between Aphrodite and Stavros, to defuse the tension, and to help out her friend Kiki, caught in a humiliating situation. Still, Anna's encouragement to her husband is not exactly what one would normally expect of a skeptical wife, especially if she had perceived—as Artemis had— that not just Stavros but her husband, too, was "somewhat aroused" by Aphrodite's dancing. Whether Anna was sincere at the time, and only later, in retrospect, came to feel resentful at Aphrodite's behavior; or whether she was already, during the party, feeling resentment, we do not know. By the time Anna had talked to Mara, the first informant in a three-person chain of gossip (Mara–Artemis–myself), the event was over. The repercussions of the party were probably already influencing Anna's original perceptions of the interaction.

Though any reflections on Anna's motives are necessarily speculative, these reports of her actions raise important issues concerning the ambiguities of sociability as an activity that is ideally spontaneous and guileless yet in practice a social accomplishment requiring knowledge, skill, give and take, and even deception. If the first interpretation—of Anna's initial sincerity and subsequent resentment—is the more accurate one, her reaction recalls the disappointment Dimitra expressed: Anna's remarks imply that she felt that her optimistically generous impulses on behalf of collective pleasures were cynically exploited for selfish ends. But if the second interpretation holds, a very different dynamic is suggested. Here, there is a rift between Anna's public gesture of generosity (a kind of performative "utterance" saying "we really *are* all together; here, dance with my husband! I don't mind!") and her private sentiments of suspicion and, perhaps, jealousy. Anna's gesture suggests that in a situation where sociability is the explicit rationale—as Aphrodite's table certainly, "officially" was—one can feel obliged to act with duplicity. "Go on, dance with her!" Anna urges her husband; but when Aphrodite dances with him, she reinforces her own image as promiscuous seductress. And had Aphrodite refused, wouldn't she have caused offense? Both Anna and Aphrodite are trapped; both act, more or less skillfully, according to the conventions of "making *parea*," yet the success of their shared project is doomed by suspicions of bad faith and ulterior motives.

Yorghos quotes Nikos, Aphrodite's alleged former lover, but also offers some of his own reactions: both indicate how the situation is viewed from a male perspective. Nikos, he reports, is "just waiting" for another man (Stavros) to succumb to Aphrodite's charms (and, implicitly, for this to become public knowledge). The remark suggests that Nikos has himself suffered criticism for his own liaison with her and would be glad to see another man subjected to the same.[32] For his part, Yorghos both condemns Aphrodite and playfully suggests he would have an affair with her if he could get away with it. He first embellishes the story of Aphrodite, the "promiscuous woman," with

[32] Despite the ideology that men are naturally inclined to pursue sex whenever possible, there was intense community disapproval of this affair. A man's extramarital liaisons are tolerated, even expected, if he must be absent from home for long periods for work or business, but Nikos and his wife were living together in Sohos. His affair with Aphrodite must have seemed unnecessary and, therefore, insulting to his wife. Probably more important, townspeople expressed the fear that the family, which included two young children, would be broken up. They may have suspected that Nikos' wife, also a reasonably well paid civil servant, had the wherewithal, unusual for a Sohoian woman, to support two children on her own, if necessary.

his own anecdote, inviting his wife Mara and Artemis to collude with him in laughing at her. Then he jestingly tries to elicit their sympathy, "complaining" to them about how tedious monogamy is for him.

CONFLICTING INTERPRETATIONS AND CONTRADICTORY VALUES

These verbal accounts do not so much diagnose the truth of a situation as construct an interpretation of it. The individual constructing each account is not involved in an abstract, objective exercise in social analysis, but speaks from a particular position, with particular interests. This construction is also a social process: personal accounts that themselves draw upon more broadly held assumptions are exchanged both in gossip and in the ethnographic interview. Shared and compared, they provide the possibility for revised interpretations.

What I have presented here no doubt represents only a fraction of what was said about Aphrodite's party. Even so, it reveals a celebration of enormous complexity. Quite a lot was going on, though some of what occurred was emphasized as more significant than other aspects of the evening by those trying to make sense of the event. What is initially most striking is the degree to which the different participants agree in their assessments. Overwhelmingly, they blame Aphrodite for the fact that the party failed. Nearly all cite her "deployment of sexuality," as Foucault would term it, as problematical.[33] Most describe her as "provocative," "lascivious," "going too far," as the aggressor initiating a sexual quest, though one, Stavros, pleads her ignorance—"she didn't know what was happening"—and criticizes her mostly for drinking too much and hence failing to remain circumspect. In almost all cases she is deemed responsible for the men's responses; in almost no case is her own sexual desire deemed legitimate in itself. The images used—of an orgy, of her simultaneous pursuit of several men and the voracious appetite this implies—portray feminine sexuality as powerfully destructive. The male teachers come in for criticism for their deviousness and antisocial selfishness, but the reaction to them is mild compared with the scorn heaped upon Aphrodite.

The vehemence of the responses to Aphrodite indicates how deeply entrenched is the idea that female sexuality is "dangerous to society" and that any woman seen to express sexual desire openly deserves harassment and punishment. Though Aphrodite was never given the chance to clarify her intentions verbally, the celebrants drew on their

---

[33] Being a "foreigner," Aphrodite does not wholly share the bodily orientations of the locally defined habitus. Even her everyday demeanor was regarded as unusually coquettish, by local standards, and her transgression may have seemed especially outrageous.

knowledge of her previous behavior and inferred—perhaps preferred to infer—that her body language was clear.

This said, it is nonetheless not entirely satisfactory to analyze this situation only in terms of the hegemonic gender codes of everyday life. Though hardly irrelevant, it is inadequate for understanding the particular dynamics of such a party, in which, especially for young people, "letting go" is acknowledged to be a value, and sensuality (expressed through dancing), flirtatious banter, and teasing are acceptable and valued elements of sociability, elements that are encoded in practices. This is acknowledged in the accounts themselves. Thus within the resounding chorus of condemnation of Aphrodite's behavior is an unmistakable murmur of quiet, thoughtful dissent. Listening closely, one hears not only disagreements among various celebrants about what went wrong and whose fault it was but also ambivalences within individual interpretive accounts. "Maybe it's good, because she wanted to get it all out," says Artemis. "But everybody dances *tsifte teli*," says Thomas (see figure 24). Alexandros' account ("too bad for her") and Stavros and Kiki's hospitality when Aphrodite is too frightened by the late-night doorbell ringing to sleep at home show some sympathy toward her plight. The accounts reveal the speakers' ambivalence, uncertainty, or shifting stance about culpability, about reasonable and justifiable actions, and about what the purposes of such a party were and should be.

It is not simply that the party, as a framed context, has its own, totally different assumptions and rules about what social actions are permissible and what they mean. Rather, the meanings of actions are unstable and uncertain because values of individual pleasure and collective sociability, spontaneity and obligation, flirtatious sexuality and serious seduction, all of which may be recognized as legitimate in the party context, are potentially incompatible and contradictory. In successful situations, celebrants skillfully negotiate between them; when the celebration breaks down, the contradictions become exposed.

Aphrodite's erotic history, as understood by the other celebrants, outside the frame undoubtedly fueled suspicions that her flirtation within it was more than playful. In addition, her ignorance of or refusal to submit to the subtle self-censorship required to sustain unity and sociability certainly contributed to the progressive collapse of even the façade of sociability. At the same time, the already existing antagonisms among the other celebrants played their part in undermining attempts to invent a putative unity. In the accounts that try to make sense of what went wrong, Aphrodite is made to shoulder what seems more than her share of the blame. Yet the fact that some interpreters entertain a moment of doubt about the legitimacy of this blame point

24. Recalling, perhaps, examples like that of Vasso, here enjoying herself at the Businesspeople's dance, Thomas insists that "everybody dances *tsifte teli!*"

to the contradictory values coexisting within the celebratory frame. Although some voices deny them, a few explicitly recognize the duplicities and double binds that these contradictory values set up, most notably for girls and, here, particularly for Aphrodite, who seems both culprit and victim.

CHAPTER NINE

Because of the Dance

. . . sociability may easily get entangled with real life.

—Georg Simmel, "Sociability"

I HAVE been concerned in this book to explore how gender and sexuality are socially constructed, particularly in the dance. I have looked at the ways they are physically constructed—the ways they are embodied—individually and collectively, in the conventionalized poses, postures, and gestures Sohoians assume when they are celebrating: at the table, on the dance floor, in the streets. I have considered how they are verbally constructed in the talk within and about dance-events, both spontaneous talk and that elicited by myself as ethnographer, exploring what Sohoian women and men, girls and boys, say about dancing and noting the terms in which they are admired, enjoyed, criticized, or blamed as dancers. I have insisted that the celebrant who both witnesses and participates in the sociable practices of a dance-event (in which gender ideas and relations are visibly and palpably rendered) and in the discursive practices (in which stories of the event are collectively fabricated) inevitably experiences the dance-event in a gendered way. Engaging in these practices, she or he is also, more or less, engaged—or bound, sometimes even trapped—by them. The problems that the dance-event presents to the individual celebrant may themselves provoke reflection on the tensions, ambiguities and contradictions of social experience that go beyond questions of gender: for instance, the relations between individual and society. Nonetheless, social experience always includes questions of gender; the celebrant always encounters the world as a female or a male subject.

Dance-events are set apart from the mundane preoccupations of everyday life, but the degree to which that everyday reality can be bracketed is always tenuous. Each person brings to the dance-event goals, interests, desires, fears, grudges, a past, a reputation, a cluster of identities. People come to watch, evaluate, and criticize others; but also to enjoy themselves, forget their worries, "get outside" of themselves. Perhaps nowhere more than in dancing do Sohoians realize—both comprehend and make real—the pleasures of collectivity, especially in those rare and transcendent moments when *kefi* is achieved and individual distinctions cease to matter. In this sense, the dance-event—with the dance line composed of bodies moving in harmonious unison as its most succinct emblem—is a utopian image of the collective at its most joyous, sensuous, and orderly best. Creating it—the labor of "making *parea*," for example—is a utopian project. "We ate, we drank, we laughed, we danced, we had a wonderful time!", Sohoians typically tell each other after a dance they have enjoyed. But if these experiences are highly valued and desired, they are also difficult to create and sustain.

Dance-events are bounded spheres, and it is by pushing at or playing with this boundary between the dance and the everyday that a man finds out what it is to be male and a woman what it is to be female. They discover, I emphasize, *not* what to be male or female "is" in any essential or metaphysical sense, but what it means or implies given the ideas and relations of gender dominant in Sohos today. When the boundaries break down, perhaps because a man or a woman, a youth or a girl, has gone—or is deemed to have gone—"too far," conflicts and misunderstandings result. This identification of transgression and of misunderstanding proceeds according to a gendered logic. It reflects the different ways in which males and females are constituted as social persons outside the dance-event and the different ways they are expected to act within it. Inasmuch as male and female dancing bodies are read in different, gendered ways, dance presents different problems for the male and female subjects who both "are" and "have" these bodies. Dance is problematical for men and for women, but in different ways.

For youths and men the problematic of dancing coalesces around the culturally configured conflict between the individual male self and society, as expressed in the notion of *eghoismos*, or self-regard. Male *eghoismos* is conceived to balance delicately at the juncture between individual will and social demand. *Eghoismos* is viewed not as either positive or negative in dance-events, but rather as both positive and negative. On the one hand, if dance-events are to be sustained (and men, for various reasons, do both want and feel obliged to try to sustain them), each individual male must put aside antagonisms toward other men and participate in the collective production of sociable pleasures. Each does this by engaging in practices that simultaneously symbolize and create unity and reciprocity. The ritualized sharing of alcoholic spirits is a quintessential practice of sociability, though also a fundamentally ambiguous one. Drinking with other men facilitates the release from shame and self-consciousness that keeps a man separated from other men, a release ideally realized in the altered state of *kefi*.

On the other hand, a man must be constantly vigilant that in his participation in collective pleasures he is not denied—whether by oversight or design—the social recognition, or "meaning," that he feels is his due. Alternatively, he may use this opportunity to assert his precedence. Males who encounter each other in the dance site are united, divided, and hierarchically ordered on the basis of their socioeconomic group, their political faction, and their age. They are, in other words, differentiated; these are distinctions of position. The framed, "as if" quality of dance-events enables the negotiations of positioning to occur with some fluidity, but they can sometimes lead to misunderstandings. Conflict "because of the dance" among men nearly always revolves around issues of order—of serial positioning and of the ordering (requesting) of dances. These issues directly concern social order in both the practical and the philosophical senses.

The man who feels snubbed, or the protagonists of a group who sense they have been challenged, may not necessarily react dramatically on the spot; but this does occasionally occur. Sohoians view such quarrels with ambivalence. They value the collective generation of *kefi*, the sensual intensity and release that emerge when everybody is "all together." They become angry at the disruption that "spoils the *kefi*" and ruins the *ghlendi*. People often say that such quarrels are "over nothing," "over stupidities," that the slights that provoke them are trivial, perhaps imaginary, possibly even invented. They attribute them to the surfeit of drink that takes over a man ("it's the ouzo talking," they say). Yet at the same time they also seem to enjoy the man's disruptive acts, which are evidence of his "liveliness," his demand to be taken seriously "as a man."

The ways in which dance is problematical for girls and women also have to do with their collective position in the everyday world. Females in this community are not a homogeneous group, and each celebrant also competes to differentiate herself (in relation, of course, to a fairly strict norm) from others of her own gender. But she tends to do this in ways much quieter than those of her male counterparts. She differentiates herself especially through her bodily presentation: her clothing, her hairstyle, and the ways she uses her body as she dances. However, although the distinctions that she asserts are not unimportant, the fundamental distinction that shapes how her dancing body is read by her fellow celebrants in the dance-event is that she is a woman and not a man. For in the Sohoian social world, the defining feature of a woman is her sexuality: how and with whom she expresses it is central to how people define who and what she is.

It is worth placing these notions in a broader cultural and historical perspective. Although Sohoian "ways of seeing" men and women and, here, of "reading" their dancing bodies, originate in a specific milieu— a Greek Macedonian provincial town—they are not wholly unfamiliar to those from sites further west. The social subordination of women and the identification of woman as the locus of sexuality are components of a historical legacy of patriarchy that Western societies share. Perhaps it is not surprising that John Berger's reflections, based on his study of the representation of male and female bodies in the Western art tradition, on how those in the West learn to "see" men and women, resonate so strongly with situations I have described:

> The social presence of a woman is different in kind from that of a man. A man's presence is dependent upon the promise of power which he embodies. If the promise is large or credible his presence is striking. If it is small or incredible, he is found to have little presence. The promised power may be moral, physical, temperamental, economic, social, sexual—but its object is always exterior to the man. A man's presence suggests what he is capable of doing to you or for you. His presence may be fabricated, in the sense that he pretends to be capable of what he is not. But the pretense is always toward a power which he exercises on others.
>
> By contrast, a woman's presence expresses her own attitude to herself, and defines what can and cannot be done to her. (1972:45–46)

Female Sohoians look forward to dances as a place where they can "escape" and "forget" their relatively restricted everyday lives, and where they are encouraged to do precisely this in order to be good, carefree celebrants. Yet the conditions of a girl's or woman's participation often militate against this kind of engrossment. She is acutely aware of herself as both subject and object, as one who acts and is acted upon, who sees and is seen; this acuity of self-awareness is necessary because her failure to manage her presentation of self can have serious consequences for her. Her efforts to obtain release are necessarily mediated by her need to be seen to retain control of her self and her body. In many ways, she has already internalized this bodily control through habitus. Her expressions of "letting go" play at the boundaries of, but rarely transgress in any fundamental way, the limits of bodily expression she has already buried deep in the fibres of her flesh.

Playing with that boundary between "good" and "bad" sexuality in the dance-event, a Sohoian female finds out what it is to be female. In this dance space, ambivalent attitudes toward female sexuality are juxtaposed. Girls and women are not necessarily expected to mute or hide their sexuality. Flirtation, energy, the display of beauty, even subtle seduction are acknowledged and valued aspects of female performance in these events. This is particularly true for unmarried girls who, Sohoians believe, naturally want to be noticed by potential husbands. A performance with novelty and "swagger" wins male (and often, female) admiration, and a female dancer may enjoy this attention and the sense of power that it entails. But being the center of attention is always potentially problematical. A girl who is thought to lack control—of her body, her emotions, her sexuality—who "fails to uphold her position" (*dhen kratai tin thesi tis*) can be misunderstood. A girl wants to avoid misunderstandings, not only for the sake of her reputation, but also for the sake of her relations with others, and not least with other girls. If she is misunderstood, she can seldom respond directly, because the misinterpretations themselves tend to be diffuse and implied; they are articulated not through direct accusation but through innuendo and gossip. A female celebrant's experience of the dance, then, is rooted in her position in gender relations, but it is not only men who keep her "in her place." Women do, as well. Only when she believes that everybody is truly "all together" can the female celebrant really feel free to let go; for girls, everybody being "all together" is both the precondition for and the expression of collective *kefi*.

This is a far cry from the effortless conviviality of Greek dancing presented in films, in tourist brochures, and in the polished performances of professional dance troupes. Such representations render the Greek dancer a transparent Other: spontaneous, guileless, passionate, at once sublimely individualistic and superbly sociable. They deny the complexity of the dancer's life in society. In emphasizing the possibilities for conflict, I do not mean to imply that Sohoians are especially factious or quarrelsome. Nor do I mean to deny—for men and women alike—the pleasures of the dance. I do mean, however, to complicate them.

THOUGH this book stands, self-contained, as an ethnographic study about gender and sexuality, about the body politic and the politics of the body, and about dancing and dance-events in a particular community, it can also be read as an attempt to complicate our ways of approaching these ideas and relations theoretically and methodologically and of representing them textually.

In the opening pages of this book, I asserted that a "consensus" model of culture concerned with beliefs, values, and roles is inadequate for exploring a realm of ideas and relations that is complex and deeply embedded in the habitus and yet, paradoxically, also unstable and at least sometimes contested. I distinguished my analysis from those that portray the gender ideas and relations of the Other as unproblematically coherent and consistent "in their own terms." To some extent, the historical conditions of my fieldwork in Greece—in particular, the campaign for "Equality" promoted by a new socialist government and the consequently increased awareness of the "woman question" among Sohoians—forced such an approach upon me. But my treatment of these issues also, of course, reflects a theoretical persuasion that predated my fieldwork, and that in turn resulted in particular choices about ethnographic practice and writing. Thus I chose not to work in a small or remote village and not to focus on the traditional (as opposed to the "traditional") aspects of village society. Moreover, making sexual and gender asymmetry the central problem, approaching this through the notion of hegemony, and tracing how both consent and dissent are articulated through symbolic manipulations of a highly complex contemporary identity has entailed portraying complexity, cacaphony, and change as ontological features of the local reality, and therefore as central and ongoing themes of the analysis.[1]

Anthropologists working in many places in the world acknowledge, of course, that gender ideas, roles, and relations can and do change. Often, however, they draw uncritically upon models of urbanization, modernization, or Westernization to describe and account for processes of change in this realm. These models, because they treat the community and its culture "as an isolate with outside forces of market and state impinging upon it" (Marcus and Fischer 1986:77), simplify such processes and present them as overly determined. Ultimately they offer few conceptual tools for understanding how both reproduction and change within sex and gender systems are linked to the socially constructed desires, needs and interests of (and conflicts among) particular individuals and groups.

When discussing gender and sexuality, as well as other aspects of Sohoian culture, I have therefore avoided as much as possible using such dichotomies as traditional and modern, indigenous and foreign, rural and urban, Greek and non-Greek, and Sohoian and non-Sohoian as analytical distinctions that in and of themselves analyze or explain anything. Such distinctions all too easily reify and essentialize "Us" and "Them." They obscure the social differentiation and ideological disagreement to be found within the community of Others, and they also obscure the ways that ideas and relations found in this small Macedonian town bear certain similarities to, and are (today more than ever but in the past, too) politically, economically, and ideologically affected by and intertwined with, our own. Perhaps most important the use of these dichotomies as analytical or explanatory terms obscures the ways that they have become appropriated by Sohoians for

---

[1] This strategy contrasts with approaches that discuss social change or competing ideologies in the final section of a portrait of an Other way of life. See, for example, du Boulay's final chapters. "Past and Present" and "Epilogue" (1974:233–58), and Herzfeld's final chapter, "Transformations" (1985a:259–74).

use as symbolic terms within local discourses, both verbal and nonverbal. Understood in this different sense, as a vocabulary of symbols through which individuals and groups negotiate identities, positions, and power relations, they must be taken very seriously indeed.

This perspective arose as I struggled to see how, as in Bourdieu's formulation of habitus, the symbolic universe is incorporated into and expressed by the body. Yet, because the Sohoian symbolic universe is not monolithic, I soon recognized that no single dance-event or form of dancing can be seen as a "quintessential" or "truly authentic" expression of the body politic. Rather, dance-events in Sohos are characterized by multiple idioms, and in this multiplicity is manifested the ideological complexity of contemporary identity. Gender, as a component of ideologies and practices of identity, of "who we are," is an important and sometimes highlighted element within such idioms. Coexisting as they do in the community's celebratory life, these idioms do not operate quite as Herzfeld's "disemic" formulation (1982, 1985c) would seem to imply. Herzfeld argues that there are two sides to contemporary Greek identity, the Hellenic and the Romeic, the first emphasizing idealized qualities of the collective self and a public, externally directed orientation, the second emphasizing the ethnically impure, morally flawed qualities of the collective self and a private, internally directed orientation. Yet it would be wrong to identify the *horoesperidha*—"Hellenic" in its European inflections—as an externally directed performance for the benefit of (Western) outsiders, and the wedding—"Romeic" in its local amalgam of Greek, Turkish, and Slavic symbols—as internally directed for fellow Sohoians and intimates. Though the idioms that characterize the two events can be seen in Hellenic-Romeic—or, at least, in European-Macedonian—terms, both are public spectacles.[2] Moreover, both performers and audience (though these roles are not always clearly distinguished) are largely Sohoians. Whatever performances of individual and collective self are being undertaken in these events, they are being directed primarily to other Sohoians. Finally, such a formulation portrays these idioms as inversions of each other and thus obscures their shared, though differently inflected, elements, such as the patriarchal configuration of gender and sexual relations.[3] The patriarchal configuration common to

[2] Indeed, one could argue that the event celebrating the "Macedonian" self, the wedding, is the more public in local terms, and that it is the equally "traditional" local Carnival that attracts foreign visitors and brings fame and prestige to the community.

[3] Thus Herzfeld presents an episode of a wife playfully slapping her husband as evidence that male authority "is transformed into a measure of subordination in the family home," and portrays it as a Romeic reality "more familiar—and certainly more embarrassing—than most writers acknowledge" (1986:220). Although acknowledging that women may enjoy certain powers in the domestic sphere, I think Herzfeld's point is in

both idioms enables celebrants to move from one to the other and to experience this move, at least with respect to gender relations, as relatively uncontradictory.

By the same token, the celebratory forms explored here, each with its distinct idiom, are not in themselves associated with or used exclusively by specific social groupings of class, kin, or political party in Sohos. Many of the same families and individuals who join in the *patinadha* or "dance the bride" in the churchyard or dress as *karnavalia* in the Carnival celebrations also attend *horoesperidhes*. Some manipulation of symbols and practices nevertheless does occur within these shared forms, especially within *horoesperidhes*, in order to express particular ideological positions: thus, the female-dominated and Left-identified Sohos Youth Association appoints a female emcee to welcome its celebrants, and the local PA.SO.K. activists hire a progressive musical ensemble and play down the hierarchical ordering in the "first dance" so prominently displayed in the *horoesperidha* of the right-wing Orpheus.

Regarded in another way, the multiple celebratory idioms reveal a certain archaeology of the Sohoian collective self, though this, too, requires a complicated reading of history in Sohoian bodies. The various ensembles of social/musical/dance practices that constitute Sohoian dance-events emerged within, or were brought to, the town in particular historical moments. Yet as contemporary events, they must be interpreted with cognizance of the ideological, social, and political climate of the more recent moment of fieldwork and analysis: the wedding (and also the Carnival, see Cowan 1988b) connoting a local history and tradition at a time when, in national-level discourse, these very terms were being delivered from the taint of backwardness by the newly triumphant Panhellenic Socialist Movement, whose rhetoric invited a "return to our roots"; the *horoesperidha* (and in similar ways the *kafeteria*) recalling the long legacy of Western hegemony and the continued prestige of its symbols in a community that has always seen itself as more than "just" another village; and finally, Aphrodite's party reiterating (here, by its failure) the ideals of the table—unity, play, the absence of instrumental attitudes—among celebrants who reside in the same town but are bound neither by kinship, club, nor ties of place.

---

other ways misleading. To identify public postures of male authority as Hellenic and Western, and to suggest that the Romeic reality inverts this male authority, risks trivializing the significance of indigenous patriarchal forms that have long perpetuated systematic violence against women. Indeed, such violence has usually occurred inside the house, a place idealized not only in Greek thought but in Western liberal thought as, in Lasch's (1977) words, a "haven in a heartless world." It seems to me unhelpful to challenge the progressive assumptions of models of modernization or Westernization simply by shifting the blame for gender inequalities from East to West. We ought, rather, to look at their common features and their historical and ideological interpenetrations.

Symbolically resonant and sometimes politically valorized, dance-events are also intense sociable, sensual, and aesthetic experiences. Sohoians find such events exciting and participation in them rewarding. But at the same time, these events are configured by power relations. Relations of inequality both situational and systemic—of gender, of ethnicity, and among political factions—are subtly embedded in celebratory practices.

These relations of inequality are continually contested, but there are limits to how they may be contested. The most prevalent form of contestation—misunderstandings among men—is itself a conventionalized articulation of the dominant gender ideology. But is a more subversive contestation possible? Irony in performance and in descriptions of it is one strategy to call a particular performance into question. As we have seen, however, this can be used to reassert, as well as to subvert, existing power relations.

Paradoxically, the heightened sensuality and significance of the celebration may itself discourage gestures of contestation. Though Sohoians may behave themselves at a dance-event out of fear of sanctions, they undoubtedly also do so because they derive pleasure from the songs, the dancing, and the chance to have a good time with their family and friends, or because they feel a sense of loyalty to those who sponsor the event or to some of the things it stands for. The very fact that a celebrant values the dance-event, and the fact that it is valorized by significant others, may make the celebrant reluctant to contest the practices that constitute it.[4]

I have argued that by engaging in the social and bodily practices of dance-events, celebrants literally embody particular ideas and relations. This raises the question of the relation between collective forms and individual articulations.[5] Are these merely poses that present a public self while masking an interior, private one? Or are the shared, public forms—bodily conventions, even clichés—constitutive of the gendered persons who articulate relations through these forms? If phrased as either/or, the question itself is wrongly posed, replicating

[4] The point I am making here about the difficulty of negotiation differs from that made by Bloch (1974), whose well-known claim that "you can't argue with a song" (or a dance) has been widely criticized, and indeed, characterized by one writer as "Stalinist" (Karp 1988:40). Bloch's claim is based on the supposedly "restricted" nature of the codes of song and dance. My questions allude to people's emotional, aesthetic, and political attachments to and uses of celebratory forms and the implications of these for gestures of contestation.

[5] Beidelman (1986:200–215) discusses this question in reference to Kaguru social experience with sensitivity and insight, though in pursuing it by contrasting the Durkheimian and the Simmelian approaches, and finding the latter's emphasis on individual creativity more amenable, his discussion accepts and remains within the terms of Western bourgeois sociology.

at the level of analysis an opposition between individual and society, and a compulsion to identify one or the other as ontologically prior, that many—Marx and Bakhtin among them—have shown to be a conundrum of Western bourgeois ideology. I see collective bodily and social forms and individual articulations as mutually determining. The dancer comes alive as a social and a sociable person by feasting and dancing in collectively recognizable ways; through such usages, these celebratory practices are enlivened as collective forms. This process is not, however, merely circular. Sometimes the dancer may feel a lack of fit between pose and experience. Since this may (though it certainly does not always) lead to innovations in poses and practices, and since the meanings of these are always subject to negotiation, the process is, in fact, dialectical.[6]

The dialectical nature of the relation between collective forms and individual articulations is a feature of all realms of social life. Yet, the set-apart qualities of the dance frame alter the dynamics of this dialectic, differentiating it from that which obtains within taken-for-granted dispositions and practices of everyday habitus. In the dance-event, the forms themselves are highlighted, elaborated, played with. Nevertheless, the dance-event is an arena not only of creativity, exaggeration, and release but also of norms, conventions, and sanctions. Here, the nature of gendered persons and the relations among them are articulated and negotiated, and the themes of freedom and constraint, desire and obligation, self-containment and association are posed and explored. As Sohoians profoundly recognize, the expressive discourse of dance-events is also a moral discourse. Dance for them is thus compelling, in every sense of this word. As they explain, "if you enter the dance, you must dance."

---

[6] Sugarman (1989) comes to a similar conclusion in her superb analysis of singing and gender among Prespa Albanians.

Abu-Lughod, Lila. 1986. *Veiled Sentiments: Honor and Poetry in a Bedouin Society*. Berkeley: University of California Press.

Alderson, A. D., and Fahir İz, eds. 1959. *The Concise Oxford Turkish Dictionary*. Oxford: Clarendon Press.

Alexiou, Margaret. 1974. *The Ritual Lament in Greek Tradition*. Cambridge: Cambridge University Press.

Anderson, Benedict. 1983. *Imagined Communities: Reflections on the Origin and Spread of Nationalism*. London: Verso.

Ardener, Edwin. 1975. Belief and the Problem of Women. In *Perceiving Women*, ed. Shirley Ardener, 1–27. London: Malaby Press.

Asad, Talal. 1979. Anthropology and the Analysis of Ideology. *Man* 14:603–627.

Auerbach, Susan. 1984. Song, Lament and Gender: Musical Meaning in a Northern Greek Village. M.A. thesis, University of Washington.

Austin, J. L. 1975. *How to Do Things with Words*. Cambridge, Mass.: Harvard University Press.

Bakalaki, Alexandra. 1984. The History and Structure of a Feminized Profession: Hairdressing in Athens and Thessaloniki. Ph.D. dissertation, State University of New York, Buffalo.

Bakhtin, Mikhail. 1984. *Rabelais and His World*, trans. Helene Iswolsky. Bloomington: Indiana University Press.

Bateson, Gregory. 1958. *Naven*. Stanford: Stanford University Press.

———. 1972a. A Theory of Play and Fantasy. In *Steps to an Ecology of Mind*, 177–193. New York: Ballantine Books.

———. 1972b. Double-Bind, 1969. In *Steps to an Ecology of Mind*, 271–278. New York: Ballantine Books.

Bauman, Richard. 1977. *Verbal Art as Performance*. Rowley, Mass.: Newbury House.

Beidelman, T. O. 1986. *Moral Imagination in Kaguru Modes of Thought*. Bloomington: Indiana University Press.

Berger, John. 1972. *Ways of Seeing*. New York: Penguin Books.

Berger, Peter, and Thomas Luckman. 1967. *The Social Construction of Reality*. Garden City, N.Y.: Doubleday.

Bernstein, Richard. 1976. *The Restructuring of Social and Political Theory*. Philadelphia: University of Pennsylvania Press.

Blacking, John, and Joann Kealiinohomoku, eds. 1979. *The Performing Arts: Music and Dance*. The Hague: Mouton.

Bloch, Maurice. 1974. Symbol, Song and Dance, or Is Religion an Extreme Form of Traditional Authority? *European Journal of Sociology* 15 (1):55–81.

Boon, James. 1973. Further Operations of "Culture" in Anthropology: A Synthesis of and for Debate. In *The Idea of Culture in the Social Sciences*, ed. Louis Schneider and Charles Bonjean, 1–32. Cambridge: Cambridge University Press.

Bourdieu, Pierre. 1977. *Outline of a Theory of Practice*. Cambridge: Cambridge University Press.

Brandes, Stanley. 1980. *Metaphors of Masculinity: Sex and Status in Andalucia*. Philadelphia: University of Pennsylvania Press.

Butterworth, Katharine, and Sara Schneider. 1975. *Rebetika: Songs from the Old Greek Underworld*. Athens: Komboloi Press.

Campbell, J. K. 1964. *Honour, Family and Patronage: A Study of Institutions and Moral Values in a Greek Mountain Community*. New York: Oxford University Press.

Caraveli, Anna. 1982. The Song beyond the Song: Aesthetics and Social Interaction in Greek Folksong. *Journal of American Folklore* 95 (376):129–58.

———. 1985. The Symbolic Village: Community Born in Performance. *Journal of American Folklore* 99 (289):260–86.

Caraveli-Chaves, Anna. 1980. Bridge between Worlds: The Greek Women's Lament as Communicative Event. *Journal of American Folklore* 93 (368):129–57.

Carrithers, Michael, Steven Collins, and Steven Lukes, eds. 1985. *The Category of the Person: Anthropology, Philosophy, History*. Cambridge: Cambridge University Press.

Cavounidis, Jennifer. 1983. Capitalist Development and Women's Work in Greece. *Journal of Modern Greek Studies* 1 (2):321–38.

Clark, Mari. 1983. Variations on Themes of Male and Female: Reflections on Gender Bias in Fieldwork in Rural Greece. *Women's Studies* 102:117–33.

Clifford, James, and George E. Marcus. 1986. *Writing Culture: The Poetics and Politics of Ethnography*. Berkeley: University of California Press.

Clogg, Richard. 1979. *A Short History of Modern Greece*. Cambridge: Cambridge University Press.

Connolly, William. 1983. *The Terms of Political Discourse*. Princeton: Princeton University Press.

Cousinery, M.E.M. 1831. *Voyage dans la Macédoine*. Paris.

Cowan, Jane K. 1986a. Winking Geishas and Mexican Hats: Contested Symbols and the Politics of Tradition in a Macedonian Town. Paper presented to the Postgraduate Seminar, Centre for Byzantine Studies and Modern Greek, University of Birmingham.

———. 1986b. "Somewhere Else" in Greek Women's Construction of Experience in a Macedonian Town. Paper presented at the Symposium on Horizons of Current Anthropological Research in Greece and the Establishment of a Department of Social Anthropology at the University of the Aegean, Mytilene, Greece, September 1–5.

———. 1988a. "Embodiments: The Social Construction of Gender in Dance-Events in a Northern Greek Town." Ph.D. dissertation, Indiana University.

―――. 1988b. Folk Truth: When the Scholar Comes to Carnival in a "Traditional" Community. *Journal of Modern Greek Studies* 6 (2):245–60.

―――. 1989. Defiant Poses: *Zeibekiko* as Embodied Rhetoric and Social Practice. Typescript.

Crapanzano, Vincent. 1986. Hermes' Dilemma: The Masking of Subversion in Ethnographic Description. In *Writing Culture: The Poetics and Politics of Ethnography*, ed. James Clifford and George E. Marcus, 51–76. Berkeley: University of California Press.

Crosfield, Domini. 1948. *Dances of Greece*. London: Max Parrish and Co.

Dakin, Douglas. 1966. *The Greek Struggle in Macedonia, 1897–1913*. Thessaloniki: Institute for Balkan Studies.

Danforth, Loring M. 1978. The Anastenaria: A Study in Greek Ritual Therapy. Ph.D. dissertation, Princeton University.

―――. 1979a. The Role of the Dance in the Ritual Therapy of the Anastenaria. *Byzantine and Modern Greek Studies* 5:141–63.

―――. 1979b. Women's Strategies and Powers: A Rural Greek Example. Paper presented to the 1979 meeting of the American Anthropological Association, Cincinnati.

―――. 1982. *The Death Rituals of Rural Greece*. Photographs by Alexander Tsiaras. Princeton, N.J.: Princeton University Press.

―――. 1983. Power through Submission to the Anastenaria. *Journal of Modern Greek Studies* 1 (1):203–224.

―――. 1984. The Ideological Context of the Search for Continuities in Greek Culture. *Journal of Modern Greek Studies* 2 (1):53–85.

de Lauretis, Teresa. 1984. *Alice Doesn't: Feminism, Semiotics, Cinema*. Bloomington: Indiana University Press.

Denich, Bette. 1974. Sex and Power in the Balkans. In *Woman, Culture, and Society*, ed. M. Rosaldo and L. Lamphere, 243–63. Stanford: Stanford University Press.

Dimen, Muriel. 1983. Servants and Sentries: Women, Power and Social Reproduction in Kriovrisi. *Journal of Modern Greek Studies* 1 (1):225–42.

Divry, George C., ed. 1979. *Divry's Modern English–Greek and Greek–English Desk Dictionary*. New York: D. C. Divry.

Douglas, Mary. 1966. *Purity and Danger: An Analysis of the Concepts of Pollution and Taboo*. London: Routledge and Kegan Paul.

―――. 1973. The Two Bodies. In *Natural Symbols*, 93–112. New York: Penguin Books.

Dubisch, Jill. 1983. Greek Women: Sacred or Profane? *Journal of Modern Greek Studies* 1 (1):185–202

―――, ed. 1986. *Gender and Power in Rural Greece*. Princeton: Princeton University Press.

du Boulay, Juliet. 1974. *Portrait of a Greek Mountain Village*. Oxford: Clarendon Press.

Ekaterinidhis, Yiorghios. 1979. Ta Karnavalia tu Sohu Thessalonikis. In *Praktika tu Tritu Simposiu Laografias tu Vorioelladhiku Horu*, 13–24. Thessaloniki: Institute of Balkan Studies.

Errington, Frederick. 1984. *Manners and Meaning in West Sumatra: The Social Context of Consciousness*. New Haven: Yale University Press.

Eudes, Dominique. 1972. *The Kapetanios: Partisans and Civil War in Greece, 1943–1949*. New York: Monthly Review Press.

Fabian, Johannes. 1983. *Time and the Other: How Anthropology Makes Its Object*. New York: Columbia University Press.

Femia, Joseph V. 1981. *Gramsci's Political Thought: Hegemony, Consciousness and the Revolutionary Process*. Oxford: Clarendon Press.

Flax, Jane. 1987. Postmodernism and Gender Relations in Feminist Theory. *Signs* 12 (4):621–43.

Foucault, Michel. 1978. *The History of Sexuality*. Vol. 1, *An Introduction*. New York: Random House.

——. 1979. *Discipline and Punish: The Birth of the Prison*, trans. Alan Sheridan. New York: Random House.

Friedl, Ernestine. 1962. *Vasilika*. New York: Holt, Rinehart and Winston.

——. 1967. The Position of Women: Appearance and Reality. *Anthropological Quarterly* 40 (3):97–108.

——. 1970. Fieldwork in a Greek Village. In *Women in the Field*, ed. Peggy Golde, 195–220. Chicago: Aldine.

Gallagher, Catherine, and Thomas Laqueur, eds. 1987. *The Making of the Modern Body: Sexuality and Society in the Nineteenth Century*. Berkeley: University of California Press.

Geertz, Clifford. 1973a. *The Interpretation of Cultures*. New York: Basic Books.

——. 1973b. Deep Play: Notes on the Balinese Cockfight. In *The Interpretation of Cultures*, 412–53. New York: Basic Books.

Giddens, Anthony. 1976. *New Rules of Sociological Method: A Positive Critique of Interpretative Methodologies*. London: Hutchinson.

——. 1979. *Central Problems in Social Theory: Action, Structure and Contradiction in Social Analysis*. London: Macmillan.

——. 1984. *The Constitution of Society: Outline of the Theory of Structuration*. Cambridge: Polity Press.

Giovannini, Maureen J. 1985. The Dialectics of Women's Factory Work in a Sicilian Town. *Anthropology* 9 (1–2):45–64.

Goffman, Erving. 1959. *The Presentation of Self in Everyday Life*. New York: Penguin Books.

——. 1974. *Frame Analysis: An Essay on the Organization of Experience*. New York: Harper and Row.

Golde, Peggy, ed. 1986. *Women in the Field: Anthropological Experiences*, 2d ed. Berkeley: University of California Press.

Gramsci, Antonio. 1971. *Selections from the Prison Notebooks*, ed. and trans. Q. Hoare and G. Nowell-Smith. London: Lawrence and Wishart.

——. 1978. *Selections from Political Writings, 1921–26*, ed. and trans. by Q. Hoare. London: Lawrence and Wishart.

Handman, Marie-Elisabeth. 1983. *La Violence et la Ruse: Hommes et Femmes dans un Village Grec*. Aix-en-Provence: Edisud.

Hanna, Judith Lynne. 1979. *To Dance Is Human: A Theory of Nonverbal Communication.* Austin: University of Texas Press.

———. 1988. *Dance, Sex, and Gender: Signs of Identity, Dominance, Defiance, and Desire.* Chicago: University of Chicago Press.

Haug, Frigga et al. 1987. *Female Sexualization.* London: Verso.

Herzfeld, Michael. 1980a. Honour and Shame: Problems in the Analysis of Moral Systems. *Man* 15:339–51.

———. 1980b. The Dowry in Greece: Terminological Usage and Historical Reconstruction. *Ethnohistory* 27:225–41.

———. 1981. Performative Categories and Symbols of Passage in Rural Greece. *Journal of American Folklore* 94 (371):41–57.

———. 1982. *Ours Once More: Folklore, Ideology, and the Making of Modern Greece.* Austin: University of Texas Press.

———. 1983a. Looking Both Ways: The Ethnographer in the Text. *Semiotica* 46 (2–4):151–66.

———. 1983b. Semantic Slippage and Moral Fall: The Rhetoric of Chastity in Rural Greek Society. *Journal of Modern Greek Studies* 1 (1):161–72.

———. 1985a. *The Poetics of Manhood: Contest and Identity in a Cretan Mountain Village.* Princeton: Princeton University Press.

———. 1985b. Gender Pragmatics: Agency, Speech and Bride-Theft in a Cretan Mountain Village. *Anthropology* 9 (1–2):25–44.

———. 1986. Within and Without: The Category of "Female" in the Ethnography of Modern Greece. In *Gender and Power in Rural Greece*, ed. Jill Dubisch, 215–33. Princeton: Princeton University Press.

———. 1987a. "As in Your Own House": Hospitality, Ethnography, and the Stereotype of Mediterranean Society. In *Honor and Shame and the Unity of the Mediterranean*, ed. D. D. Gilmore, 75–89. Washington, D.C.: American Anthropological Association Special Publication, no. 22.

———. 1987b. *Anthropology through the Looking-Glass: Critical Ethnography on the Margins of Europe.* Cambridge: Cambridge University Press.

Hirschon, Renée. 1978. Open Body/Closed Space: The Transformation of Female Sexuality. In *Defining Females*, ed. Shirley Ardener, 66–88. New York: John Wiley and Sons.

———. 1981. Essential Objects and the Sacred: Interior and Exterior Space in an Urban Locality. In *Women and Space*, ed. Shirley Ardener, 72–88. London: Croom Helm.

———. 1983. Women, the Aged, and Religious Activity: Oppositions and Complementarity in an Urban Locality. *Journal of Modern Greek Studies* 1 (1):113–30.

———. 1989. *Heirs of the Greek Catastrophe: The Social Life of Asia Minor Refugees in Piraeus.* Oxford: Clarendon Press.

Holden, Rickey, and Mary Vouras. 1965. *Greek Folk Dances.* Newark, N.J.: Folkcraft Press.

Holst, Gail. 1977. *Road to Rembetika.* Limni and Athens: Anglo-Hellenic Publishing.

Holst, Gail. 1980. *Theodorakis: Myth and Politics in Modern Greek Music.* Amsterdam: Adolf M. Hakkert.

Irigaray, Luce. 1974. *Speculum de l'Autre Femme.* Paris: Minuit.

Jackson, Michael. 1983. Knowledge of the Body. *Man* 18:327–45.

Jameson, Frederic. 1981. *The Political Unconscious: Narrative as a Socially Symbolic Act.* London: Methuen.

Jelavich, Charles, and Barbara Jelavich. 1977. *The Establishment of the Balkan National States, 1804–1920.* Seattle: University of Washington Press.

Kaberry, Phyllis. 1939. *Aboriginal Women: Sacred and Profane.* London: Routledge and Kegan Paul.

Kaeppler, Adrienne. 1967. The Structure of Tongan Dance. Ph.D. dissertation, University of Hawaii.

———. 1978. Dance in Anthropological Perspective. *Annual Review of Anthropology* 7:31–49.

Karp, Ivan. 1980. Beer Drinking and Social Experience: An Essay in Formal Sociology. In *Explorations in African Systems of Thought,* ed. Ivan Karp and Charles Bird, 83–119. Bloomington: Indiana University Press.

———. 1986. Agency and Social Theory: A Review of Anthony Giddens. *American Ethnologist* 13 (1):131–37.

———. 1988. Laughter at Marriage: Subversion in Performance. *Journal of Folklore Research* 25 (1–2):35–52.

Karp, Ivan, and Martha Kendall. 1982. Reflexivity in Fieldwork. In *Explaining Human Behavior,* ed. P. Secord, 249–73. Los Angeles: Sage Publications.

Kealiinohomoku, Joann. 1973. Culture Change—Function and Dysfunctional Expressions of Dance: A Form of Affective Culture. Paper presented at the Ninth International Congress of Anthropological and Ethnological Sciences, Chicago.

Keesing, Roger. 1987. Anthropology as Interpretive Quest. *Current Anthropology* 28 (2):161–76.

Kenna, Margaret. 1976. Houses, Fields and Graves: Property and Ritual Obligation on a Greek Island. *Ethnology* 15:21–34.

———. N.d. Saying "No" in Greece: Some Preliminary Thoughts on Hospitality, Gender, and the Evil Eye. In *Mélanges en l'Honneur de John Peristiany,* ed. S. Damianakos and M. E. Handman. Forthcoming.

Kitromilides, Paschalis. 1983. The Enlightenment and Womanhood: Cultural Change and the Politics of Exclusion. *Journal of Modern Greek Studies* 1 (1):39–61.

Kofos, Evangelos. 1964. *Nationalism and Communism in Macedonia.* Thessaloniki: Institute for Balkan Studies.

Kortsidhas, Haralambos. 1980a. Imeroloyio Antistasis Sohu ke Periferias. *Ethniki Antistasi* 24:52–77.

———. 1980b. Imeroloyio Antistasis Sohu ke Perifereas. *Ethniki Antistasi* 25:65–79.

Kutsimanis, Stefanos. 1974. *Antilali apo ton Sohon ke tin Periohin tu.* Thessaloniki: Evangelos Kaspakis.

Kyriakidhu-Nestoros, Alki. 1978. *I Theoria tis Ellinikis Laoghrafias.* Athens: Moraitis School.

Laing, R. D. 1969. *Self and Others*. New York: Penguin Books.

Lakoff, Robin. 1975. *Language and Woman's Place*. New York: Harper and Row.

Lambiri, Ioanna. 1968. The Impact of Industrial Employment on the Position of Women in a Greek Country Town. In *Contributions to Mediterranean Sociology*, ed. John Peristiany, 261–68. Paris and the Hague: Mouton.

Lange, R. 1975. *The Nature of Dance: An Anthropological Perspective*. London: MacDonald and Evans.

Lasch, Christopher. 1977. *Haven in a Heartless World: The Family Besieged*. New York: Basic Books.

Leake, William. 1835. *Travels in Northern Greece*. Vol. 3. London: J. Rodwell.

Leigh Fermor, Patrick. 1966. *Roumeli: Travels in Northern Greece*. London: John Murray.

Loizos, Peter. 1975. *The Greek Gift: Politics in a Cypriot Village*. Oxford: Basil Blackwell.

Loizos, Peter, and Akis Papataxiarchis, eds. Forthcoming. *Gender and Kinship in the Anthropology of Greece*. Princeton: Princeton University Press.

Lomax, Alan. 1968. *Folk Song Style and Culture*. New York: American Association for the Advancement of Science.

Loutzaki, Rena. 1979–80. Hori tis Orinis Serron: Katagrafi meti methodo "Kinisiografias tu Laban." *Ethnografika* 2:97–128.

———. 1985. O Ghamos os Horeftiko Dhromeno: I Periptosi ton Prosfighon tis Anatolikis Rumelias sto Mikro Monastiri Makedhonias. *Ethnografika* 4–5 (Nafplion).

Lukes, Steven. 1974. *Power, A Radical View*. London: Macmillan.

MacCormack, Carol, and Marilyn Strathern. 1980. *Nature, Culture and Gender*. Cambridge: Cambridge University Press.

Makreas, Mary. 1979. Cretan Dance: The Meaning of Kefi and Figoures. M.A. thesis, Indiana University.

Marcus, George E., and Michael M. J. Fischer. 1986. *Anthropology as Cultural Critique: An Experimental Moment in the Human Sciences*. Chicago: University of Chicago Press.

Martin, Emily. 1987. *The Woman in the Body: A Cultural Analysis of Reproduction*. New York: Beacon Press.

Martis, Nikolaos. 1984. *The Falsification of Macedonian History*. Athens: Ikaros.

Marx, Karl. 1977 (1844). *Economic and Philosophic Manuscripts of 1844*. London: Lawrence and Wishart.

Marx, Karl, and Friedrich Engels. 1947 (1845–46). *The German Ideology*, trans. R. Pascal. New York: International.

Mauss, Marcel. 1935. Les Techniques du Corps. *Journal de Psychologie Normale et Pathologique* 35:271–93.

———. 1967 (1925). *The Gift: Forms and Functions of Exchange in Archaic Societies*, trans. Ian Cunnison. New York: W. W. Norton.

———. 1985. A Category of the Human Mind: The Notion of Person, The Notion of Self. Trans. W. D. Halls. In *The Category of the Person: Anthropology, Philosophy, History*, ed. Michael Carrithers, Steven Collins, and Steven Lukes, 1–25. Cambridge: Cambridge University Press.

Mead, Margaret. 1949. *Male and Female: A Study of the Sexes in a Changing World*. New York: William Morrow.

Moore, Sally Falk. 1976. Uncertainties in Situations, Indeterminacies in Culture. In *Symbol and Politics in Communal Ideology*, ed. Sally Falk Moore and Barbara G. Myerhoff, 210–39. Ithaca: Cornell University Press.

Moore, Sally Falk, and Barbara G. Myerhoff, eds. 1977. *Secular Ritual*. Amsterdam: Van Gorcum.

Mosse, George. 1985. *Nationalism and Sexuality: Respectability and Abnormal Sexuality in Modern Europe*. New York: Howard Fertig.

Mouzelis, Nicos. 1978. *Modern Greece: Facets of Underdevelopment*. London: Macmillan.

Ollman, Bertell. 1971. *Alienation: Marx's Conception of Man in Capitalist Society*. Cambridge: Cambridge University Press.

Ortner, Sherry B. 1978. *Sherpas through Their Rituals*. Cambridge: Cambridge University Press.

———. 1984. Theory in Anthropology since the Sixties. *Comparative Studies in Society and History* 26:126–66.

Ortner, Sherry, and Harriet Whitehead. 1981. *Sexual Meanings: The Cultural Construction of Gender and Sexuality*. Cambridge: Cambridge University Press.

Papagaroufali, Eleni. 1986. Ellinidhes Feministries: Idheoloyia ton Filon ke Praktiki se Sinikiakus Silloghus ke tin Ikoyenia. Paper presented at the Symposium on Horizons of Current Anthropological Research in Greece and the Establishment of a Department of Social Anthropology at the University of the Aegean, Mytilene, Greece, September 1–5.

Papataxiarchis, Akis. 1986. I Nomi tu Filu: Andhriki Sinestiatiki Filia ke Singenia se mia Kinotita tis Eyeiakis Elladhas. Paper presented at the Symposium on Horizons of Current Anthropological Research in Greece and the Establishment of a Department of Social Anthropology at the University of the Aegean, Mytilene, Greece, September 1–5.

———. N.d. The Dancing Efes: Notions of the Male Person in Aegean Greek Fiction. Typescript.

Peristiany, John. 1966. Honour and Shame in a Cypriot Highland Village. In *Honour and Shame: The Values of Mediterranean Society*, ed. J. Peristiany. Chicago: University of Chicago Press.

Petrides, Ted. 1975. *Folk Dances of the Greeks*. Jericho, N.Y.: Exposition Press.

———. 1980. *Greek Dances*. Athens: Lycabettus Press.

Petrides, Theodore, and Elfleida Petrides. 1974. *Folk Dances of the Greeks*. Folkestone: Bailey.

Petropoulos, Ilias. 1972. *Rebetika Traghudia*. Athens.

Piault, Colette. 1985. *Familles et Biens en Grèce et à Chypre*. Histoires et Perspectives Meditérranéenes. Paris: l'Harmattan.

Pitt-Rivers, Julian. 1961. *The People of the Sierra*. Chicago: University of Chicago Press.

Raftis, Alkis. 1985. *O Kosmos tu Elliniku Horu*. Athens: Politipo.

Reiter, Rayna R. 1975. *Toward an Anthropology of Women*. New York: Monthly Review Press.

Rheubottom, David. 1980. Dowry and Wedding Celebrations in Yugoslav Macedonia. In *The Meaning of Marriage Payments*, ed. J. Comaroff, 221–49. New York: Academic Press.

Rice, Timothy. 1980. A Macedonian *Sobor*: Anatomy of a Celebration. *Journal of American Folklore* 93:113–28.

Richards, Audrey. 1956. *Chisungu*. London: Faber and Faber.

Romaios, K. A. 1973. Elliniki Hori ke Idhietera o Kalamatianos. *Lavirinthos* 1:49–57.

Rosaldo, Michelle. 1974. Woman, Culture, and Society: A Theoretical Overview. In *Woman, Culture, and Society*, ed. M. Rosaldo and L. Lamphere, 17–42. Stanford: Stanford University Press.

Rosaldo, Michelle, and Louise Lamphere, eds. 1974. *Woman, Culture, and Society*. Stanford: Stanford University Press.

Royce, Anya Peterson. 1977. *The Anthropology of Dance*. Bloomington: Indiana University Press.

Scarry, Elaine. 1985. *The Body in Pain: The Making and Unmaking of the World*. Oxford: Oxford University Press.

Schiefflin, E. L. 1976. *The Sorrow of the Lonely and the Burning of the Dancers*. New York: St. Martin's.

Schneider, Jane. 1971. Of Vigilance and Virgins. *Ethnology* 9:1–24.

Schutz, Alfred. 1970. *On Phenomenology and Social Relations*, ed. and with introduction by Helmut R. Wagner. Chicago: University of Chicago Press.

Schutz, Alfred, and Thomas Luckman. 1973. *The Structures of the Life World*. Evanston: Northwestern University Press.

Seeger, Anthony. 1987. *Why Suyá Sing: A Musical Anthropology of an Amazonian People*. Cambridge: Cambridge University Press.

Simmel, Georg. 1971a. Sociability. In *On Individuality and Social Forms*, ed. Donald Levine, 127–40. Chicago: University of Chicago Press.

———. 1971b. The Stranger. In *On Individuality and Social Forms*, ed. Donald N. Levine, 143–49. Chicago: University of Chicago Press.

Singer, Alice. 1974. The Metrical Structure of Macedonian Dance. *Ethnomusicology* 18 (3):379–404.

Skouteri-Didaskalou, Nora. 1984. *Anthropoloyika Ya to Yinekio Zitima (4 Meletimata)*. Athens: Politis.

Spencer, Paul. 1985. *Society and the Dance: The Social Anthropology of Process and Performance*. Cambridge: Cambridge University Press.

Stamiris, Eleni. 1986. The Women's Movement in Greece. *New Left Review* 158:98–112.

Stavrianos, L. S. 1958. *The Balkans since 1453*. New York: Holt, Rinehart and Winston.

Stewart, Charles. N.d. Honour and Sanctity: Two Levels of Ideology on a Greek Island. In *Mélanges en l'Honneur de John Peristiany*, ed. S. Damianakos and M. E. Handman. Forthcoming.

Stoianovich, Traian. 1960. The Conquering Balkan Orthodox Merchant. *Journal of Economic History* 20 (2):234–313.

Stone, Ruth M. 1982. *Let the Inside Be Sweet: The Interpretation of Music Event among the Kpelle of Liberia*. Bloomington: Indiana University Press.

Strathern, Marilyn. 1981. Culture in a Netbag: The Manufacture of a Subdis-
cipline in Anthropology. *Man* 16 (4):665–88.

———. 1987a. An Awkward Relationship: The Case of Feminism and Anthropology. *Signs* 12 (2):276–92.

———. ed. 1987b. *Dealing with Inequality: Analysing Gender Relations in Mela-
nesia and Beyond.* Essays by Members of the 1983/1984 Anthropological
Research Group at the Research School of Pacific Studies, the Australia
National University. Cambridge: Cambridge University Press.

Stratou, Dora. 1966. *The Greek Dances.* Athens: Angelos Klissiounis.

Sugarman, Jane. 1989. The Nightingale and the Partridge: Singing and Gender among Prespa Albanians. *Ethnomusicology* 33 (2):191–215.

Sutton, Susan Buck. 1986. Family and Work: New Patterns for Village
Women in Athens. *Journal of Modern Greek Studies* 4 (1):33–49.

Svoronos, Nikos. 1986. *Episkopisi tis Neoellinikis Istorias.* Athens: Themelio
Press.

Turner, Bryan. 1984. *The Body and Society.* Oxford: Basil Blackwell.

Turner, Victor. 1957. *Schism and Continuity in an African Society: A Study of
Ndembu Village Life.* Manchester: Manchester University Press.

———. 1969. *The Ritual Process: Structure and Anti-Structure.* Ithaca: Cornell
University Press.

———. 1974. *Dramas, Fields, and Metaphors: Symbolic Action in Human Society.*
Ithaca: Cornell University Press.

Vacalopoulos, Apostolos E. 1973. *History of Macedonia, 1354–1833.* Thessaloniki: Institute for Balkan Studies.

Vance, Carole S., ed. 1984. *Pleasure and Danger: Exploring Female Sexuality.*
Boston: Routledge Kegan and Paul.

Williams, Drid. 1978. Deep Structures of the Dance. *Yearbook of Symbolic Anthropology* 1:211–30.

Williams, Raymond. 1977. *Marxism and Literature.* Oxford: Oxford University Press.

Zotiades, George. 1961. *The Macedonian Controversy.* Thessaloniki: Eteria
Makedhonikon Spudhon.

PRINCETON MODERN GREEK STUDIES